From Free to Fair Markets

From Free to Fair Markets

Liberalism After Covid-19

Richard Holden and Rosalind Dixon

OXFORD
UNIVERSITY PRESS

OXFORD
UNIVERSITY PRESS

Oxford University Press is a department of the University of Oxford. It furthers
the University's objective of excellence in research, scholarship, and education
by publishing worldwide. Oxford is a registered trade mark of Oxford University
Press in the UK and certain other countries.

Published in the United States of America by Oxford University Press
198 Madison Avenue, New York, NY 10016, United States of America.

© Oxford University Press 2022

CIP data is on file at the Library of Congress

ISBN 978–0–19–762598–9 (pbk.)
ISBN 978–0–19–762597–2 (hbk.)

DOI: 10.1093/oso/9780197625972.001.0001

1 3 5 7 9 8 6 4 2

Paperback printed by Marquis, Canada
Hardback printed by Bridgeport National Bindery, Inc., United States of America

Contents

Contents

PART I
THE CRISIS IN NEOLIBERALISM

1

Introduction

As we write this book the world is grappling with a public health crisis of a magnitude not seen in decades. While vaccination rates and associated freedoms are increasing in many countries, Covid-19 has proven to be a devastating public health event, with the virus able to expand its reach exponentially. Health officials have expressed joy when the number of people infected in a country goes from doubling every three days to doubling every week—the latter being a rate at which 100 infections would turn into 16.5 million in six months.

It has also caused a major economic crisis, with large parts of the economy shutting down, or being forcibly closed, to slow the spread of the infection. This has led to ripple effects throughout economies—with these "supply shocks" (reductions in the amount that the economy produces) translating into reductions in demand for goods and services of the type and magnitude seen in the Great Depression.

The Covid-19 crisis has also laid bare the imperfections of liberal democracies that already existed. Even before 2020, it was already clear that there was a fundamental crisis in work and wages and that many countries' healthcare systems were dysfunctional. There were records levels of economic inequality, and we had failed to tackle perhaps the greatest challenge of our time: climate change. Covid-19 made these imperfections even more stark and significant.

Globalization and automation had already led to a crisis in work and wages well before Covid appeared. Globalization and free trade had promised to expand the economic pie in a way that could be divided to make everyone better off. However, for a lot of manufacturing workers in the United States and other advanced economies, it has meant the loss of their jobs to overseas markets. And while in some cases other jobs have appeared, they have often tended to be less well-paid and have less attractive benefits.

Many workers have found that they are unable to find new work, or at best can find casual or part-time work with few, if any, benefits. These impacts have often been highly geographically concentrated and have led to the collapse of many rural and regional towns and cities. This collapse has itself contributed to a further spiral of hardship—in the United States especially, unemployment or under-employment of this kind has deprived many towns and cities of the tax base they need to provide core public services.

The worry, for those who see what this has done to some rural and regional areas, is that automation—or the robot era—will hasten and spread these effects across the economy. While estimates vary, almost all experts agree that robots and artificial intelligence are likely to cause a substantial loss of jobs in coming years. Self-driving vehicles and automated checkout lines threaten millions of jobs in relatively low-skilled occupations. In many instances—such as truck driving—this is already happening.

Even for those workers not in an industry that has been affected by global-ization or automation, there is also a very real sense that while the economy has been growing and society has become richer overall, workers are being left behind. It is a staggering fact that in the last 40 years, the average worker's income has not increased in real terms. While it is possible to explain away wage changes in isolated industries as the unfortunate victim of progress and to point to assistance programs that can ameliorate the effects, it is hard to deny a structural failure in the entire liberal project when the average worker is not sharing in the gains of prosperity over a period of nearly two generations.

Recent decades have likewise seen a secular trend toward the replacement of many previously full-time jobs, with relatively generous benefits, with a larger number of part-time or casual jobs offering few if any benefits. And the new technologies encouraged and embraced by liberals in the neoliberal era have only accelerated these trends: the so-called gig economy that involves companies such as Uber and TaskRabbit all depend crucially on technology for their business models. They also create new forms of part-time, casualized work—or self-employment—that offers few of the same benefits as traditional forms of full-time work.

And while the causes of this decline are still being debated, many suggest that they include the same forces driving an increase in unemployment and under-employment in many advanced economies—namely, globalization, casualization, and automation.

The crisis in work and wages was also only *one* part of the deficiency of lib-eralism pre-Covid-19. One of the long-run trends going into 2020 was the rise in the power of large firms. Indeed, in the two years prior to Covid-19, "trillion-dollar" firms began to exist as the technology giants Apple, Amazon, and Microsoft achieved market capitalizations previously hard to imagine. This also has impacts on competition in labor *and* product markets, thereby affecting the welfare of both workers and consumers. Indeed, the effects of globalization, automation, and "gigification" in many countries have been amplified by the combined effects of a decline in the power of labor unions and a rise in the number of large firms enjoying monopoly power in hiring.

There has likewise been a steady rise in many countries in the level of income and wealth inequality. As numerous left-leaning commentators and intellectuals have pointed out, even prior to 2020 the distribution of income and wealth was already more unequal than at any point in recorded modern history. The degree of wealth inequality was so extreme that in 2019, the eight wealthiest people in the world controlled more wealth than the poorest 3.6 billion. The United States was no exception, with the average income of the top 10% of earners nine times as much as the bottom 90%.[1]

Finally, despite decades of warnings from scientists about the gravity of human-induced climate change, as well as an overwhelming consensus among economists about the appropriate ways to deal with it (through a carbon tax or emissions-trading scheme), governments around the world have done very little to address the problem.

The Covid-19 pandemic has also exacerbated many of these trends. It has made starkly clear how fragile many people's jobs and livelihoods are. It has led to more people being unemployed and under-employed, more downward pressure on wages, and more workers without key benefits such as health-care at the time they arguably need it most. It has amplified economic and racial equalities. And despite, or perhaps was arguably evident at, the United Nation's most recent climate conference in Glasgow, COP26, it has further undermined the willingness of many countries to put climate action at the top of the political agenda.

At the same time, in many countries Covid-19 has sparked the kind of bold policy responses that might yet save liberalism from itself or mark the beginnings of a new and fairer market-based model. In many countries, government-funded wage-replacement programs have sought to maintain the relationship between employers and employees. There has been a significant expansion of unemployment benefits—both in who is eligible and how much recipients are paid. In addition, many governments have provided paid leave to those forced to stay home to care for children due to closures of schools and daycare facilities. And strikingly, in the early months of his presidency, Joe Biden has embraced a suite of policies—underpinned by nearly $1.9 trillion of Covid-19 relief spending and $4.1 trillion of proposed social, economic, and environmental spending—that largely comport with the "fair markets" approach we advocate in this book.[2]

One might ask why the pandemic is likely to produce any lasting change in countries' longer-term economic growth or lead to the embrace of a vision of this kind. The answer lies partly in the capacity for a crisis to catalyze broader social, economic, and political change. Sometimes, this is because such a crisis can cause us to change or experiment in ways that, afterward, it would be strange, or at least politically difficult to reverse. Citizens may come to enjoy and rely on forms of support, which, as voters, they are then reluctant to relinquish. Economists and social psychologists associate this with a common behavioral bias known as the "endowment effect": people are generally more reluctant to part with what they have than they are to pay to obtain those things in the first place.[3]

Or, it may be because crises—especially crises such as this one—give us an opportunity to pause and reflect on our existing ways and how they might be improved upon. For many, as we outline in subsequent chapters, Covid-19 has been a time of enormous economic and personal stress. The pandemic has involved continued work in essential services, combined with an increased "second shift" or responsibility for homeschooling.[4] For others, it has meant an extended period of enforced or self-enforced social isolation: it has forced us into new routines and rhythms, with less opportunity for distraction and more time for contemplation. It has given us the opportunity to think about what we prize about our current economic and political system and how we could make it work better in the service of public health and economic inclusion. And in some cases, it has made us realize that we have habits that threaten our planet and our democratic liberal ideas that we can actually do without.

This disruption—or spur to contemplation—may thus be an opening for those who have long sought—and continue to seek—a newer, more radically democratic form of liberalism, or a fair over free markets–based approach.

But this is far from a foregone conclusion: in democracies at least, it depends on persuading democratic leaders and voters that the best path out of the Covid-19 crisis is simultaneously to expand and to scale back the immediate policy responses to the crisis to make them more long-term, targeted, and sustainable, and yet essentially similar in aim and effect—that is, effective in creating a more compassionate and competitive form of liberalism, or a fair rather than free market model.

Another possible path out of the pandemic could well involve a form of "radical rollback"—that is, a complete retreat from all of the policy and environmental gains made during the pandemic to a similar or even more imperfect form of liberal paradigm. There is some concern that the response to Covid-19 may lead to an even more radical form of neoliberal "whiplash" to radical austerity—a retreat from even a limited form of liberal cosmopolitan order, and environmental deregulation and "revenge pollution" rather than increased regulation and reduced carbon emissions.

A key aim of this book is to make the case for a form of graduated expansion and taper as the preferred path for market-based economies as they seek to achieve a more democratic form of liberalism, as opposed to this more regressive form of rollback or return to previous neoliberal approaches.

A. Toward a More Democratic Form of Liberalism

What do we mean by "liberalism" or liberal democracy in this context? Democracy is generally a relatively well-understood idea. It is a model of collective self-government based on regular, free, and fair multiparty elections. For this model to be meaningful, a constitutional order must guarantee political rights and freedoms and provide a system of checks and balances adequate to ensure that elections are actually free and fair, and political rights and freedoms are respected. In this sense, it is also impossible for a system to be truly democratic and yet fail to respect minimum commitments to deliberation, the rule of law, and democratic constitutionalism.[5] But it need not necessarily go beyond this constitutional "minimum core" to live up to live up to democratic ideals or requirements.[6]

Liberal ideas of democracy, however, go much further and suggest that a great deal more is required for a democratic constitutional system to be legitimate: democracies must also guarantee a broad set of individual rights beyond the political sphere.[7] Liberalism as a philosophy is committed to the freedom, equality, and dignity of all individuals; and this extends to constitutional protections for these rights.[8]

John Rawls, for example, argued for four interconnected principles of justice in a liberal society: (i) the principle of "equal basic liberties" for all citizens; (ii) fair value of the political liberties; (iii) substantive equality of opportunity; and (iv) the difference principle. Scholars such as Amartya Sen and Martha Nussbaum likewise emphasize the centrality to liberal ideas of justice of individual freedom, dignity and equality—or equal dignity or "capabilities" for all.[9]

Liberalism's commitment to individual freedom, dignity, and equality also extends to all areas of social and economic as well as political life. And this entails a commitment to some degree of market-based ordering as a means of structuring *economic* life.

In the post–World War II era, liberalism has also generally been understood to encompass a commitment to economic and geopolitical freedom or openness—namely, free markets, global or multilateral forms of cooperation, and the relatively free movement of goods and persons across national borders. Liberal theorists often disagree as to how much freedom there should be in this context. Many political liberals, for example, defend the idea of the nation state, national sovereignty, and the ability of the state to determine the composition of its own people, as opposed to a principle of global open borders.[10] Almost all liberals, however, endorse the idea that there should be some degree of freedom and openness both economically and globally.

Liberalism, however, can also be understood in a range of ways: as it was understood by the classical liberals of the 18th and 19th century; as neoliberal in approach; or as embracing the more social, egalitarian form of liberalism that began with thinkers like T.M. Greene and Leonard Hobhouse in the progressive era, or early 20th century.[11] It is also this more social, egalitarian, democratic form of liberalism that is the focus of this book.

Democratic forms of liberalism, we suggest, emphasize notions of equality and dignity, as well as freedom for all citizens. They likewise emphasize the importance of democratic input into or "correction" of the various ways in which free markets fail to promote social welfare. Indeed, it suggests that government has a crucial role to play in: (i) guaranteeing access to a public baseline of core goods, or access to a generous social minimum to all citizens, regardless of market outcomes; (ii) ensuring equality of access to certain "relative goods"; (iii) regulating market power or sources of monopoly power; and (iv) responding to or "internalizing" negative externalities or social costs associated with private market behavior.

At the same time, we argue, democratic liberalism is also liberal in one key sense: it maintains a strong commitment to individual choice, to national and global markets, and to the flexibility and efficiency gains they offer. In this sense, it remains distinctive from rival proposals for a turn after Covid-19 toward a more radically democratic socialist or economic nationalist approach to economic regulation.

In effect, democratic liberalism calls for policies that advance the operation of "fair" rather than "free" markets—or markets that protect and promote the dignity and interests of citizens, workers, and consumers, not just that of multinationals, employers, or producers.

Often, the two are mutually dependent, as markets depend for their success on innovation and efficiency by producers. But where they conflict, democratic liberalism suggests that consumers and workers should take priority because the point of markets is to promote individual freedom and dignity—not for individuals to sacrifice that dignity in the service of generating returns for wealthy individuals or large corporations.

B. Concrete Proposals for Policy Reform

To illustrate these ideas, we further offer six key proposals consistent with the notion of democratic liberalism or a fair markets–based approach:

1. A universal jobs guarantee, which pays decent wages, is flexible, gives preferences to environmental or "green" projects but does not crowd out private-sector employment, and is complemented by policies designed to boost private-sector jobs and wages;
2. A significant increase in the minimum wage, but accompanied by a meaningful increase in government wage subsidies in the form of a generous earned income tax credit, wage earner equity schemes, and wage subsidies for new industries in towns with high unemployment;
3. Universal healthcare for all citizens, based on a two-track model of public and private provision, involving a strong and universal *public baseline*;
4. A similar public baseline for childcare and basic leave benefits (or holiday, sick, and parental leave for all workers), coupled with equality of access to quality education, from preschool to university, through a mix of special taxes and subsidies;
5. A new critical infrastructure policy for nation states to sit alongside a commitment to global free trade; and
6. Universal pollution taxes, with all proceeds returned directly to citizens by way of a green dividend.

The common theme of all the policies is that they combine a commitment to markets with democratic commitments to equal dignity for all citizens, and the regulation of markets in line with majority interests and understandings— or the idea that markets should be both free and fair and well-functioning, as opposed to simply "free." Because of this, they are also policies that are "blue," "pink," and "green."

They take seriously the needs and concerns of traditional blue-collar workers left vulnerable by the Covid-19 pandemic and recent neoliberal versions of liberalism. They emphasize a commitment to gender equality, or the need to ensure that caring responsibilities are put at the center of economic policies in liberal societies, so as to promote the interests of children and broader goals of gender equality both inside and outside the home. And they are consistently "green" in focus: they seek to align economic responses to problems of disadvantage in ways that ameliorate rather than worsen problems of environmental pollution and degradation.

Perhaps the best example of this is the jobs guarantee we propose: it is a policy that aims to guarantee decent work, wages, and benefits to any worker unable to find private-sector employment. In this sense its aims are fundamentally blue. However, in its design, the policy is also pink and green—namely, flexible and focused on environmental projects and remediation in ways that give it a broader social purpose. Other democratic liberal policies, however, also reflect this overlapping or intersectional approach to the democratic liberal project: for example, in addressing environmental externalities, we argue that all policies must be carefully designed to avoid worsening economic disadvantage and inequality.

C. Fair Economic and Political Markets

This vision of liberalism is quite distinct from neoliberal understandings that argue for completely free, *unregulated* markets and the withdrawal of the state as both economic regulator and guarantor of a generous social minimum, and regulator of market power and externalities. Instead, the idea of democratic liberalism is that markets can and should be regulated in order to serve citizen and consumer interests in guaranteeing a public baseline of core goods and regulating and overcoming market power and externalities, and in some cases even delivering actual equality, not just sufficiency of access to certain "relative" goods.

Democratic liberalism emphasizes liberal democratic commitments to dignity and equality, as well as freedom or autonomy. It also takes seriously the idea of economic and political self-government – that is, democratic decision making about what constitutes a dignified social minimum or externality, or how these and other forms of market failure should be addressed. This, in turn, means that it takes seriously the idea of both fair economic and political markets.

Unlike neoliberal approaches, democratic liberal (or fair market) approaches also reject the idea that the state should be "small" or retreat from large-scale welfare or spending programs. The age of austerity was dead long before Covid-19. If the 2008 global financial crisis taught us anything, it was that too little state regulation and spending can do just as much harm as too much state intervention. Covid-19 and the rise of "secular stagnation" have underlined that lesson.

But we also discuss how to make these policies economically and political sustainable—by proposing ways to fund them, and proposing democratic reforms consistent with a democratic liberal approach. Specifically, we argue for:

1. A new approach to debt, deficits, and government accounting that takes seriously the need to reduce long-term public sector debt, while also allowing for governments to invest in physical, social, and human capital and to respond to economic crises and "secular stagnation"; and
2. Competitive corporate tax rates, moderate taxes on capital and progressive income, *and* value added taxes as a means to pay for these policies.

Democratic liberalism, in this sense, is based not only on normative ideals but what is economically and politically sustainable—and achievable. Indeed, as we write this book we are heartened by signs that the United States—the world's largest market-based economy—is in fact moving toward a more fair markets–based approach. Despite Republicans in Congress railing against the Affordable Care Act, it has proved popular with voters, being viewed favorably by a 53%–34% margin.[12] And, the Biden administration has, in its early months, proposed initiatives that address, at least in part, our six policy proposals outlined above.

Whether our specific proposals are in fact viable or achievable will, of course, depend on the economic and political context and the level of democratic support for change. In some systems, there may also be especially large obstacles to achieving change because political as well as economic markets are "unfair" or poorly functioning and, therefore, tend to undermine momentum for more democratic liberal economic policies.

We seek, however, to lay out what a viable and pragmatic reform path could look like, in the hope that some political leaders and activists may see it as an appealing vision that is worth fighting for, within the constraints of their own political systems.

Finally, we make the case for these policies based on gaps and flaws in the liberal model in many countries prior to Covid-19, but especially in the United States. This reflects our experiences living and working in the that country. Current US economic and political debates are also referenced throughout the book, as a guide to understanding how our ideas translate into current real-world political debates. The cast of the 2020 Democratic presidential primary race features prominently in our story: we draw on both affinities and contrasts, at various points, with ideas proposed by Senators Bernie Sanders and Elizabeth Warren, President Joe Biden, and tech entrepreneur Andrew Yang.

D. Fair Markets and the Australian (Centrist?) Model

We also draw at various points on the experiences of our current home country, Australia. Australia is not fully democratically liberal, nor is democratic liberalism unique to Australia. Indeed, our hope is that the book will be read and considered by readers in a wide range of countries, many of whom will recognize the seeds of a democratic liberal approach within their own economics and politics. It is simply that the "Australian model" is often closer to our conception of the democratic liberal ideal than either the democratic socialist model that predominates in much of Europe or the laissez-faire capitalist model that prevails in the United States.

Australia's minimum wage is north of US$15 per hour, and unions have strong legal protections, but the employment system retains a significant degree of flexibility for employers. Australians are entitled to unemployment benefits without any hard end-date or time limit, and without having made any tax-based contribution to the system. But they are increasingly required to satisfy quite demanding work requirements in order to receive these benefits and are encouraged to return to work wherever possible. Australia has universal healthcare, but not a single-payer system. Australia has privatized many formerly state-owned enterprises, but control of water and prisons remains in government hands. Childcare in Australia is heavily subsidized but largely privately provided. The tax and transfer system is strongly progressive, reducing pretax income inequality substantially, but the tax-to-GDP ratio is 27.8% compared to the OECD average of 34.0%.

That is not to say that Australia has all the answers, or that it is unique in the answers it does offer. Rather, we see the Australian model as a framework that provides an antidote to the ills of liberalism, while preserving the power and virtues of markets. As such, it is likely to be of broad interest to those looking for new approaches to the economic and political challenges of the 21st century—but within a liberal rather than democratic socialist framework.

In this sense, the book offers a policy blueprint for an increasingly endangered part of the political spectrum for those who identify as independents, moderates, or within the political center. Both the current "left" and "right" will find much to hate, as well as some things to love, among the ideas we propose. The hope, however, is that these ideas will resonate with those in the United States and elsewhere looking for a new middle path or "third way" between the current political extremes.[13]

For many economists and political theorists, the ideas will be quite familiar. This is not a work of economic or political theory, nor an attempt to create a wholly new approach to liberalism or democratic constitutionalism. All of the ideas we propose are in some way novel or have some distinctive democratic liberal twist to them. But for the most part, our aim is to synthesize, explain, and refine the ideas offered by proponents of a capabilities approach and "progressive capitalism"—in the hope that greater numbers of policymakers and voters may engage with them more seriously.[14]

E. Structure of the Book

The remainder of this book proceeds as follows. Part I of the book provides the theoretical and contextual backdrop to the project. Chapter 2 explores ingoing fault lines within liberalism and the current free market economic paradigm. Liberalism, it suggests, is ultimately a theory that promises citizens equal freedom and dignity. Yet liberalism in recent decades has taken a distinctly "neoliberal" or free market turn, which has failed to deliver on this promise in at least four ways. First, forces of globalization, automation, and "gigification" have led to a long-term decline in access to decent work, wages, and entitlements for large portions of workers. Second, there has been a rise in the share of income and wealth, and slice of market power, enjoyed by the most wealthy and powerful individuals and corporations. And third, there has been a steady rise in environmental pollution and degradation, most notably in the form of carbon emissions, which now pose an existential threat to the planet but which most countries have done little to address. It also explores how the Covid-19 pandemic has exacerbated many of these fault lines within liberalism (i.e., worsened existing problems of unemployment, wage and job insecurity, and economic inequality).

Chapter 3 then considers the different potential philosophical responses to this crisis in liberalism, and the contrast between non-liberal ideas that reject the role of national and global markets (democratic socialism and economic nationalism) and what we label a "democratic liberal" approach: namely, one that starts with a commitment to individual freedom and free markets but seeks to respond to the failures of neoliberalism by asserting a more democratic form of liberalism, which affirms the importance of individual dignity and democratic regulatory control of markets to the legitimacy of the liberal project. This also entails four quite specific limits or "fetters" on free markets: (i) a commitment to ensuring universal access to a generous social minimum, or access to a public baseline of core goods; (ii) equal access to certain "relative" goods; (iii) democratic regulations to define and counter social costs, or externalities, arising from market-based transactions; and (iv) democratic regulation of markets to address the dangers of market or monopoly power. It also explains how these ideas apply to political as well as economic markets, and the precedent for (or beginning of) this kind of fair markets approach in many countries' response to the Covid-19 pandemic—and especially the early policies of the Biden administration.

Part II turns to the specific proposals we make for a more democratic rather than neoliberal approach, or to designing fairer, better-functioning markets now and in the future. It seeks to illustrate the three key components of a fair markets approach by reference to four concrete case studies.

Chapter 4 begins with a focus on work and unemployment. It makes the case for a response to the current crisis in work and wages and the likely acceleration of that crisis in the age of automation in the form of a universal jobs guarantee. It outlines how a fair markets approach could inform the design of such a guarantee: first, by pointing to the need for such a program to provide decent wages and benefits to all workers on a flexible basis, and to focus on meaningful projects with real social returns that offer workers a sense of dignity and purpose; and second, by ensuring that there remains an incentive for private-sector work. It also explores how governments could enhance this second aspect of a jobs guarantee by adopting a range of other policies designed to boost private-sector wages, including a generous earned income tax credit, incentives for universal wage earner equity, and appropriately targeted place-based policies involving wage subsidies.

Chapter 5 turns to a focus on healthcare and the idea of a public baseline of healthcare provision, as distinct from either a public option or public system of provision. Critics of neoliberalism have rightly highlighted the moral imperative of providing universal access to healthcare as a basic human right. The chapter argues, however, that it is a mistake to equate the need for universal access to healthcare with the need for universal government provision via a single-payer Medicare-style model. Instead, the chapter argues, there are strong arguments for combining a system of private health insurance and a model of basic state provision along the lines of the Australian healthcare model—that is, a public baseline level of healthcare topped up by private insurance. This approach, we argue, is both more affordable and sustainable than proposals in the United States for "Medicare for all," and more respectful of individual choice—especially choices to keep current insurance plans or current choice of doctor. The chapter also considers how similar principles could inform the development of a public baseline model of childcare and paid leave, and the differences as well as similarities between these "core" goods and relative goods such as elementary and secondary education.

Chapter 6 addresses questions of monopoly power and, from a democratic liberal or fair markets perspective, highlights the dangers of uncontrolled market power in free markets. It shows how monopoly power can lead to higher prices for consumers and, in some cases, shortages of core goods—including the Covid-19 vaccine. It also explains how market power in the form of informational power can lead markets to be inefficient or even break down, and how mandates for information provision can help prevent this unraveling. It further explains how a democratic liberal approach generally favors regulating the exercise of market power and preventing further market concentration, not "breaking up" existing firms; and how in some markets, especially technology markets, market power may in fact be more fragile than it first appears. In addition, it points to a form of strategic manufacturing of core goods such as food, medical supplies, and electricity to avoid problems of "holdup" by foreign allies and adversaries alike—but not to broader forms of economic protectionism.

Chapter 7 focuses on the environment as an illustration of the need for liberal societies to address problems of externalities. Climate change arguably poses an existential challenge not just to liberal societies, but to life on the planet as we know it. Responding to it is therefore a pressing global political priority. The chapter, however, explores the idea of a market-based approach that relies on carbon pricing or markets as the best solution, as well as ways of mitigating the potential dangers this poses to the enjoyment of a generous social minimum—through the redistribution of the proceeds of such a tax in the form of a "carbon dividend." It also considers other potential examples of this same approach, including in the context of a congestion tax and other forms of pollution regulation.

Part III then turns to considering how we pay for a shift from neoliberalism to democratic liberalism, or from free to fair markets. Some of our proposals are not cheap, which raises the obvious question of how they can be funded. We begin by exploring debt, deficits, and budgeting, and how governments and voters can distinguish between sustainable and "good" versus "bad" forms of government debt over the longer term. We also discuss a range of new approaches to tax—approaches that preserve commitments to markets and liberalism but effectively expand the revenue available to fund democratic liberal policies. Specifically, we propose the idea of a "progressive value-added tax" along with various increased compliance efforts and reliance on progressive income taxes and a meaningful, if competitive, corporate tax rate and increased taxes on capital, as preferable to reliance on wealth or estate taxes or extremely high personal income taxes. While we take the position that debt is cheap to service and likely to remain so in a post-Covid world, it is essential that—to be consistent with a commitment to markets and liberalism—the policies on which democratic liberalism rests are fiscally sustainable. This implies the importance of finding new, sustainable sources of revenue, though we reject other more radical proposals to increase taxes or rely on so-called modern monetary theory (MMT).

Chapter 9 offers a brief conclusion, focusing on the degree to which the ideas offered in the book are likely to appeal to voters in different countries and with different philosophies, and the extent to which they could be considered realistic, utopian, or apologist in nature. In doing so, it also considers the necessary democratic politics required to sustain a true form of democratic liberalism, and the connection between competitive economic and political markets.

2
The Crisis in (Neo)Liberalism

2022 is arguably a tough time to be a liberal. From the streets of Paris to the voting booths of England and the corridors of power in Washington, DC, the liberal ideas that have underpinned modern Western democracies are under attack. They are attacked by supporters of politicians on the left and the right, by urban voters and rural, by millennials and by seniors.

And, although the financial crisis of 2008—the "Great Recession" as it has become known—did not bring the same economic destruction that the Great Depression did 80 years earlier, it unleashed a wave of political upheaval of historic proportions. In the wake of the Great Recession, the United States elected an anti-establishment, isolationist, and openly protectionist president. Britain voted to leave the European Union and put the entire European project in jeopardy. A French president seemed at first confused by, but quickly capitulated to, "yellow-vest" protests against a gas tax that became about much more than that.

Indeed, institutions associated with free markets are now routinely vilified. The International Monetary Fund and the World Bank—two cornerstones of the 20th-century economic order—were blamed by *The Guardian* for both Brexit and the rise of Donald Trump.[1] The so-called Washington consensus involving financial liberalization, privatization, and fiscal balance is often held responsible for a range of ills across the developing world.

And the increasing concentration of income and wealth are routinely criticized as yet another sign that markets, and liberal democracy, are failing: the rock-star *du jour* of American politics, Democratic Socialist Alexandria Ocasio-Cortez, in fact suggested that "every billionaire is a policy failure."[2]

Contrast each of these facts with those a decade or two earlier. Both sides of US politics were pro–free trade, and President Bill Clinton signed the North American Free Trade Agreement (NAFTA). Years later President Barack Obama negotiated the Trans-Pacific Partnership (TPP), which was set to become the world's largest ever free trade deal, covering 40% of the world economy.

The world's first comprehensive climate change agreement—the Paris Agreement—bears the name of the city in which it was negotiated in December 2015, aiming, in the words of Barack Obama, to leave our children with "a world that is safer and more secure, more prosperous, and more free."[3] And, far from being "policy failures," no fewer than four media and technology billionaires (Ted Turner, Andy Grove, Jeff Bezos, and Mark Zuckerberg) were celebrated as *Time Magazine*'s Person of the Year.

A. Why the Crisis in Liberalism?

What, then, explains this recent turn against liberalism? Liberalism has always had its critics—on the right, communitarians have long pointed out the limits to liberalism in promoting feelings of community and belonging and membership among groups of individuals, and promoting individual duties and responsibilities as well as rights. And on the left, critics of liberalism have also highlighted its racist and imperialist origins, its failure to interrogate family and private life, and its failure to provide economic justice.

For instance, liberalism has been criticized for placing far too much emphasis on the individual and downplaying the importance of individuals' connection to their families and communities. Feminists, for example, have criticized liberal philosophy for failing to pay adequate attention to the family as opposed to the state, and for failing to interrogate the ways in which the "private" domain is often a site of injustice for women.[4] Feminist scholars such as Jennifer Nedelsky have likewise suggested that liberalism needs radically to be rethought in light of the importance of human relationships and interconnectedness.[5]

Others challenge liberalism for its emphasis on individual rights and freedoms over our individual duties and obligations. Mary Ann Glendon suggests that liberalism has become a discourse that promotes individual rights over obligations and, in the process, has eroded notions of civic duty, civic responsibility, and collective social life.

Others challenge liberalism and its commitment to market-based forms of ordering as placing too much emphasis on material over spiritual well-being, and as fundamentally failing to respect other nonhuman species and the planet. The age of liberalism has been the age of the "anthropocene": a period in which human activity has dominated other species, and our environment and has led to lasting forms of environmental damage and degradation.[6] Many environmental critics also link this to the inherent consumerist, anthropocentric biases within liberalism.

Many social democratic—and certainly Marxist—critics of liberalism note its tendency to produce, and reproduce, structures of economic inequality—or systematically to privilege capital over labor.

And critical race and post-colonial scholars highlight the connection between liberalism, racism, and colonialism. For much of its history, liberalism effectively celebrated the freedom of white propertied men and failed to embrace norms of equality for indigenous people or other racial minorities. The critical left has long highlighted the capacity of liberal legal and economic models to legitimate injustice, not just counter it.

These criticisms also all have powerful bases and are worthy of serious consideration. For any modern political philosophy to be attractive, it must certainly take seriously the importance of family and community, social obligations as well as individual rights, environmental stewardship, racial, global, and economic (in)equality. And classical liberalism is surely in need of renovation: the ideas of the 18th and 19th centuries do not provide an adequate basis for responding to the challenges of globalization, the robot age, or indeed climate change as an existential threat to current democratic liberal systems.

Liberals, however, have responded to these criticisms by showing the potential for liberal theories to adapt to include deeper commitments to gender, sexual, and racial equality, to provide space for civic organizations that promote community and greater equality and inclusion, and to support various forms of economic redistribution through democratically enacted "tax and transfer" policies. Many of these answers have been imperfect and incomplete, but they have still persuaded many on the right and left that it is better to continue to work within the liberal tradition to reform it than to abandon it in favor of wholly illiberal or non-liberal alternatives.

The crisis facing liberalism in 2022 is thus of a new magnitude and urgency, and arguably more recent origin. We focus on three central areas in which liberalism has gone wrong in recent decades: first, the decline in work, wages, and entitlements; second, the rise of the mega-corporation and income and wealth-based inequality; and third, the failure to tackle social costs—including the most pressing "externality" of our time, namely the existential threat posed by climate change. As we explain below, at least the first two of these failures have also been dramatically worsened by the Covid-19 pandemic and its wide-ranging health and economic impacts.

(i) Trend 1: The Decline in Work, Wages, and Entitlements

By almost any measure the world economy has become radically more inter-connected over the past several decades. There have been numerous attempts to create indices that quantify the extent of globalization, using a wide range of factors. One widely cited index[7]—which points to increasing interconnec-tedness—includes measures of international trade, financial market integra-tion, participation in United Nations peacekeeping missions, international voice traffic, tourism, international student flows, even the global spread of IKEA and McDonald's.

One of the more profound consequences of globalization has been that more than two billion people in the developing world have been lifted out of extreme poverty. The World Bank has reported that the proportion of people worldwide that live in extreme poverty has now fallen below 10% (from 37% in 1990) for the first time.[8]

In advanced economies, consumers have seen a drastic improvement in the value-for-money of the goods and services they purchase. From kids' toys to refrigerators, television sets to clothing, globalization has consistently led to significantly increased variety, higher quality, and lower prices of consumer products, just as economic theory predicts.[9]

At one level it is fairly obvious why this is a good thing for consumers—they can access better products at lower prices. But there is a broader impli-cation of this fact. The social minimum is not simply about a specific amount of money, it is about access to a particular bundle of goods and services. Consequently, it is linked to purchasing power, which is determined both by one's income and also the cost of that consumption bundle. Viewed through this lens, one effect of globalization has been to make the social minimum more attainable.

The price of this gain to consumers, however, has been a loss of manufacturing jobs in many advanced economies. Figure 2.1 shows the dra-matic fall in US manufacturing employment from nearly 21 million persons in the late 1980s to around 13.3 million in 2010—a fall of more than a third. There has been some rebound since the depths of the Great Recession, yet manufacturing employment still stands at just 14.6 million. Moreover, this re-bound has largely been in more advanced manufacturing which, while posi-tive and encouraging, has tended to benefit higher-paid workers.[10]

Worse still than the large loss of manufacturing jobs has been the geo-graphic concentration of those losses. Industries tend to cluster geograph-ically. Perhaps the most famous illustration of this is the technology and

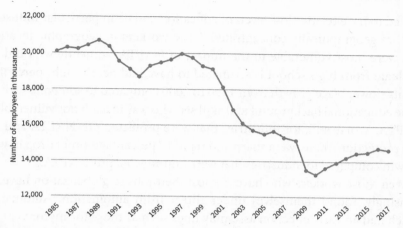

Figure 2.1 US Manufacturing Employment, 1985–2017

venture capital sectors in Silicon Valley, but manufacturing in states like Michigan, Wisconsin, Ohio, and Indiana is similarly concentrated.

So, when the Great Recession hit and the US car industry was hammered, unemployment in Detroit rose to 28.4%. At the time of writing, it still stood at 9.5% compared to less than 4% for the United States as a whole.[11] And while unemployment overall in the so-called Rust Belt has continued to fall, so have wages. The $25 per-hour manufacturing jobs with good benefits have routinely been replaced by $12 per-hour service sector jobs with fewer or no benefits.[12]

This can be seen most starkly in the manufacturing sector, which is highly exposed to the pressures of globalization and the rise of countries such as China. The growth of manufacturing in China has been extraordinary. In the 20 years beginning in 1991, China went from having 4.1% of worldwide manufacturing, in value-added terms, to 24.0%.[13] One country that was particularly impacted by this was the United States. A recent study by MIT economists identified a causal relationship between globalization—the rise of China in particular—and the contraction of employment as well as plant closures in the United States.[14] Related work demonstrates that one-quarter of the decline in US manufacturing employment can be attributed to competition from imports.[15]

The effect of globalization is also not confined to the manufacturing sector, or even just tradeable goods, nor is China the only "culprit." Both Donald Trump and Bernie Sanders railed against NAFTA in the 2016 presidential campaign, and there is persuasive empirical evidence NAFTA has had a causal effect on the employment prospects (and wages) of certain US workers. But again, the pockets of workers that have been hit hardest by NAFTA have tended to have relative low levels of education and be in particular industries that are geographically concentrated.[16] For workers in geographic locations that were most vulnerable to the impact of NAFTA, someone who did not graduate from high school is estimated to have had nearly eight percentage points slower wage growth from 1990 to 2000 compared to someone with the same educational background and skill set who was in a job not vulnerable to NAFTA. Worse still, for industries that were protected pre-NAFTA and lost that protection, there was a sharp and rapid 17 percentage-point drop in wage growth compared to industries that were unprotected pre-NAFTA.[17]

Even those workers who have not lost their jobs to globalization have, increasingly, found themselves under threat from automation. Automation, which had an early effect on assembly lines such as those for motor vehicles, has emerged as a threat to the jobs of millions in a wide variety of sectors.

For instance, 2.4 million people in the United States drive trucks for a living. Add to that 500,000 school bus drivers, 160,000 transit bus drivers, and 340,000 taxi or Uber drivers, and one quickly sees a threat to 3.4 million American jobs from autonomous vehicles. Amazon Go's checkout-free shopping technology could put 3.5 million cashiers out of work in the United States if it was applied widely.

More broadly, it has been estimated that up to 14% of jobs in OECD countries are highly subject to automation, and a further 32% could face significant changes to how they are carried out.[18] Some studies paint an even bleaker picture. Carl Benedikt Frey and Michael A. Osborne estimate that 47% of all people employed in the United States are currently working in jobs that could be performed by computers and algorithms within the next 10–20 years.[19] According to PwC, in the United Kingdom up to 30% of jobs could be at high risk of automation by the early 2030s, compared to 35% in Germany, 38% in the United States, and 21% in Japan.[20] For Europe as a whole, it is estimated that the share of jobs at risk of automation ranges between 45% to more than 60%, with southern European workforces facing the highest exposure to a potential automation.[21]

Perhaps due to the readily identifiable job losses and unclear job gains, this has led many people to speculate that automation could have a potentially catastrophic effect on employment. Moreover, these effects may be particularly concentrated. Whatever the impact of automation, it seems quite likely that it will be far from uniform—even within industries. Certain tasks lend themselves to automation, whereas others might be able to resist even sophisticated machine-learning algorithms. If so, those with high levels of human capital will be insulated from the downsides of automation, while others with lower levels of human capital bear the brunt of it. As Erik Brynjolfsson and Andrew

McAfee put it in their acclaimed work *The Second Machine Age*, "there's never been a better time to be a worker with special skills or the right education, because these people can use technology to create and capture value. However, there's never been a worse time to be a worker with only 'ordinary' skills and abilities to offer, because computers, robots, and other digital technologies are acquiring these skills and abilities at an extraordinary rate."[22]

This adds up to a depressing picture of shrinking overall employment—and radically shrinking employment prospects for the less skilled. Yet, there have been equally genuine concerns in the past about the prospect of automation wiping out swathes of jobs but providing insufficient replacements. As MIT economist David Autor points out, in the early 1960s *Time Magazine* ran a story called "The Automation Jobless" in which they observed "automation is beginning to move in and eliminate office jobs too . . . . In the past, new industries hired far more people than those they put out of business. But this is not true of many of today's new industries . . . . Today's new industries have comparatively few jobs for the unskilled or semiskilled, just the class of workers whose jobs are being eliminated by automation."[23]

This type of concern even led to President Lyndon Johnson, in 1964, empaneling a "Blue-Ribbon National Commission on Technology, Automation, and Economic Progress." In light of this, it is reasonable to ask why this time is different. If technological progress from the time of the printing press has led to disruptive job losses but net job gains, won't the same thing happen in the current era?

There are good reasons to believe that this time is, indeed, different. The advent of huge amounts of data and the computing power to process it means that automation through machine-learning algorithms is qualitatively different from the mechanized automation of the past. Machines of the past were able to plow fields and hammer nails more efficiently than humans could. Modern machines can do much more than that.

There is a vertical-efficiency dimension to modern automation that is arguably *quantitatively* different from the past. There are physical limits—perhaps quite stringent ones—to how efficient a mechanical plow can be. Mechanical power is limited by Newton's laws. Computing power, by contrast, seems to know almost no limits. The famous and roughly-empirically-accurate fact of Moore's Law—that computing power doubles every two years—has seen, literally, the exponential growth of the ability of machines to perform a wide range of tasks. The tantalizing prospect of a widely used quantum computer suggests that computing power is limited by the laws of Einstein, not Newton.

Practical applications of this have already had significant impacts on employment—even of individuals with seemingly high human capital.

For instance, legal discovery is now routinely performed, in large part, by computers rather than law school graduates. Baseball scouts have been largely replaced by Moneyball-type statistical analysis. Financial advisors are increasingly being replaced by so-called robo advisors like Wealthfront.[24]

Yet, machine learning offers not only the prospect of performing tasks more efficiently, but also helping define what the relevant tasks themselves are. This represents a *qualitative* break from the past history of automation. One step in this direction is *unsupervised machine learning*, which identifies commonalities in data and uses them to process new data, rather than being instructed how data are to be classified or "labeled."

Among the more dramatic labor-displacing technologies in recent decades have been robots. These robots came to dominate manufacturing lines many years ago, but now offer the prospect of replacing workers who drive trucks or, possibly, even perform surgery for a living. In fact, modern robots that can perform complex tasks—like driving trucks or altogether replacing scanners at supermarket checkouts—utilize artificial intelligence. In that sense, the term *robot* is, sometimes appropriately, used as a catchall. And sometimes, when people talk about a "robot tax" they really mean a tax on the use of artificial intelligence (such as that used in text recognition) as well as when a physical robot is involved.

There do seem to be limits to the reach of automation, and there is a vigorous debate about exactly what those limits are. David Autor, for instance, coins the term *Polanyi's Paradox* after the notable polymath who, in 1966, observed "We know more than we can tell." For Autor, this means that tasks "demanding flexibility, judgment, and common sense" are the most challenging to automate.[25] Surely there is a good deal of truth to this, and it suggests that the qualitative break whereby machine learning and artificial intelligence not only perform tasks but define them may come slowly, if at all.

Wherever the automation revolution stops, it is definitely a bad time to be a bus driver or cashier. And although these people may find other work, the skills they possess may mean that those new jobs are also at risk from other new technology.

One of the more remarkable trends in theUnited States in recent years has been the rise of the so-called gig economy. A 2018 Gallup report documented the extent of the gig economy. Taking a fairly broad definition of what constitutes a "gig worker" to include independent contractors, online platform workers, those who work for labor-hire and contract firms, as well as on-call and temporary workers, Gallup concluded that as many as 57 million Americans are part of the gig economy. This represents 36% of the American workforce and nearly a quarter of full-time workers.[26]

Both the gig economy and offshoring of workers have been called "fissuring" by David Weil—a term that usefully highlights that all of these jobs would once have been performed by employees of corporations.[27] As Cynthia Estlund points out, the gig economy workers we have in mind here are one part of a broader phenomenon of fissuring.[28] While some of these workers are relatively fortunate—working as well-paid and self-employed contractors— others are in a much more precarious position involving uncertain work, low wages, and minimal if any benefits. Indeed, the term *gig economy* is often used in a somewhat pejorative manner, indicating relative low pay, the absence of benefits like healthcare, and lack of job security.

Taken together, these factors have put meaningful downward pressure on wages—particularly for workers with lower levels of formal education. It is these workers whose jobs are more readily "offshored" to workers in lower-wage countries, and whose jobs are more likely to be able to be automated. It is then no surprise, though it is a major concern, that workers in jobs like truck driving, supermarket cashiering, or warehouse stacking and picking have seen both their jobs and their wages come under significant pressure.

Wages are determined by the "outside option" that workers and firms have, and by their relative bargaining power. Automation and globalization have given firms better alternatives or outside options, and workers worse ones.

(ii) Trend 2: Mega-corporate Power and Rising Economic Inequality

In addition, there has been a marked shift in the relative bargaining power of workers and firms, due in large part to the decline of trade unions and the rise of the "mega-corporation." One thing that trade unions do is give workers more bargaining power than they might otherwise have. The ability to bargain collectively often puts workers in a stronger position than they would be bargaining as individuals. Over the last several decades, there has also been a striking decline in rates of unionization in the United States.

The proportion of workers now belonging to a trade union now stands at 10.5%, compared to 20.1% in 1983.[29] In the private sector, rates are even lower—around 7%, which is a lower level than at any point since the early 1930s. And this phenomenon is not limited to the United States. Unionization rates are at historic lows in many countries around the world, standing at 7.9% in France, 14.6% in Australia, and 17.0% in Germany.[30]

On the other side of the wage-bargaining table, there has been an increase in the rise of mega-employers such as Walmart and Amazon. These corporations have substantial power as employers of huge numbers of workers, and this additional bargaining power means that even unionized workers bargaining collectively can have a hard time getting an increase in real wages.

But this is not the only change in the employment landscape. There has been a surprising return to highly concentrated local labor markets, even if those employers aren't behemoths like Walmart or Amazon. The late 19th century witnessed the rise of the "company town," where firms like railroad car manufacturer Pullman essentially built towns next to their factories and often acted as both landlord and employer.

As literally the only employer in the town, this put companies like Pullman in an incredibly strong bargaining position. Workers wanting better conditions would have to credibly threaten to leave. But how credible could that threat be if it meant having to move—with their whole family—to a completely different town?

Although the 19th-century version of the company town rarely exists any more, a modern version has taken its place. Healthcare workers, such as nurses and doctors who live outside of major urban areas, often have only one or two potential employers within a reasonable commute of their home. Similarly, in industries ranging from agribusiness to livestock processing, a single employer often dominates local communities. Switching jobs often means uprooting families and lives—and employers know that.

There are plenty of anecdotes, from chicken processing plants to healthcare clinics, attesting to this trend. More concretely, José Azar, Ioana Marinescu, Marshall Steinbaum, and Bledi Taska assembled data on essentially all online US job vacancies and calculated how concentrated labor markets are using the standard economic measure (the Herfindahl-Hirschman index or "HHI") for every US commuting zone. They found that 54% of labor markets are highly concentrated by the Department of Justice and Federal Trade Commission definition. These highly concentrated markets account for more than one-sixth of all employment in the United States.[31]

This labor market concentration is troubling enough on its face, but it has also been shown to lead to exactly what economic theory and common sense suggests it would—lower wages. In other work by an overlapping set of authors José Azar, Ioana Marinescu, and Marshall Steinbaum show that the causal effect of moving from the 25th percentile to the 75th percentile in concentration is a 17% decline in wages.[32]

Even more than this, there is an interaction effect between labor market concentration and levels of unionization. Efraim Benmelech, Nittai Bergman, and Hyunseob Kim use census data from 1977 to 2009 to offer evidence consistent with that of Azar, Marinescu, and Steinbaum that there is a negative relationship between local-level employer concentration and wages.[33] Moreover, this is getting worse over time, and finally the negative relationship between labor market concentration and wages is more pronounced in areas where unionization rates are low. Indeed, these authors claim that when one adds two additional empirical facts—that productivity growth and wage growth is stronger when labor markets are less concentrated, and exposure to greater import competition from China leads to more concentrated labor markets—most of the wage stagnation of recent decades can be explained. As they put it "These five results emphasize the role of local-level labor market monopsonies in influencing firm wage-setting behavior and can explain the stagnation of wages in the United States over the past several decades."

Concentration is one thing, but unlawful restrictions on the mobility of workers is quite another. Suresh Naidu, Eric A. Posner, and Glen Weyl have recently argued that antitrust law—particularly the analysis of the anticompetitive effects of mergers—needs to be seriously rethought in light of these issues.[34] But there is also ample evidence of behavior by certain employers restricting labor mobility that is already unlawful.

So-called no-poaching agreements, where employers agree not to hire each other's workers, have become infamous in Silicon Valley since news surfaced of exchanges between Steve Jobs and Sergey Brin.[35] Apple and Google were prosecuted in 2010 for these kinds of agreements.[36] However, the practice extends beyond highly paid software engineers. Bloomberg reported no-poaching agreements among fast-food restaurants and tax-preparation firms.[37] Beyond this there is the increasing prevalence of "non-compete" clauses in employment contracts. These clauses were once largely reserved for senior executives, often in fields with a substantial client/customer base or significant intellectual property, but have now become widespread in employment contracts for relatively low-level employees, as Evan Star, J.J. Prescott, and Norman Bishara have documented.[38]

A striking example they cite is Amazon warehouse employees or "packers" who are seasonally employed but are required to sign the following: "for 18 months after the Separation Date, Employee will not . . . engage in or support the development, manufacture, marketing, or sale of any product or service that competes or is intended to compete with any product or service sold, offered, or otherwise provided by Amazon."

The authors conducted a nationally representative survey of more than 11,000 workers and found that in 2014, around one in five workers were bound by non-compete clauses and that nearly two in five have been bound at some point in their life. They also found that while such clauses are more prevalent in high-skill jobs, they are quite common in low-skill jobs—as in the case of Amazon. Shockingly, fewer than 10% of employees negotiate over the clause—suggesting they are unaware of it or lack sufficient bargaining power to resist the imposition of it. Worse still, around one-third of such clauses are signed *after* an employment offer has been accepted, suggesting opportunistic "hold-up" behavior on the part of the employer.[39]

By removing the possibility of the most natural source of alternative employment, these clauses severely weaken the bargaining positions of workers and effectively put a lid on wage increases. A senior executive may find it easy—perhaps desirable—to take a two-year break after leaving his or her position, somewhat nullifying the bargaining impact of the non-compete clause. Relatively low-level employees typically just cannot afford to be out of the workforce for an extended period of time—and the employers who demand that they sign these contracts know it when considering changes to their wages, benefits, and conditions.

Indeed, one of the long-run trends going into 2020 was the rise in the power of large firms. David Autor and coauthors have documented the rise over the last 30 years of what they call "superstar" firms that have come to dominate markets.[40] For instance, the five largest publicly traded firms in the world are currently: Apple, Google/Alphabet, Amazon, Microsoft, and Facebook.

In August 2018 Apple became the first company to have a market capitalization of more than $1 trillion.

These firms all operate in markets with significant "network externalities." That is, the more people that consume their products the more attractive they become to other people. Amazon is attractive to consumers because there are more than 500 million products available on the US site, and because there are lots of customers, this makes it attractive to sellers to participate in Amazon Marketplace. Facebook is popular in no small part because there are so many other people (more than 2 billion) on Facebook. Google's search engine is popular because it returns very accurate searches, and the accuracy of its algorithm is improved by machine learning applied to a huge volume of searches.

Moreover, this is not just limited to markets with strong network effects—such as technology platforms like Uber, Amazon, or Facebook—but is broadly true across different sectors and industries.[41] In financial services, large firms are able to access wholesale funding more cheaply than smaller firms and offer the prospect of a "one-stop shop" for many customers. This has not only led to the "too big to fail" problems so acutely highlighted by the financial crisis in 2008, but also to concerns about banks pushing customers into their own wealth-management products and into inferior financial arrangements because of internal incentives and pressure.

Gauti Eggertson, Jacob Rollins, and Ellen Wold provide evidence that since the 1980s, economic rents—which are precisely the returns earned by firms above what would be earned in a competitive market—have risen from 3% of income to 17%.[42] Consistent with both of these findings, Jan De Loeckeer, Jan Eeckhout, and Gabriel Unger use firm-level data to show that markups—the ratio of the price that firms sell goods for over their marginal cost of production—has risen from 21% in the 1980s to 61% today. Despite there being some debate about what the exactly correct measure of "marginal cost" is,[43] even the most optimistic interpretation is that there has been a continued rise of markups since 1955 that has gone uninterrupted.

In the two years prior to Covid-19, "trillion dollar" firms began to exist as the technology giants Apple, Amazon, and Microsoft achieved market capitalizations previously hard to imagine. Indeed, during the early days of the Covid-19 crisis, with tech firms seeing expanded opportunities because of remote work and the increased demand for online shopping and electronic commerce, pundits began to muse about which company would become the first "$2 trillion firm."

Together with globalization, automation, "gigification" and decline of unions, this rise of the mega-corporation has also meant that there has been a quite clear, secular trend toward increased economic insecurity for ordinary workers combined with economic *security*—indeed riches—for an ever-smaller proportion of citizens.

In the United States, the top 1% of households now hold more wealth than the entire middle class (Figure 2.2). Since the Great Recession of 2008, it is

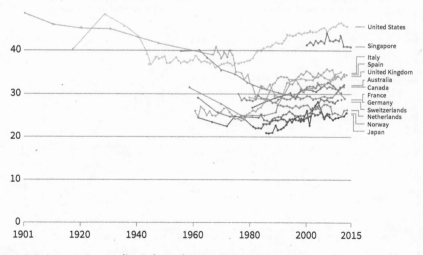

Figure 2.2 Income Inequality Selected Countries, 1901–2015

only the wealth of the top one-fifth of households that has bounced back.[44] And, famously, three Americans have more wealth than the entire bottom half of their compatriots.[45] This pattern is also replicated, albeit to a somewhat lesser degree, in countries around the world.

Part of this income inequality (Figure 2.3) involves the very large incomes earned by a very small number of people. This extreme wealth has also been growing markedly in recent decades in certain countries.

Why? In a somewhat unlikely bestseller, *Capital in the 21st Century*, the celebrated French economist Thomas Piketty pointed out that when returns to capital exceed the rate of economic growth in the economy, there is upward pressure on income inequality.[46] This suggests that inequality is not merely a feature of the United States or some particular group of economies, but that there is an underlying tectonic force that pushes advanced economies toward increased inequality. That conclusion has been sharply disputed, and that debate is an important one, for it speaks directly to what are the appropriate policy responses to inequality.[47] But it is important to acknowledge the increase in inequality in many countries around the world, as an undeniable and secular trend in many liberal democracies.

One point that bears emphasizing in this context, however, relates to "net" versus "gross" measures of inequality. While there have been varying degrees of increases in pre-tax-and-transfer income inequality around the world, countries with progressive taxation and redistribution systems have not seen such a sharp rise in the effective level of income inequality.[48]

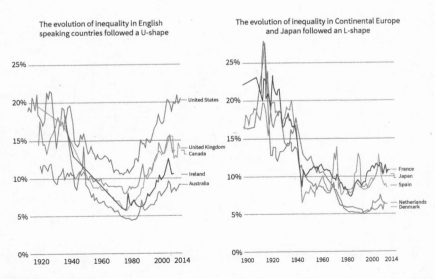

Figure 2.3 Top Incomes

Inequality of this kind also makes the crisis in work and wages worse in at least three ways: it has a "miner's canary effect," or tells ordinary workers that the current crisis is an avoidable one; it has spillover effects on the affordability of certain core goods, where consumption is inherently rivalrous; and often it undermines the political pressure for change to current policies on work and wages.

The extreme wealth of the few certainly suggests that there is enough wealth to go around—that the question is one of distribution, not scarcity per se. Further, extreme wealth tends to drive up the price of a range of core goods in ways that further compound the economic pressures on individuals caused by a decline in work and wages. It can also undermine the equal enjoyment of core goods—such as education and housing close to areas of work and study—that have an inherently rivalrous or tournament-like quality.

Often, as US presidential candidates such as Senators Bernie Sanders and Elizabeth Warren have repeatedly emphasized, it can also undermine the likelihood of achieving the political change needed to address problems in liberalism—by giving wealthy political donors disproportionate influence over legal and policy outcomes.

The combination of economic inequality driving a larger number of extremely high-net-worth individuals and the January 2010 *Citizens United* decision of the United States Supreme Court, has led to an explosion of money in US politics.[49] Not all of this increase comes from high-net-worth individuals, and not all of the increase occurred after the *Citizens United* decision. But it is hard to dispute, and the 2020 Presidential election cycle bore out the point, that there is an extraordinary amount of money from wealthy individuals and powerful vested interests seeking to influence the outcomes of elections in the United States.

(iii) Trend 3: The Environment

It has been apparent for decades now that humans have been having a significant effect on the planet's climate through carbon and other emissions. As far back as 1896, Swedish scientist Svante Arrhenius suggested that burning of fossil fuels such as coal—which increased the amount carbon dioxide gas in the earth's atmosphere—would raise the planet's average temperature. This, of course, is the famous "greenhouse effect," and Arrhenius provided the first calculation of its magnitude.[50]

Although it took time for the science of global warming to prove out Arrhenius's initial claim, we have witnessed for nearly half a century now—from the 1970s to today—increasingly credible, precise, and dire warnings about the calamity that climate change represents. And, to match those warnings we have seen, from a policy perspective, what can only be described as profoundly inadequate action from countries around the world.

As long ago as 1975, the phrase "global warming" was used in a peer-reviewed academic journal—a *Science* article by geochemist Wallace Broecker of Columbia University's Lamont-Doherty Geological Observatory: "Climatic Change: Are We on the Brink of a Pronounced Global Warming?"[51]

In 1979 the US National Academy of Sciences launched a report—often known as Charney Report after its chairperson, Massachusetts Institute of Technology professor Jule Charney—stating that "if carbon dioxide continues to increase, [we find] no reason to doubt that climate changes will result and no reason to believe that these changes will be negligible."[52]

On June 23, 1988, James Hansen of the NASA Goddard Space Institute gave testimony to the US Senate Committee on Energy and Natural Resources about global warming, summarizing the research of he and his colleagues that emphasized three conclusions. First, the earth was warmer in 1988 than at any point in history. Second, there was a causal relationship between greenhouse gas emissions and global warming. Third, the greenhouse effect was large enough in magnitude to affect the probability of extreme weather events.[53]

In 1989—in what now seems like an extraordinary thing for a conservative leader to say—the prime minister of the United Kingdom, Margaret Thatcher, delivered a speech to the United Nations calling for a global treaty on climate change and saying that "We are seeing a vast increase in the amount of carbon dioxide reaching the atmosphere . . . The result is that change in future is likely to be more fundamental and more widespread than anything we have known hitherto."[54]

Some 30 years ago in 1990, the International Panel on Climate Change (IPCC) issued a report warning that the world faced an average likely increase in global temperatures of 0.3°C per decade: 1.0°C by 2025 and 3.0°C by the end of the century.[55] And, as predicted, the average temperature of the earth's surface has in fact increased by about 0.6 degrees Celsius (1.0 degrees Fahrenheit) in the last three decades, and global sea levels have risen by around 3mm per year in recent decades, largely due to an increase in CO_2 and other human-emitted greenhouse gases in the atmosphere.[56]

The changing climate is also understood to have a range of current and potential impacts. These include an increase in the number and intensity of natural disasters, the loss of large tracts of habitable land, the extinction of animal and plants species, and significant implications for human health due to, for example, increased air pollution.[57]

B. Fault Lines in Liberalism after Covid-19

Each of these trends demonstrates aspects of the failure of liberal democracies to live up to the true meaning of their ideals, or as economist John Quiggin puts it, that "the economic system we have used to allocate resources and investments for the last forty years is no longer fit for purpose."[58]

The decline in work, wages, and entitlements has meant that hard work is no longer a guarantee of economic self-sufficiency in ways that are contrary to democratic liberalism's focus on a generous social minimum, along with work as a source of community and dignity. Linked to this has also been an increase in income inequality in most advanced economies in recent decades, and the rise of the "superstar firm" and "mega-corporation" that has led to a reconfiguration of bargaining power throughout these economies. And the failure to appropriately account for social costs as part of the market mechanism has led to a systematic failure to address climate change.

Moreover, many of these ingoing fault lines in liberalism have only become wider, and worse, during the Covid-19 pandemic. By the time the pandemic is brought under control globally, a significant proportion of people in liberal democracies will have lost their jobs, and some of those jobs will never return in economies that are structurally changed by the crisis. In some instances that will be an acceleration of ingoing trends in certain sectors and industries, and in other cases the prospect of another major public health crisis will lead businesses to transform how they operate. As we go on to discuss later in this book, the social ills from unemployment are very significant and can have a large impact on individuals, households, and communities.

It is, at this point, too early to provide definitive statistics, but the isolation and anxiety—both economic and social—caused by the Covid-19 crisis will lead many people to turn to drugs and alcohol as a coping mechanism. There is already compelling evidence that poor economic prospects and communities in economic decline in parts of the United States contributed to the opioid epidemic that has killed tens of thousands of people every year though the abuse of various substances, including prescription opioids and fentanyl, although recent work by Janet Currie and Hannes Schwandt shows that specific features of the US healthcare market played a very significant role.[59]

The pandemic has also put healthcare systems in advanced economies—systems that were once thought robust—under massive strain. And this strain revealed deep flaws in the structure of those healthcare systems in many countries, especially the United States. The large number of infections quickly overwhelmed hospital systems in countries like Italy and Spain. Even in New York City, home to some of the best hospitals in the world, the healthcare system could not keep up. Perhaps no fact better captures the impossible pressure hospitals were under than Spain using an Olympic ice rink as a temporary morgue and a park in New York City being dug up to temporarily inter the dead.

So stretched were hospitals in the United Kingdom that the official catchphrase used by the government, urging people to abide by stay-at-home orders once they were enacted, was, "Stay home, save lives, protect the NHS," referring to the National Health Service's ability to cope with the influx of Covid-19 cases.

The US hospital system was so overrun by the virus that by mid-May 2020, the US Army Corps of engineers had built 37 field hospitals in convention centers around the country to deal with the surge in hospitalizations due to Covid-19.

Not only has the availability of hospital beds been overwhelmed by Covid-19, but testing resources have failed to keep up with the number of tests needed to have an adequate picture of the course of the pandemic and to take appropriate measures for those who are infected. An interactive *New York Times* chart shows the evolution of testing rates per capita in a number of countries with some of the most advanced and well-resourced healthcare systems in the world. Even by mid-May 2020—well into the pandemic and with many countries beginning to reopen from lockdowns—only one country (Denmark) was conducting more than 150 tests per 100,000 people per day, and only four were conducting more than 100 such tests per day. Yet, the best epidemiological advice suggested that 152 tests per 100,000 people per day was the minimum level required to safely reopen an economy from lockdown.[60]

Some healthcare systems performed well during the crisis—Australia, Taiwan, Singapore, and New Zealand are notable examples—but that was in no small part due to the fact that in those countries the response to the pandemic was sufficiently rapid and comprehensive that their healthcare systems were never tested with a large caseload. As we shall see in Chapter 4, most of these countries also all have a form of democratic liberal approach to healthcare.

On one level, there was a sense in which the virus did not respect wealth in its impact. Nobody was immune from it, and in many ways all people had to abide by shelter-in-place orders. In some ways the virus flattened inequality because it seemed to affect all people—or at least have the potential to do so. High-ranking government officials like US President Trump, UK Prime Minister Boris Johnson, Canadian Prime Minister Justin Trudeau, German Chancellor Angela Merkel, and Australian homeland security minister Peter Dutton all had health scares to varying degrees early in the course of the pandemic. In Australia and New Zealand, some government officials were stood down for breaching shelter-in-place orders that needed compliance by all.

In other very important ways, there was a material increase in inequality stemming from the pandemic. Many of the job losses due to lockdown provisions have been concentrated in the services sector among people toward the lower end of income distribution. Waiters, taxi and Uber drivers, and other people whose jobs involve close physical contact were the first to see their jobs essentially banned by government fiat.

To a first approximation, it was the people most likely to be living paycheck-to-paycheck who lost their paycheck first. In countries like the United States, where benefits such as healthcare are often tied to the employment relationship, this has had an additional destructive effect.

By contrast, the jobs most likely to be able to be performed from home are generally those held by higher-income earners who need little more than a computer and Internet connection to be able to be productive. And although these people experience isolation, too, they have work to occupy their time and give them a sense of purpose, and a greater ability to avoid infection by not needing to leave their homes. On top of all of this, the homes of the more affluent are obviously more comfortable places in which to be confined. They tend to be larger, better equipped, and are more likely to have what has now become a precious commodity—high-speed Internet access.

Cell-phone location data released by Google and Facebook also sheds some light on who is able to stay home. Although these data have been anonymized to the point that individual-level demographics are not available, it is possible to look at the movements of people in poorer versus more affluent neighborhoods in particular cities. For instance, Reuters noted that, based on Facebook data, "In New York, for example, researchers found mobility dropped significantly on the weekends but crept back up on weekdays, when many people—particularly those living in low-income neighborhoods—are still required to work."

On top of this were the stark differences in the experience of shelter-in-place orders as a function of wealth. In New York City, it was again widely observed that more affluent residents of the city could quite readily escape to vacation homes, while the less affluent obviously could not do so—let alone leave the place where they needed to perform their essential-service jobs.[61] It's fair to say that sacrifices made during the pandemic were sharply different depending on one's wealth, job security, and ability to perform jobs remotely.

And the experience of the pandemic has shone a light once again on the extent of unequal access in so many countries to the economic baseline necessary for a life worthy of full human dignity.[62] Or perhaps more to the point, existing structural inequalities were put on stark display.

Of the first 100,000 people to die in the United States due to Covid-19, more than 23% were African American, despite the fact that African Americans make up just 13% of the population.[63] In Louisiana, blacks accounted for 70% of the deaths but 33% of the population. In Alabama, they accounted for 44% of the deaths and 26% of the population.[64]

The Center for Disease Control (CDC) has pointed out that disparities in living and working conditions play a fundamental role in these health outcomes.[65] And the CDC goes on to point out that racial and ethnic minorities typically live in more densely populated areas and thus find it harder to comply with physical distancing guidelines. Economic geography and what is sometimes called "racial residential segregation" is strongly associated with health disparities and underlying conditions, which are comorbidities associated with worse outcomes when facing Covid-19. Multi-generational households are also more common in these communities, making physical distancing harder or borderline impossible, and exposing seniors to greater health risks. And, sadly, racial and ethnic minorities are overrepresented in prisons, where infections have spread rapidly.

And, of course, underlying health conditions that are due to multiple factors, but certainly including lack of access to healthcare, are known to play an important role in Covid-19 mortality rates. The social and economic effects of the crisis will make the task of binding up the wounds from racial injustice, and redressing the economic inequality that came with it, all the more difficult.

Similarly, in poorer countries the devastating combination of high-density cities, poor access to healthcare, large informal sectors of the economy, and a weak social safety net combined to make efforts to combat Covid-19 extremely challenging.[66] Across Latin America the virus continued a seemingly irrepressible march throughout 2020 and into 2021, even as it was being brought under control (to varying degrees) in wealthier countries. This brought huge suffering to countries like Mexico, Chile, and Peru. And, of course, to Brazil, where the illiberal president Jair Bolsonaro made light of the disease, did little to check its rise, and indeed helped transport it across international borders with a delegation that he was part of, testing positive after meeting with President Trump at Mar a Lago in early 2020.

There has been clear inequality within countries in dealing with the public health crisis brought on by Covid-19. This inequality will continue into the post-Covid-19 era. Even in countries with relatively generous government assistance packages, many people will have taken on increased personal debt to get through the crisis, and many people will have accumulated rent or mortgage debt in the course of it. Even in jurisdictions where mortgage payments or rent could be postponed without foreclosure or eviction for some period of time, the mortgage and rent payments have still accrued. Those who own their homes outright are in a very different position than those who have a mortgage or rent. And among those renters and mortgage holders, some will have been able to keep their jobs and perform them from home, while others will have been on some form of relatively modest government assistance.

These effects also differ across countries, as the ingoing fiscal position of countries has determined their capacity to mount an aggressive fiscal response. A country like Australia, which had net debt less than 20% of Gross Domestic Product (GDP), had a large amount of "fiscal space" to support its citizens during the crisis with wage replacement and increased unemployment benefits.[67] The United States had much higher ingoing debt levels—with net debt/GDP approaching 100%—but being the world's so-called reserve currency has meant that foreign investors continue to find US dollar denominated securities issued by the US Treasury to be attractive, allowing the United States to continue to borrow cheaply and mount a significant fiscal response, as it did early in the crisis with its initial US$2 trillion CARES Act.[68]

Other countries like Italy and Spain, already with high debt levels and with economies that had still not really recovered from the Great Recession of 2008, have been able to do much less to help their citizens. Those two countries, of course, were among the hardest hit by the Covid-19 pandemic in health terms, and also in economic terms.

The future of an entire generation in these countries is grim. With youth unemployment going into the crisis above 30% in Spain and at 29% in Italy, economic prospects for this generation were already limited.[69] The damage done to the economy during the crisis has only exacerbated this already troubling outlook for young people.

For some school children who spent months or even a year in home schooling, the effects of the containment measures will be long-lasting. The fortunate, with relatively affluent parents able to spare the time to facilitate their home schooling/online learning, and to provide the information-technology equipment and resources to make it more effective and enjoyable, will have survived the crisis from an educational standpoint. But even they will have largely missed a significant period of social contact with classmates and friends. Some will have formed stronger bonds with their parents and siblings as partial compensation, but will need to re-establish other social connections post-crisis.

Children from less advantaged socioeconomic backgrounds will have suffered both educational and social losses from the crisis. Some—seeing bleak economic and employment prospects in front of them—will never return to school, forever reducing their skills and human capital and, as a consequence, their lifetime earning potential.

There is also the fact that many young people entering the workforce in the wake of the Covid-19 crisis may do so with the economy in deep recession. Many of them will not be able to find jobs—even in economies with far lower levels of unemployment and youth unemployment than Italy or Spain. Economists have demonstrated that there are persistent, negative causal effects on employment outcomes for those who enter the workforce during a recession.[70]

Covid-19 has also arguably only increased the market power of many large firms, including large tech firms such as Facebook and Amazon. Even before Covid-19, there were serious concerns about the influence of large technology companies on modern economies, and societies more generally. Not only have companies like Facebook and Amazon generated fabulous wealth for their founders, they have had substantial influence over both commerce and politics.

Facebook was heavily criticized for its role in potentially facilitating the spread of disinformation during the 2016 US presidential election and for not taking a stronger stance on hate speech propagated on its platform. Companies like Amazon were seen as controlling the marketplaces they created and giving themselves an unfair advantage in the sale of their own products on those platforms. Ride-sharing platforms like Uber were criticized for exploiting their drivers and paying them inadequately. And the data-retention and use policies of many large technology companies was called into question on both commercial and ethical grounds.

But during the pandemic, these companies have become even more essential and profitable. Apple and Google have been an important part of some contact-tracing efforts. Amazon Fresh, Uber Eats, and other services have contributed to efficient and safe food-delivery efforts. And in China, the Alibaba Group played a key role in a range of activities from public health to the provision of basic services and data analysis.

While there are certainly great opportunities for big tech to play a valuable and constructive social and economic role post-Covid-19, there is also a legitimate fear that they will become further entrenched in our economy and our politics in ways that only increase their already considerable market power.

For the most part, as the next chapter notes, the natural environment was an accidental beneficiary of the Covid-19 crisis.[71] Yet, all the environmental challenges that were present pre-Covid-19 remain. Moreover, there tends to be a significant bounce-back in emissions after recessions. The likelihood of this "dirty restart" to the world economy is particularly troubling in light of the fact that around seven million people a year die due to air pollution.[72] But worse still is the possibility of pollution and emissions returning to levels *above* those pre-Covid-19. With a number of governments around the world using the Covid-19 crisis as the basis for providing government support to fossil fuel industries, this is certainly not out of the question.[73] The overall impact of these types of energy stimulus plans depend on the degree to which they are linked to improvements in efficiency and reductions in emissions. For instance, Canada's $1.7 billion aid package to the oil and gas industry involved requirements to reduce methane and clean up contaminating oil and gas wells.[74]

Perhaps worse still, in some countries the pressing need to stimulate the economy in the wake of Covid-19 has led to the removal of important environmental regulations. For example, in the United States, the Trump administration weakened rules—so-called safe affordable fuel-efficient (SAFE) vehicles rules[75]—established during Barack Obama's time in office that require automakers to produce more fuel-efficient vehicles.[76]

Other countries have used the economic impact of Covid-19 as a rationale for reneging on their climate change commitments. Even by mid-March 2020, it was clear that certain European countries were pushing back on efforts to reduce emissions, in favor of economic stimulus.[77]

Thus, the environment challenge post-Covid-19 is twofold. First, preventing further environmental damage done either in the name of economic stimulus and recovery or merely through unconstrained private behavior—as in the purest case of "revenge pollution." And second, addressing the massive challenges that existed pre-Covid-19 but in a world where economic growth is at even more of a premium, and any measure that has overall social benefit—such as reductions in greenhouse gas emissions—but that comes at a direct economic cost is seen as "unaffordable."

C. Neoliberalism as Cause?

Some of these challenges or failures are the product of broad social and technological changes that have occurred against the backdrop of a system of economic and/or political liberalism. And, while some link Covid-19 to the failure of liberal societies to protect against environmental degradation, many see it as largely an exogenous "shock" to liberal democratic and authoritarian systems alike.

At least some of these changes, however, are linked more directly to recent "neoliberal" approaches to liberalism and the role of the state, and to an emphasis on small government and unregulated markets over a more egalitarian or "progressive" model of capitalism.[78]

In some ways, the term *neoliberalism* is everything and nothing. It has, in common parlance, come to be a generic and derogatory term used to criticize anything that involves markets and free enterprise. This usage is so pervasive that even center-left commentators on popular mainstream podcasts like *The Argument* and *FiveThirtyEight Politics* routinely use phrases like "not to sound like a neoliberal shill, but . . . " as a preemptive defense of positions involving the idea that markets sometime have virtues. If one took this type of discourse at face value, then it would be tempting to define neoliberalism as anything that is partially pro-market. But this is vastly over-inclusive.

A more helpful, if no less critical, definition of the phenomenon can be found in David Harvey's highly cited *A Brief History of Neoliberalism*. He characterizes it this way:[79]

> Neoliberalism is in the first instance a theory of political economic practices that proposes that human well-being can best be advanced by liberating individual entrepreneurial freedoms and skills within an institutional framework characterized by strong private property rights, free markets, and free trade. The role of the state is to create and preserve an institutional framework appropriate to such practices. The state has to guarantee, for example, the quality and integrity of money. It must also set up those military, defence, police, and legal structures and functions required to secure private property rights and to guarantee, by force if need be, the proper functioning of markets. Furthermore, if markets do not exist (in areas such as land, water, education, health care, social security, or environmental pollution) then they must be created, by state action if necessary. But beyond these tasks the state should not venture. State interventions in markets (once created) must be kept to a bare minimum because, according to the theory, the state cannot possibly possess enough information to second-guess market signals (prices) and because powerful interest groups will inevitably distort and bias state interventions (particularly in democracies) for their own benefit.

This is an extremely useful definition of neoliberalism because it captures all of the key features of the free-market fanaticism associated with Ronald Reagan and Margaret Thatcher. Unpacking Harvey's characterization, notice that it has three key features: a belief in the protection of property rights through appropriate legal structures (and by force if necessary); a belief in the expansion of markets as a means of regulating complex social problems;

and, most important, a minimal role for the state in the *regulation* (rather than guarantee) of market-based forms of ordering.

The protection of property rights through appropriate legal structures is a core feature of all liberal approaches, from the classical liberalism of the 18th century, to the neoliberalism of the 1980s, to our own concept of democratic liberalism. The only question in a democratic liberal approach is how broad or strong those protections should be, not whether they should exist.

There is likewise a good argument for viewing markets—such as markets for "land, water, education, health care, social security, or environmental pollution"—as potentially helpful rather than harmful to the effective democratic regulation of those spheres. Often, creating markets for environment pollution and water are examples of attempts to correct market failure. Creating a market for pollution—either through taxing output or granting tradeable permits—is the canonical example of recognizing and addressing the problem of social cost through internalizing an externality, as we discussed previously. Similarly, markets for water help address overuse of common resources and the so-called tragedy of the commons.[80]

The major failing of neoliberalism, as defined by Harvey and others, is its emphasis on unregulated forms of capitalism—or *"free"* markets without any real form of regulation by the state to address various forms of market failure. But linked to this has also been an insistence on the idea of a small and shrinking state.[81] At least from the progressive era onward, liberalism in most major democracies was tempered by a commitment to a strong and generous welfare state, which guaranteed access to a range of core goods and a dignified social minimum for all citizens. This form of "social liberalism" often involved the state providing access to certain goods, as well as funding or subsidizing access. It also involved the state maintaining a level of tax and spending necessary to underpin this form of public good provision and social safety net.

Neoliberalism, however, directly challenged these kind of social-liberal, welfare-state commitments. It insisted on private over public ownership, regardless of the argument for state provision of public goods – that is, the potential for markets to fail to provide an adequate quantity or quality of such goods. And it held that state spending was almost always bad, regardless of the degree to which that spending sought to overcome fiscal crisis or address economic disadvantage.

This commitment to privatization and austerity was at odds with both earlier classical-liberal and social-liberal accounts of the state as both a guarantor of individual dignity and broader economic prosperity. And, together with an insistence on unregulated markets, this commitment to a small and shrinking state has been a major contributor to the three trends underpinning the current crisis in liberalism.

By abandoning the traditional (neo-*classical*) liberal emphasis on competitive economic ordering, neoliberals have often made liberalism seem like an ideology that is pro-business rather than pro-market—and thus incapable of promoting the interests of ordinary workers and consumers. By abandoning a commitment to recognizing and responding to market failure, neoliberalism has likewise promoted the view (no matter how mistaken) that liberalism entails a commitment to laissez faire economics—rather than well-functioning, orderly markets. And by abandoning the more egalitarian, pro-social elements of the liberal tradition, neoliberalism has led to a perception that liberalism is in fact all about freedom for and of the wealthy, when in fact it is equally committed to the dignity of the least well off and, in some forms at least, true equality of access to certain opportunities and goods.

These failings in the neoliberal model have also simply been exacerbated—and laid bare—by crises such as Covid-19. In the United States, poorer communities—often with a significant proportion of people of color—were hit hardest by and were less able to deal with the coronavirus pandemic. Many performed low-paid service jobs that gave them significant exposure to the virus, while at the same time typically not having access to high-quality healthcare that would help them survive if they were infected. Both on the employment side and on the healthcare side, the market fanaticism of neoliberalism left people in these communities tremendously vulnerable.

Of course, the real question is how we move from neoliberalism to democratic liberalism, and it is to that which we now turn.

3
From Neoliberalism to Democratic Liberalism

A. Why Save Liberalism?

Why attempt to save or reimagine liberalism in the wake of the Covid-19 pandemic? Why not use Covid-19 as a moment to reconsider our fundamental commitment to liberalism and adopt a more radically social democratic or communitarian approach? Neoliberalism has certainly more than had its day. And as Chapter 2 notes, there are many on both the left and right who would be happy to see a commitment to liberalism go.

We argue, however, that many of the core ideas in liberalism retain the same relevance and value post-Covid-19 as pre-Covid-19. Liberalism may not be the most attractive philosophy, but as Winston Churchill said in relation to democracy, it may be the least-worst alternative we have when it comes to protecting individual freedom and dignity—including "economic dignity."[1]

Liberalism is a philosophy that prizes individual freedom and dignity, and that has helped generate the kind of economic prosperity that can sustain access to a dignified social minimum in countless countries around the world. For instance, one of the more profound consequences of globalization has been that more than two billion people in the developing world have been lifted out of extreme poverty. The World Bank has reported that the proportion of people worldwide that live in extreme poverty has now fallen below 10% (from 36% in 1990) for the first time.[2]

In advanced economies, consumers have also seen a drastic improvement in the value-for-money of the goods and services they purchase. Turning away from global free trade, therefore, would also imply a significant loss in the purchasing power and living standards of large numbers of citizens.

A turn away from liberalism would also entail a loss in freedom and equality, or the opportunity of new, previously disadvantaged groups to enter the market. Uber, for example, has tended to be far more open to racial minorities than traditional taxi companies. And TaskRabbiters are often women combining work and significant family responsibilities in a way that traditional work makes difficult if not impossible.[3]

What we seek to do in the remainder of the book, therefore, is to reimagine liberalism in a way that takes more seriously commitments to individual dignity and equality, as well as freedom, within the liberal tradition; and that places the democratic citizen—and her claim to equal dignity as well as freedom—at the center of a liberal approach. We call this a "democratic" as opposed to "neoliberal," or "fair" as opposed to "free" market approach.

In many ways, this vision of liberalism is old rather than new: it harks back to an earlier, more progressive "social" form of liberalism, before liberalism was coopted by neoliberal forces and understandings. Indeed, it shares many of the same principles as the "social" liberalism or egalitarian liberalism of the early 20th Century. L.T. Hobhouse, for example, suggested in 1911 that liberalism should be understood as entailing a commitment to both liberty and equality, and that "as time has gone on, men of the keenest Liberal sympathies have come not merely to accept but eagerly to advance the extension of public control in the industrial sphere, and of collective responsibility in the matter of the education and even the feeding of children, the housing of the industrial population, the care of the sick and aged, the provision of the means of regular employment."[4]

The key difference is that "democratic liberalism" explicitly celebrates liberalism as an ideal, and one that entails a commitment to more than markets or capitalism alone, but also to individual freedom and self-government. It also seeks to develop ideas of social liberalism that can meet the challenges of new technologies and environmental challenges, in a post-neoliberal world.

The remainder of the chapter explores these ideas in five parts. The first characterizes democratic liberalism. The second describes the relationship between democratic liberalism and the state. In the third we compare and contrast democratic liberalism with democratic socialism. The fourth discusses democratic liberalism and globalization. The fifth connects the idea of democratic liberalism to the idea of fair markets.

B. Toward Democratic Liberalism

The idea of *liberal democracy* is that free and fair elections are not enough to guarantee individual freedom and equality: we also need constitutional rights protections for minorities, and a philosophical commitment to markets.

The idea of *democratic liberalism,* in contrast, is that markets alone are not enough to guarantee true freedom or equality. Rather, true economic freedom and dignity depends on a central role for the state in both supplementing and regulating markets, and democratic input into both when and how this should occur.

(i) Guaranteeing a Public Baseline or Generous Social Minimum

First, and perhaps most important, a democratic liberal approach seeks to ensure that all individuals have access to a range of "core goods," including a minimum level of (1) food, (2) clothing, (3) clean water, (4), electricity, (5) housing, (6) healthcare, (7) education, (8) rest and leisure, including as a worker and a senior, and (9) time with family, including as a parent.

This idea of core goods draws on the work of economist Amartya Sen and philosopher Martha Nussbaum. Sen and Nussbaum jointly identified the idea of certain capabilities as necessary for a life of full human dignity. In her book *Global Justice,* Nussbaum also provided a detailed list of core human capabilities; our idea of core goods draws on this list of capabilities developed by Nussbaum, but focuses on those capabilities with some economic or material dimension.

Democratic liberalism requires that all individuals have access to minimum threshold of core goods of this kind. It does so by insisting that the government has an obligation to provide access to a public baseline—involving either the provision of or payment for these core goods for those in need.[5]

(ii) Equality of Access to Relative Goods

Democratic liberalism also takes economic inequality seriously. Economic inequality presents three problems, from a democratic liberal perspective. First, it has a "miner's canary" effect. It suggests to those experiencing economic stress or deprivation that the society in which they live has the capacity to meet their basic needs, and yet is choosing in some way not to do so. This also magnifies the expressive, or political, damage associated with a failure to provide universal access to a generous social minimum.

Second, for some core goods, there is an inherently rivalrous dimension to enjoyment of the goods. As high-income groups bid up the cost of education, or housing close to key amenities, or the technological frontier in medicine, they increase the cost—perhaps prohibitively so—to less well-off households of enjoying truly equal access to these goods. In housing, for instance, in many major cities there is a fixed supply of housing close to the central business district or downtown area, or in physically attractive areas near a coastline, waterways, or beaches. Although zoning regulations can do something to expand supply in these areas—say, through an increase in medium-density housing—the most attractive areas are in inherently limited supply due to topography and the coordination aspects of where the "center of town" is. The increase in the cost of housing in, for example, Knightsbridge in London, with a flood of foreign buyers in the last couple of decades, is an example of what can happen to house prices in sought-after areas. A similar pattern is true in many globally relevant cities, from New York to Sydney to San Francisco (and other parts of the Bay Area like Palo Alto).

In education, while it may seem that someone's child having better skills has no negative effect on another person's child, this is typically not the case, at least in the short run. It takes time for job opportunities to expand in response to increases in human capital and employee skills, so that there is often a tournament-like aspect to the job-search process. If one person has superior skills or better credentials for particular job, then they will get that job regardless of the skills and credentials of the next best applicant. In the long run, more jobs may well be created to take advantage of the skills of the applicant who misses out, but in the short run there is sometimes "no prize for second place."

Health is another area where relative consumption, not just absolute levels of care, can matter. If some people, by virtue of their wealth, have access to life-saving procedures or medications, this can cause an expressive harm to those not able to afford or to be provided with that level of medical care. Of course, the absolute level of care is extremely important, and advances in medical technology have led to a secular rise in life expectancy and quality of life in advanced economies. But those same technological forces have led to more and more expensive treatments at the frontier of medicine that are only affordable for the wealthy. And when the wealthy have exclusive access to those treatments, it in some way sends a message to the less-well-off that their lives are not as valuable as the lives of the better off.

(iii) Addressing Market Power

One of the great virtues of well-functioning markets is their capacity to aggregate and communicate information in an efficient way, through the price mechanism.[6] But most mainstream economists acknowledge that markets can also be plagued by informational asymmetries between different participants (as in many insurance markets), be subject to moral hazard (as in some financial markets), or lack sufficient competition.

The most celebrated result in all of economics—the so-called First Welfare Theorem—provides conditions under which competition leads to an optimal allocation of resources in society. Formally established by Nobel Laureates Kenneth Arrow and Gerard Debreu, this theorem embodies Adam Smith's notion that the *Invisible Hand* of the market can serve the common good— that the private self-interest of market participants can be a public virtue. But when product markets become uncompetitive, this logic breaks down. And there is persuasive evidence that, indeed, markets in the United States particularly (and elsewhere, too) have become less competitive in recent decades. For instance, De Loecker and Eckhout show that globally, sales-weighted average markups (the ratio of price to marginal costs of production) have gone from 1.1 in 1980 to 1.6 in 2016. Moreover, this increase has been most pronounced in North America and Europe.[7] And although there has been a debate about whether that is the right measure—cost-weighted average markups would be better—there is no dispute that there has been a welfare-relevant rise in markups.

Democratic liberalism also seeks to curb this form of market failure by insisting on the need for a strong role for governments in curbing and regulating this kind of market power.

Government intervention to curb market (or monopoly) power has a long history, dating in the United States to the Sherman Antitrust Act of 1890 and, in particular, active enforcement of the Sherman Act during the presidency of Theodore Roosevelt. Justice White articulated the purpose of the Sherman Act eloquently in *Spectrum Sports, Inc. v. McQuillan, 506 U.S. 447 (1993):*

> The purpose of the Act is not to protect businesses from the working of the market; it is to protect the public from the failure of the market. The law directs itself not against conduct which is competitive, even severely so, but against conduct which unfairly tends to destroy competition itself. It does so not out of solicitude for private concerns but out of concern for the public interest.

Giving the Sherman Act, and other antitrust legislation in the United States and around the world, teeth requires constant government vigilance. Indeed, *Spectrum Sports, Inc. v. McQuillan* was a case concerning what types of predatory pricing or other conduct constituted a violation of the Sherman Act and what type of (causal) link needed to be established for such conduct to constitute such a violation.

Monitoring these behaviors and understanding the appropriate definition of a "market" in different industries as they evolve over time is a crucial component of an effective antitrust regime. Indeed, the Federal Trade Commission in the United States has more than 1,100 employees and an annual budget of more than $300 million in order to perform this role.[8]

As recent discussions among commentators, regulators, and politicians concerning the technology sector have highlighted, the constantly evolving nature of business models and markets means that antitrust legislation and enforcement must constantly adapt to changing circumstances in order to be effective.

(iv) Addressing Social Costs (or Externalities)

Government also has a vital role to play in addressing the problem of social cost. The very presence of externalities—factors that are not part of the market's price mechanism—implies a role for some institution in internalizing those externalities.

Some neo-classical economists, such as Ronald Coase, have argued that in some cases institutions were not necessary, and that private bargaining could be relied upon to internalize externalities—absent "transaction costs." Coase's idea was that if the costs of identifying the counterparty, bargaining and contracting with them, and then monitoring compliance with that contrast, were low enough, then private parties could be relied upon to bargain with each other to avoid or mitigate the effect of externalities, hence making regulation unnecessary. Ideas of this kind have in recent years also been picked up and relied on by neoliberals to justify part of their deregulatory agenda.

The reality, however, is that transaction costs—namely the costs of identifying, bargaining, contracting, and monitoring a counterparty's behavior—are almost always significant. This is especially true for bargaining costs: extended forms of bargaining cost include the capacity for a counterparty to engage in forms of strategic bargaining, or "hold-up," and to be subject to "endowment effects," which cause them to place an irrationally high value on retaining current benefits or entitlements compared to obtaining new ones. Parties' own capacity to bargain may also be limited by wealth or income effects, or collective action or "free-rider" problems, which mean they cannot fully express a preference for avoiding or internalizing an externality. The Coase Theorem, therefore, does not speak to most real-world settings.[9]

Legal scholars Guido Calabresi and Douglas Melamed argue that tort law—or nuisance rules—can supplement the law of contract and property in some cases.[10] If parties that impose an externality are liable *ex post* for the damage this causes others, this can effectively internalize a range of externalities—assuming there is a plaintiff with the incentive and capacity to sue. Similarly, if parties can use injunctive remedies to force a party not to impose an externality, the tort law system can help avoid or internalize these externalities. Calabresi and Melamed even suggest that parties could be required to pay for such relief in the form of a "compensated injunction" or "reverse damages" model.

Another institution that may play a role in internalizing externalities is firms. As the modern theory of the firm, attributed to 2016 Nobel Laureates Oliver Hart and Bengt Holmstrom, emphasizes,[11] firms do a range of things more efficiently and effectively than markets do in certain circumstances. Firms, through ownership of important assets, can avoid bargaining inefficiencies at the so-called hold-up problem, which can lead to a less-than-efficient level of investment in relationship-specific activities or assets. Firms can use authority, rather than the market's price mechanism, to direct and coordinate economic activity. In environments with rapidly changing circumstances, this can be particularly valuable. Firms can structure the workplace through job design and information flows to get different parts of an organization to work together most effectively and efficiently. And firms can provide a range of implicit and explicit incentives to workers that are often not possible in decentralized markets. But firms can't do everything, and there are a wide range of externalities that are beyond the scope of firms.

For many externalities, a democratic liberal approach suggests, governments must actively intervene to regulate markets so as to internalize externalities. In some cases, where the social costs clearly outweigh the benefits, this may mean banning an activity outright. In others, where there are greater (net) social benefits, it may mean imposing limits on the time, manner, or place of economic activity—or setting a quota that effectively balances social costs and benefits. It may also involve imposing a form of "Pigouvian tax"—a special form of tax named after economist Arthur Pigou—that aims to tax the externality associated with economic activity.

The most obvious, and perhaps most important, example of regulation of this kind involves environmental regulation—that is, the attempt to internalize the various forms of pollution that can cross firms, industries, and even national boundaries in ways that cause serious damage to human health, non-human animals, and the natural environment. And, of course, the leading example of this is environmental regulation designed to address the challenge of climate change.

Not only have economists understood this problem for more than a century, they have also known how to solve it. There has been a near consensus among economists for at least a decade that a "carbon tax" is the best way to tackle climate change. William Nordhaus—who shared the 2018 Economics Nobel—began detailing the interaction between the economy and the environment in the 1970s, and laid out not only the logic of a carbon tax but also how to calculate the optimal level of it.[12] There are other ways to achieve the same economic outcome, such as an "emissions trading scheme" where permits are distributed that grant firms a right to pollute a certain amount, and they can be traded in a secondary market for such permits. This ensures that firms that can most effectively use the right to pollute buy the permits from those who can do so less effectively. Just like a carbon tax, this ensures that the marginal benefit of pollution (through economic development) is matched to the marginal cost of pollution (though environmental harm).

But the logic of all these approaches is the same: they involve governments responding to demands from democratically empowered citizens to internalize perhaps the most important externality of our time, and in ways that effectively *regulate* market-based transactions rather than bypass them. This is also the essence of a democratic liberal approach, which combines an emphasis on both democratic and market-based forms of ordering.

C. Democratic Liberalism, Politics, and the State

Democratic liberalism thus emphasizes the idea of equal human dignity, and defines dignity in a broad sense to include a level of material, physical, and psychological well-being necessary for a life of full human dignity. This is the essence of the capabilities approach developed by Sen and Nussbaum, and stands as a corrective to purely welfare- or GDP-based measures of liberalism's success.

Democratic liberalism likewise insists that equality among citizens is a core part of the liberal project and ideal. This, in turn, means both formal equality of opportunity and substantive commitments to equal dignity and ending historical forms of subordination. It also means equality of access to a range of "relative goods," where one person's enjoyment of a good is inherently linked to the level enjoyed by others.

Furthermore, democratic liberalism insists both on the power of markets and the idea that markets can fail—both by leading to forms of social costs, or externalities, and monopoly power. And where they fail, it suggests that government has a fundamental role to play in preventing and responding to these failures. It also emphasizes the powerful arguments for popular input into certain forms of economic governance that involve defining the scope of these failures and our collective response to them.[13]

These concepts, however, are not self-defining: a "generous social minimum," for example, depends on the relevant social and economic context and democratic judgments about what is reasonably necessary for a dignified life in *that context*. The idea of an externality is likewise not self-evident: rather, it depends on prevailing social understandings of the collective benefits or harms attributable to certain actions. One of the key premises of democratic liberalism, therefore, is the idea of democratic input into and regulation of markets.

Democratic processes of decision making play a critical role in determining both how we define the ideas of a generous social minimum and externalities, and how best to respond to these and other problems of inequality and market power. This also involves the idea of widespread democratic participation in economic governance, in either a direct or indirect form.

Some progressive writers suggest that direct democratic involvement is most likely to realize the goals of a fair markets approach.[14] Another approach, however, emphasizes the importance of voter enfranchisement and competition among political parties, or elites, as core to democratic liberal politics and outcomes. Economists such as Schumpter, for example, have long suggested it was more helpful to think about democratic politics as a form of competition for power and policy influence.[15] Modern election law scholars, such as Sam Issacharoff and Rick Pildes, have likewise argued that it is useful to think about democratic politics in structural terms rather than simply individual-rights terms.[16] And if we think about "politics as markets," the same principles that govern economic markets should apply to political markets.[17] That is, both economic and political markets should be fair, not simply free; and the state should adopt the regulations and structures necessary to (i) ensure universal access to the vote, (ii) address concerns about equality among citizens in the political process, (iii) regulate the existence and exercise of monopoly power, and (iv) internalize externalities. As we explore more in the final chapter, this also translates into the need for a range of electoral regulations or reforms.

One of the most important of these is also an effective system of campaign finance regulation. Money in politics isn't an inherently bad thing, and there are potential upsides to having well-funded political campaigns and candidates. But money in politics can lead to a non-level political playing field, or to inequalities in the economic sphere spilling over into the democratic sphere. If one candidate or type of candidate has a lot more money than another, they are more likely to win an election. And this kind of "inequality externality" is antithetical to the commitment to democratic equality. Especially in a market-based system that tolerates substantial residual economic inequality, it is essential to ensure that economic inequalities do not spill over into democratic politics or become sources of *political inequality*.

Similarly, where neoliberalism rejects the role of the state in both regulating the market and guaranteeing access to a dignified social minimum for all, democratic liberalism embraces a strong role for the state as guarantor of a competitive and compassionate form of market ordering. And where neoliberalism often opposes state ownership and provision on ideological grounds, democratic liberalism emphasizes the value to both public and private provision and ownership of core goods.[18]

Even the most ardent neoliberals believe that the government must provide certain "public goods" that will tend to be underprovided by purely free markets because everyone benefits from them, regardless of who pays for them. The classic example of this is national defense. But public goods that are subject to this free-rider problem extend well beyond the sphere of national defense.[19] They include many of the core goods at core of democratic liberal approach.

Democratic liberalism likewise points to a view of when public versus private provision of core goods is desirable. Ultimately, it is a question of trade-offs between quality and cost, and the degree to which contracts are a reliable means of ensuring that the state, and public, gets the quality of core good it bargains for.

It draws, for example, on the framework for thinking about public versus private provision of services is provided by economists Oliver Hart, Andrei Shleifer, and Robert Vishny, in a paper appositely titled "The Proper Scope of Government."[20] The Hart-Shleifer-Vishny (HSV) framework builds on the theory of incomplete contracts, for which Hart went on to win a Nobel Prize; and the basic premise of HSV is that government can and does pay for many things—like education, national defense, and in some countries, healthcare and other core goods—but it does not always *own* the assets required to provide those goods and services. For instance, governments can and sometimes do pay for education without running schools, through voucher programs. Sometimes governments own and run public schools. The same goes for private versus public prisons, trash collection, and even the armed services.

The animating idea behind the "incomplete contracts" approach is that there are some contingencies that contracts, no matter how detailed, can't cover. This could be because parties can't conceive of all future contingencies.

Or perhaps they understand what's at issue, but it is hard to codify that in a way a court could understand. Or it may be because ideas about the quality of core goods provision, and their relationship to human dignity, are inherently difficult to specify contractually. Where contracts are incomplete, there will also be an important role for the state in both paying for and providing—and owning the assets necessary to provide—core goods.

D. Democratic Liberalism and Fair Markets

Philosophers such as Rawls might have found a lot to agree with in our ideas, especially in the emphasis on dignity and equality for all. But our idea of "fair markets" is an ordinary, common sense, rather than a philosophical one: it is meant to convey the key four principles of market regulation that lie at the heart of a democratic liberal, as opposed to neoliberal, approach. In this sense, it has some important similarities with "fair trade" principles.

Ideas of fair trade have a long lineage, but also multiple different interpretations. One leading current definition of fair trade, however, comes from "FINE," a network that includes Fairtrade Labeling Organizations International (FLO), the International Federation for Alternative Trade (IFAT), the Network or European Shops (NEWS!), and the European Fair Trade Association (EFTA), which define fair trade as follows:

> A trading partnership, based on dialogue, transparency and respect, that seeks greater equity in international trade. It contributes to sustainable development by offering better trading conditions, and securing the rights of, marginalized producers and workers—especially in the [Global] South.[21]

This definition reveals some important differences between the idea of fair trade and fair markets. Fair trade ideas often emphasize the idea of "equity" between trading partners, and some political theorists suggest this translates into the idea of a fair or equal sharing of the gains from trade.[22] A fair markets approach, in contrast, allocates a central role to market-based forms of ordering, in ways that generally make *competitive* markets, rather than the state, the arbiter of "fair" economic value.

Fair trade ideas are likewise rooted in an "alternative trade" tradition, which sought to counter the influence of economies in the Global North.[23] And a fair markets approach aims to take seriously the economic challenges of the Global South, but without adopting a distinctly post-colonial or Global South perspective. But this idea of fair trade also reveals important similarities with fair market principles.

In their current form, fair trade principles emphasize environmental sustainability in trade and production.[24] And democratic liberalism puts strong emphasis on the need to address environmental harm—indeed, all externalities. Fair trade principles emphasize the importance of "securing the rights" and decent conditions for all workers, and especially marginalized workers, including women.[25] And democratic liberalism insists that liberalism entails a commitment to equal dignity for all—including universal access to decent work and wages, and a generous social minimum.

In this sense, a democratic liberal approach could equally be called "progressive capitalist" in nature,[26] or liberalism "blue, pink and green." It is "blue" because it takes seriously the needs and concerns of traditional blue-collar workers—or "ordinary workers"—let down by recent more neoliberal versions of liberalism. It is "pink"—or sensitive to commitments to gender equality. It takes seriously feminist arguments about the ways in which liberal market-based forms of ordering have tended systematically to privilege men over women, or male-identifying over female-identifying citizens. The distribution of income and workload in a liberal society has always been unequal in terms of gender, and part of ensuring a truly democratic form of liberalism means addressing this persistent and pervasive form of gender inequality.

And it is "green" in focus: it takes seriously the duties of current generations to ensure appropriate environmental stewardship for the benefit of future generations, nonhuman animals, and indeed the planet itself. A truly democratic liberalism is an environmentally conscious form of liberalism which insists that the environmental costs of economic activity must be "internalized" within market mechanism itself, so that environmental harms are implicitly a consideration in all of the economic choices we make—choices about how we dispose of our rubbish, our diet, the means of transport we choose, our appliances, and whether we turn off our lights.

What is central is that democratic liberalism contemplates a role for the state in guaranteeing dignity, equality, and well-functioning economic and political markets that demarcate it sharply from neoliberalism while also retaining a commitment to markets.

F. Democratic Liberalism and its Rivals

Of course, democratic politics being what it is, democratic liberalism is not the only candidate to replace neoliberalism in a post-Covid-19 world. Two other leading candidates are democratic socialism and economic nationalism. Compared to democratic liberalism, however, both of these approaches involve a much greater departure from liberal principles: instead of seeking to reform and regulate national or global markets, they often seek completely to replace them with state provision or domestic production.

(i) Democratic Liberalism versus Democratic Socialism

In response to the failures of liberalism to provide an adequate social minimum and address issues like climate change, one part of the Democratic Party in the United States has taken a sharp turn to the left. The insurgent campaign of Senator Bernie Sanders in 2016 arguably marked the start of this leftward turn, and it was only amplified in the lead-up to the 2020 Presidential election.

Several Democratic candidates for the presidency in 2020 endorsed ideas that were openly democratic socialist in approach. For instance, they argued for a policy of "Medicare for all" that involved expanding the existing Medicare program into a universal, single-payer system. They likewise argued for the elimination in $81 billion in past-due medical debt,[27] and significantly increased spending on childcare and universal pre-K education.

Sanders also promised to offer free tuition for public colleges, universities, Historically Black Colleges and Universities, Minority Serving Institutions, and trade-schools, and to cancel all student loan debt for 45 million Americans,[28] to build 10 million affordable housing units, undertake repairs on and "decarbonize" existing housing units, as well as to extend Section 8 housing vouchers to eliminate all waitlists, along with a raft of regulatory measures.[29]

A similarly ambitious democratic socialist idea is the push for a "Green New Deal." The nonbinding resolution introduced by Representative Alexandria Ocasio-Cortez and Senator Edward J. Markey takes as its stepping-off point that the world, led by the United States, needs to get to net zero carbon emissions by 2050.[30] To do that, it wants the federal government to do a range of things, some closely related, some not. Among the demands of the federal government are to dramatically reduce greenhouse gas emissions, but also to enact a jobs program to create well-paying jobs (a "green jobs guarantee") and create a kind of "Green Manhattan Project" involving a highly funded and concerted government effort to radically improve technology and drive net emissions to zero.

From a democratic liberal perspective, some of these proposals are worth embracing, and several of the ideas we develop in later chapters have important overlap with these ideas. Democratic liberalism suggests that government has an important role to play in guaranteeing access to the social minimum including, if needed, via provision of universal basic welfare or a universal jobs guarantee. The emphasis democratic liberalism places on work also makes a jobs guarantee an obvious way in which to achieve this kind of residual guarantee. And if it can address environmental problems in the process by being a "green jobs guarantee," so much the better from a democratic liberal perspective.

Similarly, it suggests that governments should intervene to prop up ordinary wages and wage growth—but in ways that retain incentives for work as the center of a democratic liberal order. That means expanding policies such as an earned income tax credit, and place-based policies that give incentives for new industries to create jobs in economically depressed or disadvantaged areas. It also means seeking to enhance the bargaining power of workers and tame that of large employers, perhaps through the use of antitrust law, as Suresh Naidu, Eric Posner, and Glen Weyl have argued.[31]

But, as we explore in more detail in the next chapter, a democratic liberal jobs guarantee will also look quite different from a democratic socialist one. The *green industry policy* component to the Green New Deal likewise has aspects that are both democratic liberal and anti-liberal in approach.

The aspect of such a policy that emphasizes innovation and the need for some form of government intervention to achieve it is entirely consistent with the field of mainstream economics known as *endogenous growth theory*, for which part of the 2018 Nobel Prize in Economic Sciences was awarded to Paul Romer.[32] Endogenous growth theory recognizes that knowledge and ideas are important drivers of economic growth, and that unregulated markets will produce ideas and innovation, but too few. This provides a case for government intervention. In many instances this is achieved through tax subsidies for research and development, but also through government funding of basic research. It is perfectly consistent with democratic liberalism for the government to directly fund climate-science innovation. It is also consistent for it to do so in a way that combats negative externalities such as climate change.

What is *not* consistent with democratic liberalism, however, is the idea that a Green Manhattan Project should become a permanent attempt to maintain certain kinds of jobs in the United States—even when markets, and global competition, suggest that those jobs are more efficiently performed elsewhere. The current turn against globalization by many in the Democratic Party is, in many ways, understandable. The great promise of that liberalism was that by expanding the economic "pie," all workers would gain. This underpinned policies like ratifying NAFTA. Yet many workers whose jobs have moved overseas in the last few decades have not found decent-paying replacement work. And wages for ordinary workers in America have stagnated.

Democratic liberalism, however, argues that it would ultimately be a mistake to turn against markets—including global markets—rather than attempt to find new ways to address problems of concentrated unemployment and general wage stagnation. Rather than abandon markets and the power they have to create prosperity, its premise is that liberalism needs to be updated and adjusted.

Democratic liberalism also points to two general concerns with how many democratic socialists propose achieving the goal of a more inclusive and sustainable model of economic development. The first-order concern with this is the level of government debt it would lead to. For example, the healthcare proposals of Sanders and Warren have been estimated to cost $30 trillion over a decade. Sanders' plan to cancel all student loan debt carried a price tag of roughly $1.6 trillion,[33] and his social housing program would have cost roughly $2.5 trillion.[34]

Borrowing rates for most governments are at historic lows, and (as we emphasize in more detail in Chapter 8) a number of countries like Australia, Canada, Germany, South Korea, and others entered the Covid-19 crisis with low levels of debt and hence a good amount of "fiscal space" for further borrowing. But if key democratic socialist proposals were adopted, debt levels could quickly become unsustainable. This would drive up borrowing costs as investors rationally become worried about the possibility of sovereign default. And high debt levels limit the ability to respond to future crises—be they the next global health emergency or a financial crisis more similar to the Great Recession of 2008.

The second concern with a democratic socialist approach, for those committed to liberal ideas of individual choice and market-based forms of ordering, is that such a dramatic increase in the size of the government sector—not for a temporary, emergency period but indefinitely—is likely to reduce incentives for private sector work and innovation throughout the economy.

In the modern economic era, the impact on private sector activity of a super–welfare state is not the traditional one of "crowding out" that was a popular, if not particularly well empirically supported, theory in the 1970s, '80s, and '90s. The idea behind crowding out is that an expanded government sector requires additional government borrowing, which leads to a rise in the real interest rate. This, in turn, makes it more expensive for the private sector to fund additional productive investments and leads to a reduction in private sector investment, innovation, employment, and growth.

Whatever the merits, or otherwise, of this view in an earlier time, in the wake of the low-growth / low-inflation economic era we find ourselves in, pushing up the very low (or negative) real interest rate is not a major concern. Indeed, it arguably will not happen at all with increased government spending. This is perhaps the most important implication of the realization that we live in an era of secular stagnation.

Indefinite funding by government of what would otherwise be private sector enterprises constitutes a real concern in our current economic circumstances, which draws human capital away from the private sector. If support from the government makes it "too attractive" for workers to work for businesses receiving that support, then other firms will have difficulty attracting talent or will have to do so a greater cost.

Similarly, some democratic socialist prescriptions could lead to a whole range of enterprises being shielded from competitive market pressure. Although one certainly wants to protect businesses from bankruptcy during a crisis, protecting those same enterprises from market competition—and the consequences of poor performance—indefinitely allows poor management and lack of innovation to go unchecked and unpunished.

The idea that market competition disciplines management has a long intellectual history, dating (as so many economic ideas do) to the writings of Adam Smith who observed in the *Wealth of Nations* in 1776 that "Monopoly . . . is a great enemy to good management."[35] Economists began taking this aphorism seriously in the context of formal models beginning with Nobel laureate (and later Sir) John Hicks's observation in his presidential address to the Econometric Society in 1937 that "the best of all monopoly profits is the quiet life."[36]

While Hicks's statement, and subsequent formal theories of the phenomenon, apply to private sector monopolies that are protected from competition, it has particular application to enterprises in the government sector that are shielded from product market competition.

Beginning in earnest with the work of Harvard economist Harvey Leibenstein (1966) economists have investigated whether competition increases the internal efficiency of firms—what Leibenstein called "X-efficiency."[37] There are reasons to believe that reduced competition makes firms less internally efficient, and there is empirical support for this proposition as well.[38]

In a democratic socialist order it is hard, if not impossible, to disentangle which businesses are under pressure because of failings of management and which are under pressure due to the virus and its complicated path through the economy. As such, government support is likely to be over-inclusive—and in any case will provide more of a crutch for bad management than would be the case in ordinary times. This leads to less "X-efficiency," in the language of Leibenstein.

Finally, where democratic socialism focuses squarely on issues of economic equality, the chief concern of democratic liberalism is with ensuring universal access to a generous social minimum for all. It takes seriously issues of economic inequality, but its chief concern in this context on the miner's canary effect and the need to expand access to the social minimum for those currently left out by the system; the economic and political spillovers associated with extreme wealth on the enjoyment of core goods such as housing and education; and on equality in the democratic process.

Of course, "democratic socialism" and "democratic liberalism" are ultimately points along a policy continuum. They share many similar objectives, and in some cases overlapping ideas about how policy should be designed. Indeed, it is worth noting that the big economic and social policy initiatives that were at the forefront of the agenda during the early months of the Biden administration were squarely democratically liberal. But they also highlighted the potential fluidity between democratic liberal and democratic socialist ideas. They draw in part on ideas put forward by the proponents of a "Green New Deal," and were designed by administration officials with democratic socialist and liberal credentials. They also met with approving nods across the democratic liberal to democratic socialist spectrums.

There are, however, still important quantitative as well as qualitative differences between the two approaches, which we seek to draw out in this book in the interest of offering both economic progressives and centrists a wide a range of policy options.

(ii) Democratic Liberalism and Globalization

Another response to the current crisis in work and wages in many countries has been a turn to "economic nationalist" ideas. In the United States, for example, a large part of Donald Trump's 2016 Presidential election campaign was animated by the idea of economic nationalism, or an emphasis on a new form of "economic sovereignty."[39] Similarly, in the United Kingdom, support for the Brexit referendum was underpinned by a desire to restore British legal and *economic* sovereignty.

One of the key planks of economic nationalism is also opposition to global free trade as part of the liberal project. For economic nationalists, free trade is a mistake because it can lead to trade deficits where the "home country" imports more goods and services from, than it exports to, a "foreign country." For instance, President Trump consistently railed against the US trade deficit with China, describing it as America "losing." For President Trump it was the trade deficit—the difference between how much we import and export—that is the big problem. There is also a concern that global free trade may leave national economies vulnerable to foreign influence or manipulation.

The Covid-19 crisis has also increased the appeal of these views in some quarters. The difficulty that many countries had in securing masks, gowns, gloves, hand sanitizer, and other personal protective equipment (PPE)—much of which is manufactured primarily in China—caused concern that strategically important sectors of the economy had been offshored in a way that not only cost domestic jobs but made it hard to deal with a public health crisis. This argument applied to testing kits as well as, perhaps most crucially, ventilators. Even food supply chains were stretched in many countries, causing concerns about the availability of food during the crisis.

In light of this, it is not surprising that there are calls in many liberal democracies for a reversal of some of the offshoring of manufacturing that has occurred in most advanced economies in recent decades. It is a natural moment for those who have been hurt by that secular trend—through job losses and community decline—to argue that it was a bad idea all along. And it provides an expanded audience for the hard-core economic nationalists, like Steve Bannon, to enlist in their ideological battle.

But it would be a serious mistake to radically about-face on the path of globalization and free trade of the last several decades. There is a strong correlation between the degree of openness of a country and its national income (e.g., GDP).

Making causal inferences about this relationship is, of course, dangerous without further evidence. For instance, countries that have low tariffs and other trade barriers are clearly expressing a view on the desirability of market-mediated outcomes, and it would thus not be surprising that they also have pro-market domestic policies such as moderate levels of regulation, relatively low corporate tax rates, and the like. This is a point understood since at least the late 1980s in work by Harvard economist Elhanan Helpman.[40]

But there is also increasingly strong evidence pointing to a causal relationship. Economists Jeffrey Frankel and David Romer, in a classic 1999 paper in the *American Economic Review*, suggested that the geographic characteristics of countries could be used to understand the causal relationship between trade and national income. They used what is known as an "instrumental variables" approach, where they show empirically that geographic characteristics are correlated with trade openness, but that (crucially) these geographic characteristics are uncorrelated with other determinants of income. In the language of modern applied microeconomics, they use geographic characteristics as "instruments." They go on to show that, even at the time of their writing, there is a strong causal relationship between trade and income.

More recent work has not only confirmed this finding; International Monetary Fund (IMF) economists Diego Cerdeiro and Andras Komaromi showed that using geographic characteristics as an instrument, and looking at data from 1990 to 2015, "a one percentage point increase in trade openness raises real income per capita by between 2 and 5 percent."[41]

The logic of these findings is also straightforward: trade between nations is not a zero-sum game, whereby if somebody wins then somebody else loses. The inescapable logic of comparative advantage, dating back to David Ricardo, is that by specializing in producing what they are relatively better at and trading, both countries are better off.

The United States imports goods like clothing, footwear, cellphones, and computers from China, where labor costs are lower and factories specialize, thereby gaining efficiencies from economies of scale. The United States exports a lot of services (as opposed to goods) to China. In everything from banking and insurance to travel and royalties, the United States enjoys a massive surplus with China. Overall, the United States exports $52.4 billion in services to China while it imports $15.4 billion.

Again, however, it is not that balance that matters. What matters is that by specializing and trading, US consumers get cheaper and better cellphones and clothing, while US producers employ millions of Americans in sectors in which the United States is relatively more efficient.

Indeed, previous tariff walls, protectionism, and industry policy have all been proven failures. Tariffs, or taxes on imports that are collected by the government, have been understood to be bad for both the importing and exporting countries since the work of British economist David Ricardo in 1817, who coined the famous term *comparative advantage*. And in the post–World War II era there had, until recently, been a steady reduction in tariffs and other related barriers to trade.[42]

Another solution sometimes proposed to address the challenges from globalization and automation is for governments to adopt a form of long-term industry policy—or adopt long-term subsidies for industries that are exposed to trade. And there is a long history of these kinds of policies. Indeed, in 1791, Alexander Hamilton in his role as the first US Secretary of the Treasury developed a proposal to aid the US manufacturing sector so that it could compete more effectively with Great Britain. Some of the principles in Hamilton's "Report in the Subject of Manufactures" that he furnished to Congress were government subsidies to particular industries, government procurement contracts for those industries, and targeted tax exemptions.[43]

Industry policy continued for various industries and in various forms under numerous presidents, including Abraham Lincoln and Franklin Roosevelt. In the modern era, there were instances of ad hoc assistance to industries under pressure from international competition including the Carter administration's Solomon Plan in 1977 designed to aid the steel industry, and 1984 Democratic presidential nominee Walter Mondale's plan for a national industry policy developed by Robert Reich.

Even Ronald Reagan—no champion of government intervention—utilized industry policy including in the pharmaceutical, semiconductor, and manufacturing industries. The Obama administration's stimulus plan in the wake of the financial crisis—the $787 billion American Recovery and Reinvestment Act of February 2009—included industry assistance targeted at agriculture, military equipment, and renewable energy, the latter to the tune of $80 billion.

President Obama's support of green energy ended famously badly, with numerous clean-energy companies that received federal loan guarantees filing for bankruptcy, including Solyndra, Abound Solar, Beacon Power, Ener1, and electric car battery maker A123.[44]

The political temptation to prop up industries that are under pressure or failing is clearly not peculiar to one side of politics in the United States. For the same reasons, it is not peculiar to the United States—in countless countries, at times of economic crisis and times of economic plenty, politicians of all stripes have succumbed to the temptation to buttress industries and to try and pick winners.

Two other instances—one from Australia and one from the UK— underscore the political temptation and economic futility of this kind of policy. The motor vehicle industry in Australia was built behind a wall of protectionism from its inception in the 1940s. The first fully Australian car, the "Holden," was produced by General Motors-Holden on New Year's Day in 1948 (named for the company's first chairman, Sir Edward Holden).

Not content with one car manufacturer in Australia, various governments from the 1960s to the 1980s subsidized not only General Motors but also Ford, Chrysler, Nissan and Volkswagen, Toyota, Mitsubishi, British Leyland, and others to produce cars in Australia and provide employment to Australian workers. Industry assistance in this era included high tariffs, import quotas that handed 80% of the car market to local producers, local content schemes for component suppliers, government procurement contracts, and export subsidies.

With high-priced, low-quality cars being produced, the Labour government led by Bob Hawke that came to power in 1983 realized that changes had to be made. Hawke and his treasurer (and later prime minister) Paul Keating were arguably the first "new Labour" or "Third Way" government, preceding Tony Blair and Bill Clinton. Yet despite scaling back and rationalizing industry assistance in many ways, the industry made limited progress. The conservative government led by John Howard provided the industry with a five-year tariff freeze in the late 1990s that many commentators and industry observers credit with triggering a further decline in international competitiveness.[45] After the tariff freeze ended, the industry could only be propped up by cash payments from successive governments on both the left and right.

This finally ended in 2017 when the Australian federal government decided to stop the clearly futile attempts to prop up the domestic car industry through explicit cash payments. With Toyota and Ford having already left, General Motors closed permanently in October 2017.

More than half a century of tariffs, subsidies, quotas, and transfer payments could not, and did not, bend the forces of globalization and comparative advantage. On the plus side, these measures did keep 10,000 or so people employed in relatively high-paying jobs—perhaps more if one takes a generous view of those employed by suppliers of the car manufacturers. But the downsides loomed large.

Consumers paid vastly more for imported cars than they would have otherwise and were pushed into buying domestic cars of inferior quality. The taxes raised to pay for the subsidies were distortionary to the economy more generally. Those taxes made individuals in other sectors pay more tax, and as all income taxes do, it distorted their labor-supply decisions. Propping up the Australian car industry imposed significant costs on Australian consumers, taxpayers, and workers in other parts of the economy. And it ultimately failed.

If it's possible, the United Kingdom has an even less distinguished history of winner-picking industry policy. Multiple governments in the 1960s and 1970s pursued policies to create so-called National Champions through mergers, preferred procurement, and outright subsidies. France also adopted similar policies in the post-war era. Perhaps the high-water mark of UK industry policy occurred in 1975, when Tony Benn, as Secretary of State for Industry in the Labour government, advocated a highly interventionist set of policies outlined in "A Ten-Year Industrial Strategy for Britain."

Britain's national champions turned out to be anything but. In car manufacturing, British Leyland was born out of a series of mergers after British Motor Corporation was formed in the 1950s, including Jaguar, Standard-Triumph, and Rover in 1966. After continued loss of market share and poor financial performance, British Leyland was first bailed out, then nationalized in December 1974.[46]

Other industries fared little better under these policies. In aviation, British Aircraft Corporation and Hawker Siddeley Aviation struggled and ended up as part of a nationalized British Aerospace in 1977. Shipbuilding, machine tooling, and electrical engineering all met a similar fate.[47]

Long-term industry policy rarely works. Part of the reason for that is that governments are particularly bad at picking winners. They typically don't have the requisite commercial and financial skills, they usually act for political or crony-capitalistic reasons, and, as baseball legend Yogi Berra once said, "Making predictions is hard. Especially about the future."

What long-term industry policy does do is provide a temporary patch to the downsides of globalization and a temporary reprieve for the workers who are exposed to the negative effects of it. And it can help with strategic industries, but it does so at a real cost. The whole reason offshoring took place was because of the comparative advantage of different countries in producing certain goods.

A democratic liberal approach, by contrast, focuses on how we can buffer the shocks from global trade—to make it fairer and better address the needs of both workers and consumers.

G. Covid-19 and a Fair Markets Approach

Covid-19 has put enormous pressure on liberal societies and highlighted longstanding weaknesses in liberalism in new and clear ways. It has put intense pressure on work and wages; indeed, in many countries it has led to significant reductions in wages and increases in unemployment. It has revealed the shortcomings of an employment system where people do not have access to meaningful benefits, and especially healthcare. Covid-19 has also revealed the extent to which big tech and other large firms exercise enormous forms of social and economic power in many liberal societies.

Yet, for democratic liberals, one of the reasons for hope coming out the Covid-19 pandemic is that in a number of countries, intimations of a more democratic liberal or fair markets approaches to economic regulation have begun to emerge.

In the United States, the Coronavirus Aid, Relief, and Economic Security (CARES) Act was signed into law by President Trump on March 27, 2020, and provided for a $1,200 per-person payment up to an income limit of $75,000; a 13-week extension of unemployment insurance (costing $250 billion);

a broadening of who is covered by such insurance to potentially include workers in the gig economy; wage subsidies of up to $10,000 for businesses of all sizes, and to small businesses specifically, under the "paycheck protection program" totaling $350 billion;[48] and a $150 billion Coronavirus Relief Fund for state and local governments.[49]

In late December 2020, President Trump signed into law a further $900 billion aid package which included direct payments to households, unemployment subsides, rental assistance, more money for childcare and school re-openings, funding for the vaccine rollout, and support for certain industries such as airlines hit hard by the pandemic.[50]

Moreover, the Biden administration used aggressive fiscal policy almost immediately after taking office. In early March 2021, Biden signed into law a sixth Covid-19 relief bill totaling US$1.9 trillion.[51] This bill included cash payments of $1,400 to a majority of Americans; extended unemployment payments of $300 per week until September 2021; and provided $350 billion to state and local governments, $130 billion for reopening schools, $49 billion for Covid-19 testing, and $14 billion for vaccine distribution.[52]

In late April 2021, Biden announced two large additional fiscal packages: a $2.3 trillion infrastructure plan and a $1.8 trillion "families plan," both to extend over a decade. The families plan included expanding the Earned Income, Child Care, and Dependent Care tax credits ($600 billion); $225 billion for parental leave; an additional $225 billion for childcare; $200 billion for expanding access to healthcare; $200 billion for universal pre-K; $109 billion for two years of free community college; and more.[53]

During the crisis, other countries essentially provided across-the-board wage replacement of between about 70% and 80% (up to a cap) for workers who might otherwise be laid off because of the pandemic (e.g., Denmark, Britain, France, Canada, Germany, Italy, and Spain). Australia provided a flat payment of A$3,000 per month to hard-hit businesses (with at least a 30% revenue drop, 50% for those with annual revenues in excess of A$1 billion) who retained their workers.

These are important measures for people who can perform their jobs, to keep businesses afloat, and to maintain the matches between workers and firms that economists typically view as very valuable (what is known as "firm-specific human capital"). But those whose jobs were extinguished because of social distancing measures needed to resort to unemployment insurance or benefits. Again, the specifics of these arrangements vary by country, but they tend to end up being much less generous than 80% wage replacement.

It is useful to unpack this response further. An alternative government policy in the face of the economic shock induced by Covid-19 would have been to eschew wage subsidies altogether and deal with the fallout to individual workers and households through the unemployment benefits system. There were good, pragmatic reasons for using wage subsidies rather than unemployment benefits—chief among them the fact that businesses small and large would face bankruptcy without the ability to keep operating at part capacity but with a subsidized wage bill. Indeed, evidence of this approach as a design principle is that the CARES Act in the United States was explicitly designed to allow firms to cross-subsidize some of their operating costs from the wage subsidies.

In addition, and perhaps more importantly for thinking about the path forward post Covid-19, is the fact that governments emphasized work as being about more than simply a paycheck. Even when the amount of work that could be performed had shrunk because of the virus's impact on consumer demand or because of containment measures imposed by governments, the wage subsidies demonstrated an emphasis on the primacy of the connection between employee and employer—of work, not simply cash. Indeed, in the United Kingdom the wage-subsidy plan was aptly named the "Coronavirus Job Retention Scheme."[54]

Furthermore, in many countries labor unions managed to gain a number of concessions in the legislation that enabled the wage subsidies. For instance, in the United States the CARES Act places restrictions on small businesses that receive assistance, requiring them to abide by existing collective bargaining agreements and to remain neutral in any union organizing effort for the term of the loan. This had almost immediate bite, with airlines who were trying to restructure their workforce being hindered in that endeavor by union action connected to provisions of the CARES Act.[55]

In the United Kingdom, labor unions and employer groups were involved in discussions with Chancellor of the Exchequer Rishi Sunak, both before the scheme was enacted and also throughout its operation, with the *Guardian* reporting that Sunak "held talks with nine of Britain's union leaders to try to reassure them plans to phase out the government's furlough scheme will be gradual and minimize the impact on unemployment" and "has also publicly thanked union bosses and business leaders for help in designing the job-retention scheme."[56]

Many countries in continental Europe already had so-called tripartite bargaining—involving government, business, and organized labor—of this kind, as part of their ordinary industrial relations landscape, and this was evident in how many of these countries responded to the Covid-19 crisis. In Denmark, the government agreed to pay 75% of wages for three months conditional on employers retaining workers, with employers covering much of the remainder, along with a contribution from employees by taking less vacation time.[57]

In Sweden, workers were guaranteed 90% of wages with the bill split evenly between government and employers. In Norway, workers got 100% wages for 20 days, with 18 of those days paid by for by government and two by the firm. In Germany, the government paid 60% of wages with employers covering the remainder.[58]

In Australia the umbrella body of the union movement—the Australian Council of Trades Unions (ACTU)—was heavily involved in negotiations around Australia's A$3000 per month flat-rate wage-subsidy scheme. Minimum wages and conditions (such as overtime pay and weekend or holiday loadings) are governed by agreements at the sector level (so-called industrial awards) and sometimes at the firm level (so-called enterprise bargaining agreements, or EBAs). The ACTU negotiated directly with the federal government to rapidly change various provisions in awards so that the wage subsidies could be legally and practically put in place, and in a timely manner. They were not only essential to being able to enact the scheme, but even extracted "an assurance they can challenge employers who do not abide by the spirit of the scheme."[59] ACTU Secretary Sally McManus described the negotiations as cooperative, saying, "The last few weeks have shown that unions and reasonable employers can work co-operatively to make the required, temporary changes needed to save jobs and keep incomes flowing during the crisis."[60] Then Industrial Relations Minister (and also Attorney General) Christian Porter described negotiations as ". . . consultative through the union movement, who have been very helpful with this process."[61]

A number of countries provided various forms of assistance for small business. One can think of the wage-subsidy programs as support for businesses in a sense, because they might not be able to make payroll otherwise and would be put under additional financial stress, possibly leading to closure or bankruptcy. But since the funds pass through directly to employees, it is other measures that are more directly supportive of small business. These include government directly providing low-interest loans, or providing loan guarantees. Governments in essentially all advanced economies moved to do this early in the crisis. These programs were often large, with the US program at US$2.3 trillion the largest of any country.[62]

Many countries also supported business (often small, but sometimes large as well) through various forms of tax relief such as reducing or removing payroll taxes and allowing deferral of company income tax payments.

Direct cash payments to certain households were common early responses in many countries. As we already mentioned, they were part of the CARES Act in the United States. Japan gave ¥300,000 to around 10 million of its 58 million households.[63] Australia (with A$1500 to welfare recipients), Belgium, Brazil, Canada, India, Japan, South Korea, and Singapore, also provided direct cash payments early in the crisis.[64]

In addition to direct cash payments, a very large number of countries provided relief to households in other ways. These included subsidies for utility bills, mortgage and rent forbearance (by placing a moratorium on foreclosure and evictions), deferred or reduced property and other tax payments to the government, subsidized or free loans (or loan guarantees) to help with immediate cash flow problems, and even food subsidies or grants.

The pandemic, along with the initial and then ongoing lack of adequate testing resources in the United States, also shone a clearer light on the importance of preventative medicine in general and the role of seemingly simple doctor visits, vaccinations, and testing. Economists have long understood the failure to have adequate preventative medicine imposes at least two types of "negative externalities"—factors that affect other people but are not captured in the market's price mechanism.

The first is that failure to prevent or quickly address health issues before they progress and become more serious is not only bad for the individual concerned, but ends up being potentially vastly more expensive for the healthcare system as a whole. In either a socialized system such as the single-payer systems in Canada, the UK, and much of Western Europe, this cost is borne by taxpayers. And in largely insurance-based systems like the United States, the cost is borne by purchasers of insurance through higher premiums. The second type of externality is the direct possibility of a sick person infecting another through exposure. This does not, of course, occur with chronic illnesses such as heart disease or diabetes, but is particularly important with infectious diseases such as the flu. Covid-19 is obviously an extreme and in many ways scary example of such a disease that is highly transmissible.

What was notable about the experience of the pandemic was that this language of externalities and public awareness of the importance of preventative medicine became a core part of public discourse around the crisis. For example, the Center for American progress observed that there are "massive" externalities surrounding epidemics, and these had the potential to alter standard economic thinking. Many things that were charged for should, in such circumstances, be provided for free—with testing being a leading example.[65]

In addition to this, the differential risk faced by older people, poorer people, and, in the US context, African Americans and members of the Latino community, showed not only the importance of preventative medicine to help reduce Covid-19 deaths but also as a cost-effective and important component of the overall healthcare system post Covid-19.

With households under financial stress, working conditions changing for many people (including working from home), and shelter-in-place orders making in-home care for children more difficult or even impossible, a number of countries moved early in the Covid-19 crisis to provide additional childcare support. Australia announced a very broad scheme in March 2020, offering free childcare during the pandemic. Canada provided an additional C$300 per child through the Canada Child Benefit scheme. Germany—which already had a fairly expansive and generous childcare system—provided expanded childcare benefits for low-income parents. Greece offered paid leave to parents with children not going to school, as did Lithuania, Malta, Montenegro, Portugal, and Switzerland. Spain offered increased funding for meals for children affected by school closures (where they would otherwise have been fed).

A number of countries provided some form of government-funded paid leave, often for those with childcare responsibilities. Although there were differences across countries, and we are aware of no instance in which every worker received an amount of "universal basic leave" (a topic and measure we will return to later) many countries did recognize that the economic dislocation caused by the Covid-19 crisis made some amount of (perhaps additional) leave necessary for many workers.

Some of the countries that provided such leave by early April 2020 were Albania (paid leave for parents), Cyprus (for parents and those with certain health conditions that would make them more susceptible to the virus), Greece (for parents with children not going to school), Latvia (sick leave payments through firms), Luxembourg (for family reasons), Russia (sick leave for those under quarantine), Sweden (funding of sick leave pay for small and medium enterprises [SMEs]), the United Kingdom (funding of sick leave pay for businesses), and the United States (2 weeks paid sick leave).[66]

In sum, Covid-19 has led to new forms of policy response and experimentation that would have been hard to imagine even 12 months before: conservative and progressive governments alike have adopted large-scale economic programs designed to preserve work and wages, and expanded access to healthcare, childcare, and other core benefits.

Covid-19 has also led to large—if temporary—reductions in economic activity; in the areas hit worst by the Covid-19 crisis, we have been offered a glimpse of a lower-carbon world. Emissions dropped by 18% in China between mid-February and mid-March. Even a one-month reduction of that magnitude equates to 250 million metric tons of carbon—half the annual emissions of the United Kingdom. In March 2020, emissions in Italy dropped by 27% compared to the same month in 2019. In the last week of March 2020, motor vehicle emissions in the United States—which make up 60% of the carbon pollution in the country—fell by 38%. And, of course, airline travel—a major source of emissions—plummeted in 2020. Britain even went for the month of May 2020 without generating any electricity from coal for the first time on record.

These are meaningful reductions, if temporary. But they have given hundreds of millions of people in large, heavily polluted cities around the world their first experience of clean air (even if lockdown provisions have made it hard to enjoy). In the Indian city of Delhi, for instance, the air quality index (AQI) is around 200 on a "good" day, and routinely above a life-threatening 900. The World Health Organization deems an AQI above 25 to be unsafe. During the early months of the Covid-19 crisis, Delhi recorded AQIs below 20 for the first time in many people's lives.[67]

As a result of the role that cruise ships had —effectively as giant petri dishes—in incubating and spreading Covid-19, the magnitude of their carbon emissions has become more widely known. A cruise ship emits 401 grams of CO_2 per passenger per kilometer. This is more than three times that of a large passenger aircraft and 36 times that of a fast passenger train like the Eurostar.[68]

There have also been recent positive signs of a shift toward a more concerted policy effort on climate change. The Biden administration's proposed infrastructure bill, for example, included significant elements of the Green New Deal— but on a more modest scale. For instance, the administration proposed $174 billion for electric vehicle incentives, $100 billion for green energy, and $35 billion for climate technology, among other things.[69]

There are, however, two broad paths coming out of the Covid-19 crisis. One is the graduated expansion and tapering of various responses to the pandemic to tailor them to the pre-existing challenges faced by liberal democracies, but more fiscally sustainable in a non-crisis setting. This path would involve looking carefully at the responses of different countries to the Covid-19 crisis and repurposing these into durable and sustainable policies that preserve the innovation, experimentation, and political change that came about during the crisis. Doing so would involve rolling back some—perhaps many—of the emergency measures that were enacted, but it would not involve doing away with them altogether. And it would involve the expansion of other programs which the pandemic has put in place as a type of experiment.

The other response is essentially to recoil against the measures—particularly the fiscal measures—put in place during the crisis and return to a neoliberal model even more damaged and discredited than before. We call this the possibility of "radical rollback" of the positive steps taken during the pandemic toward a more democratic liberal model. For instance, wage-re-placement programs could be removed in full and serve only as temporary measures that do nothing to reverse the long-run stagnation in real wages caused by globalization, automation, and changes in the bargaining power of labor.

The positive aspects of the Covid-19 response in the healthcare system could be completely rolled back, and countries such as the United States could return the system of "private insurance for some" that prevailed before the passage of the Affordable Care Act and still prevails to some extent after it.[70] It is likewise easy to imagine how, with all the priorities coming out of Covid-19, childcare reform could be pushed to the side by a somewhat strange coali-tion of those who hold "traditional" notions of the gender division of labor, those who think the current system is "good enough," and those who think that other reforms need to be prioritized.

And, all of this could be linked to calls for new austerity measures to "pay down" the debt taken on to provide the necessary and appropriate fiscal re-sponse to the crisis. In the wake of the Great Recession of 2008, there was cer-tainly a strong push to cut back government services and to attempt to move quickly to balanced budgets in many advanced economies with center-right governments. The United Kingdom and Australia were notable examples, but as Nobel laureate Paul Krugman observed: "elites all across the western world were gripped by austerity fever, a strange malady that combined extravagant fear with blithe optimism."[71] Krugman labels the focus on austerity a form of "fever" because there are very good reasons for government spending in an economic crisis of the kind created by Covid-19.

The very presence of such a large and defining event, and the fact that there have been significant public policy changes in response to it, also points to the fact that large numbers of policy questions will be "up for grabs" coming out of the pandemic.[72]

Our aim in the book is to persuade readers that the best path to follow is the first, not second path—namely, to use Covid-19 as the catalyst to embrace a more fair-market over free-market model, or democratic over neoliberal ap-proach to our shared economic future.

PART II

FROM FREE TO FAIR MARKETS

4

A Public Baseline: Toward a Green
Jobs Guarantee

It is fair to say that at the turn of the millennium—or 1990, or 2010 for that
matter—it would have been hard to find a mainstream economist who
thought that government should provide any willing worker with a job. There
was an extremely strong consensus that while the government sector plays
an important role in the provision of certain services, the private sector was
both the natural and efficient employer of the bulk of working-age population. Government had an important role to play in providing education and
training, but the private sector would put people to work.

Moreover, this consensus held that when the government did employ
people, it invariably did so inefficiently. Public airlines like British Airways
in the United Kingdom or QANTAS in Australia were privatized in the 1980s
and 1990s and became vastly more efficient both in terms of cost and the
quality of service. Public utilities like electricity generation and distribution
were privatized in many advanced economies, as were a range of other government services from railroads to postal delivery.

That is not to say that economists thought there was no role for government provision of services. In fact, quite contrary to caricature of the economic consensus of the past generation, as neoliberalism that thinks markets
are always good and government is always bad, mainstream economics has
long realized that there is an important role for government. For instance, a
canonical framework put forward by Oliver Hart, Andrei Shleifer, and Robert
Vishny emphasizes that when the government cannot write a perfectly complete contract with a private provider, then government ownership can provide superior incentives for investment in, and provision of, quality.[1]

That said, there was a time when the idea of the government stepping in
and directly providing employment to essentially anyone who was willing and
able to work was a completely conventional idea. At the height of the Great
Depression, the Works Progress Administration (WPA, later renamed the
Work Projects Administration) provided 3.3 million jobs to Americans who
would otherwise have been unemployed. This was, of course, a response to the

emergency that the nation faced with a quarter of the workforce unemployed. But it is also instructive to recall that the WPA was a key part of Tennessee Valley Authority building infrastructure for hydroelectric power in one of the poorest states in the union. The WPA even built the Golden Gate Bridge and Camp David.

Although today's economic crisis is very different in nature from the one during the Great Depression, there have been a range of calls for some kind of scheme that guarantees people a job.[2] But the concept of a jobs guarantee raises a number of threshold questions: who will be eligible, what work will be done, how much will people get paid, how will such a scheme intersect with and impact the private sector, how will it intersect with the welfare state, and more.

In the remainder of this chapter and starting in part A, we outline some answers to these questions that reflect the key principles of democratic liberalism—namely, a commitment simultaneously to preserving space for markets and the private sector, while guaranteeing universal access to a generous social minimum. In part B, we explore how this approach has foundations in the Australian unemployment model as opposed to other successful jobs guarantee programs in countries like India. In part C we explore potential alternatives, or substitutes, such as the idea of a "universal basic income" and why it is both economically unsustainable and less desirable than a jobs guarantee from a democratic liberal perspective. And in part D, we further propose a range of complementary policy ideas with the potential further to combine these commitments, including the idea of a generous earned income tax credit (EITC) for low-income workers, wage-earner equity for low- as well as high-income workers, and specific place-based policies designed to boost private sector employment in areas left behind by globalization and automation. Part E offers a brief conclusion.

A. A Green Jobs Corps: Design and Guiding Principles

A jobs guarantee that serves its purpose and does not have adverse consequences for other parts of the economy needs to be underpinned by some basic principles. First, it must be universal and apply across the economy, not merely be targeted at certain communities or certain categories of people. This matches the cause and breadth of the challenge—automation and globalization are broad challenges that must be met with a broad response.

Second, it must be purposeful, both individually and socially. At the individual level, it must provide dignity to its participants. Again, it is important to be mindful of what a jobs guarantee is replacing. It is fundamentally about providing people with the non-financial benefits of work, and thus the work itself must be as meaningful as possible.

The work performed should also be as socially valuable as possible and likely to be viewed as such. The dignity and sense of meaning people gain from work will be closely linked to its perceived social value. And although social value may be a contested concept about which there may be some reasonable disagreement, public support for such a program may also be influenced by the value it is seen to generate.

Third, it must be *incentive compatible*. Individuals will necessarily have more information than the government about whether or not they can find a private sector job. A jobs guarantee must be designed—in its pay and conditions—to ensure that to the maximum extent possible, it is taken up by those that genuinely need a government job, and not others.

Finally, it must be affordable. As we will discuss below, in an age of secular stagnation with permanently lower economic growth that is consistent with financial stability, the government has some more latitude with its finances than in previous eras. But that latitude is not infinite, and it is essential that there be a rational, clear-eyed assessment of the actual social cost as well as social benefit of the scheme.

(i) Wages and Benefits

Perhaps the most basic question one must ask about a potential jobs guarantee is what participants would be paid. A tempting starting point is to think about what people were getting paid in the job they had before it was destroyed by automation or globalization. In one sense, if the purpose of a jobs guarantee is to replace lost work and put people in the position they would have been in but for sweeping economic forces, then people should get paid their previous wage.

This is impractical at best. It is one thing to create an entitlement to have a job. But if getting paid $40 an hour at some point creates a lifetime entitlement to earn $40 an hour, then there will be huge compliance issues. One can imagine an entire cottage industry devoted to generating spurious and short-lived but high-paid employment so that people can enjoy the lifetime entitlement that would come with it. This, in turn, would spurn an administrative response to try and weed out such behavior. Determining genuine from false claims would be both imperfect and extremely costly.

In addition to these considerations about "gaming," having people working side-by-side in a Jobs Corps, performing essentially identical work for significantly different pay, would naturally breed resentment from the lower-paid participants and be challenging to manage. Together, these considerations point toward a uniform wage.

Were that wage to be set above the minimum wage, then, given that a jobs guarantee involves an entitlement, there would be an instant and dramatic outflow of workers from low-paid private sector jobs into the Jobs Corps. This would be devastating for a range of private businesses and also damaging to consumers, who would face higher prices for the goods and services purchased from those businesses.

Moreover, to satisfy the principle of incentive compatibility—having Jobs Corps jobs going only to those who really need them—it is useful to set the wage in the Corps below the minimum wage. This provides an incentive for those who can get a private sector job to do so. On the other hand, too low a wage in the Corps undermines the aim of providing dignity to participants. A reasonable view of this tradeoff might lead to a Jobs Corps wage 10% below the minimum wage.

Non-wage benefits are also an important part of the picture. As we explore in the next chapter, there is a strong case in a fair market model for universal basic benefits, including a baseline level of healthcare, childcare and paid leave. And these kind of benefits should be part of the design of any Jobs Corp: those part of the Jobs Corp should have access, for instance, to some level of paid leave. Of course, the more generous these benefits are, the more appealing the Jobs Corps will become and the more it will be a competitor with private sector employers. So, while it is important to have some level of basic benefits, leave provisions would need to be calibrated with private sector employers in mind.

(ii) Flexibility and Double-Dipping

A threshold question about any jobs guarantee is whether participation in the scheme is all-or-nothing. That is, is it possible to have a private sector job and also participate in the Jobs Corps?

Given that *under*-employment not just *un*-employment is part of the impetus for a jobs guarantee, it is natural to allow part-time participation in the Jobs Corps to supplement an insufficient amount of private sector work. There would clearly need to be some minimum amount of participation (perhaps 1 or 2 days per week), but non-exclusive participation in the Jobs Corps has a number of benefits.

First, it addresses some of the core challenges around work, such as underemployment and the rise of the gig economy. Second, it provides smooth incentives to search for suitable private sector employment. Making the Jobs Corps exclusive would tend to push people into the Corp on a full-time basis, thus making it both more challenging and costly to sustain, and harder for the individual to transition out.

Third, this would increase the flexibility of the Jobs Corps, thus making it possible for a larger number of people to avail themselves of it consistent with childcare and other responsibilities. This flexibility would also mitigate the need for the state to devote additional resources to support formal childcare as part of the jobs guarantee. Embedding this as a central design feature would not only reduce the need to provide additional resources, it would make the Jobs Corps inherently flexible and accessible, rather than containing rigidities that need to be ameliorated by other means.

Admittedly, this approach creates an important additional challenge. By its very nature, the jobs guarantee is not designed to serve as additional work and income for people beyond a certain point. The purpose is decidedly not to provide a person who already has a full-time job with additional hours. Doing so would (a) put more strain on the Jobs Corps in terms of finding meaningful work for people to perform, and (b) put downward pressure on the terms and conditions of full-time employment—pushing toward a lower-pay / longer-hours norm that is not generally desirable and is inconsistent with commitments to some form of work–life balance.

How, then, does one ensure that the Jobs Corps is not used as a "top-up" to full-time employment? The most efficient way to do so is through an *ex post* income test, rather than an *ex ante* eligibility test. An *ex post* income test would involve determining—at the time of filing an annual tax return—whether income from the Jobs Corps pushed an individual beyond a given threshold—at which point it could be taxed heavily (perhaps even at 100%). The effect of this would be to ensure that beyond a certain income level from other activities, individuals did not find it in their own self-interest to avail themselves of the jobs guarantee.

By contrast, determining eligibility *ex ante* is a resource-intensive exercise and also prone to change throughout a given year, let alone over a longer time horizon.

(iii) Intersection with the Welfare State

One important function of the welfare state is to provide benefits for people who are unemployed. Different countries have different approaches to providing such benefits, but regardless of the structure and generosity of unemployment benefits provided, a jobs guarantee raises the obvious question of whether these benefits need to be retained.

One possibility would be to abolish unemployment benefits altogether—while retaining support for those with other reasons for being unable to work such as disability. There is a certain symmetry and elegance to this approach—if unemployment benefits are meant to support people who want a job and can't get one, let's give those people a job instead of benefits.

A downside of this approach is that it pushes people more immediately into the Jobs Corps after losing or failing to find a job in the private sector. An approach more consonant with the principle that the Jobs Corps should be a fallback rather than a challenger to the private sector is to put a reasonably strict time limit on unemployment benefits. This has the virtue of encouraging search for private sector employment, limits the moral hazard problem stemming from unlimited insurance, and still provides a genuine safety net.

To make this incentive compatible—for people to want to search for private sector jobs and willing to go into the Jobs Corps and off benefits if they cannot find such a job—it would be important for the wage in the Jobs Corps to be materially higher than what could be earned on unemployment benefits. Given the other constraint on Jobs Corps wages—the minimum wage in the private sector—this implies that unemployment benefits may have to be at quite a low level, along with the time limit being reasonably stringent.

(iv) Promotion and Upside Incentives

Since the rationale for having a jobs guarantee is the permanent shift in the structure of the economy toward providing too few jobs, it is likely that at least some people will be in the Jobs Corps for an extended period of time. This raises questions about how they can be provided with promotion possibilities and "upside" incentives.

In awarding the 2016 prize in economic sciences jointly to Bengt Holmstrom, the Nobel Committee emphasized his work on "career concerns" and the role that the prospect of advancement and promotion can play in motivating workers. Motivation is key to both providing participants in the Jobs Corps with a sense of meaning about their work, and for the Corp to produce socially valuable output. It is not meant, as is famously attributed to John Maynard Keynes, to involve people "digging holes and filling them in again."[3]

The Jobs Corps as an organization will clearly need to have a layer of management to help supervise and coordinate work. One natural way to provide motivation is to allow workers in the Corp to be able to be promoted to this supervisory/managerial layer, and indeed give a preference to workers in the Corp for these positions.

It may also be the case that, depending on the type of projects undertaken, there are a range of different skills required in the Corp. This raises the possibility of workers in the Corp being able to undertake additional part-time vocational education to acquire additional skills and advance to a higher tier of work.

This would provide motivation through the prospect of career advancement and would also potentially expand the range of projects that the Corp could undertake.

(v) Taxation

It is tempting to think that, since the government is paying workers in the Jobs Corps and it is in some sense a substitute for welfare, earnings should not be taxed. But to provide the appropriate incentives to search for private sector work, it is important that the Jobs Corps and private sector be put on a level playing field.

It is also important to pay careful attention to the effective marginal tax rate that workers in the Corp are subject to. The effective rate comes from how welfare payments and other benefits phase out at different income levels. This may involve adjusting some of the thresholds for various benefits, and concessions to ensure that participation in the Jobs Corps does not lead to the loss of other benefits and therefore significantly lower the financial benefit of the jobs guarantee.

(vi) Projects

Perhaps the most important and challenging question of a jobs guarantee is what work people will actually do. It's fair to say that this is a much more complicated issue that it was in the 1930s. In that era, many of America's national parks were created by essentially providing young men with an axe and instructing them to go and clear a trail. One now has to grapple with important issues about workplace safety, as well as how workers will interact as part of a team. And one has to grapple with much more complex notions of social value, or benefit.

As we note above, the overarching criterion for selecting jobs guarantee projects should be the degree to which they involve both individually and socially meaningful forms of work. This not only holds out the greatest prospect of providing individuals with dignity, but also of garnering political support for such a program.

Part of the broader opportunity that the jobs guarantee offers is to undertake projects that the private sector would not—without a government subsidy—because there are social benefits involved that would not be factored into ordinary commercial arrangements.

This points to environmental projects as a leading possibility for the Jobs Corps. For example, the cleanup of waterways—ranging from simply removing trash to significant remediation—is a classic public goods problem where individuals will free-ride on others and markets will underprovide cleanup. There is a need in many countries for large-scale tree planting programs. And many coastal or low-lying areas require revegetation and restoration in ways that could be performed by a large green corp of workers.

Depending on the magnitude of environmental challenges in different jurisdictions and the required size of the Jobs Corps, it is even conceivable that the entire jobs guarantee could involve a Green Corps.

In some ways this would look somewhat like aspects of the Green New Deal. But as we discussed in Chapter 3, only some, not all, aspects of the Green New Deal prescription are consistent with democratic liberalism. And in some settings, either practical or political factors may mean that a Jobs Corps should go beyond green projects and focus on other projects, including "pink" projects such as eldercare and care for the disabled.[4]

Again, work of this kind is both dignified and has clear social value. This also creates a self-reinforcing cycle: it increases motivation to do the work and do it well, and thereby increases the chances that the work is seen as respectworthy and politically worthy of support.

This, at least, is one way to understand the evidence that public support for a jobs guarantee tends to increase where it is identified as focused on environmental projects. A range of polls in the United States, for example, show majority support for a jobs guarantee, but the degree of majority support increases when the program is identified as green in nature.[5]

Another important consideration is whether projects are determined at a local level, or at a state or even federal level. On the one hand, a benefit of local control is that localities will typically have better information about which projects are the most beneficial. On the other hand, control at a higher level can lead to better coordination among different projects and help ensure that the projects fit better with other governmental programs.

It seems generally unlikely that either full delegation to the local level or complete control at the national level would be optimal. One intermediate possibility is to have central control of project selection for the Jobs Corps but allow for meaningful input at the local level. This input could simply come from suggestions that are assessed by a central authority, but a way to make suggestions more credible is to give preference to projects that localities are willing to put some funding of their own behind.

This "money where the locality's mouth is" property is another form of the incentive compatibility requirement. Elements of the structure of the jobs guarantee described above cause workers to optimally reveal private information about whether they really need to take advantage of the guarantee. Giving preferential treatment to localities who partly fund projects helps those localities propose projects that they actually believe are the most socially productive.

(vii) Rate of Pay and the Minimum Wage

The type of jobs guarantee we have outlined is designed to replace work that is lost to tectonic forces like automation and globalization. What it is *not* designed to do is provide government employment on such generous terms (high wages and extensive benefits) that it either crowds out or puts substantial pressure on the private sector to match those terms.

The latter consideration underpins a number of jobs guarantee plans from progressive groups (and democratic socialists) like the Levy Institute. Randall Wray of the Levy Institute makes no secret of that, saying: "Our approach to the JG would provide new jobs in a Public Service Employment (PSE) program for approximately 15 million workers at $15 per hour, while creating an additional 4.2 million private sector jobs. It would include a package of benefits worth 25 percent of the wage bill and cover additional costs at 20 percent of the wage bill. The generous wage and benefit package would become standard across the country, as all private and government sector employers would need to match it to retain workers."[6]

As we discussed above, any jobs guarantee that has a material and negative impact on the private sector is not only unpalatable politically, it is misguided. If the private sector could provide everyone willing and able to work with a good-paying job, then the government would not need to provide a jobs guarantee, period. Democratic socialists might reasonably counter that given a federal minimum wage of $7.25 an hour with no benefits, the private sector is *not* providing all willing and able Americans with a good-paying job.

The federal minimum wage in the United States stands at $7.25 per hour, a level that has not changed since July 2009. Indeed, it has fallen in real (inflation-adjusted) terms since 1968.[7] A number of states have state laws mandating a higher minimum rate of pay, although even the most generous of these are fairly modest rates. For instance, the state minimum wage is $12 per hour in Massachusetts, $12 in California (or $11 for firms with fewer than 26 employees), $11.10 in New York, and $14 per hour in the District of Columbia (the highest in the nation). More than 40 towns and localities have enacted minimum wages above their state minimum,[8] with notable examples being New York City at $15 an hour and Los Angeles at $14.25 an hour from July 1, 2019 (going to $15 in 2020). And several states have passed new minimum wage laws that will phase in statewide $15 minimum wages. These states include California, Illinois, Maryland, Massachusetts, New Jersey, and New York.

The "Fight for 15" campaign has sought to raise the minimum wage for all workers across the country to $15 per hour, and all Democratic candidates who sought their party's 2020 Presidential nomination backed a $15 an hour federal minimum wage.[9] Based on a 40-hour work week for 50 weeks a year, that wage would provide an annual income of $30,000 to all workers. Although the cost of living differs substantially across America, a $30,000 annual income for a single person in many parts of the country is a significant contribution to a dignified social minimum. Of course, that level of income is not adequate to support a family of, say, two adults and two children at an appropriate social minimum in most if not all parts of the country. And without affordable healthcare and other benefits, even $30,000 begins to look like a paltry sum.

Even Hillary Clinton campaigned in 2016 on a more gradual approach to eventually increasing the minimum wage to $15 an hour. In many ways, the spectrum from an immediate rise to $15 an hour to a gradual rise over several years mirrors the spectrum from democratic socialism to democratic liberalism that is mentioned earlier in this book.

Joe Biden campaigned on a $15 federal minimum wage but has embraced a degree of realistic gradualism in office. In his first address to a joint session of congress on April 28, 2021, he said: "There should be a national minimum wage of $15 an hour. Nobody working 40 hours a week should be living below the poverty line."[10] He also issued an executive order raising the minimum hourly rate for federal contractors to \$15 by 2022.[11] Yet his administration pulled the \$15 minimum wage provision from the \$1.9 trillion Covid-19 relief bill in order to ensure passage of other provisions.

The main challenge to this movement—certainly the "dramatic" version and to a lesser extent the gradualist version—is that higher minimum wages may well lead to fewer people being employed. Basic economic theory tells us that when the price of something increases, less of it is demanded. Raising the minimum wage amounts to an increase in the price of labor, and it is natural to think that this will lead to a decrease in the amount of labor that employers demand.

One strand of criticism of this view holds that labor markets are somehow fundamentally different from other markets, and that people are not commodities or "goods." While most people can agree that there is an important difference between people and bananas, that difference does not automatically mean that the laws of supply and demand do not operate in the labor market.

A more important criticism of the classic theory of employment and the minimum wage is that while the direction of the impact of a minimum wage increase is clear, the magnitude is not. That is, a hike in the minimum wage will decrease employment, but it is an empirical question as to how much. This "magnitudes question" is, of course, central to understanding the key tradeoff in setting the level of the minimum wage. If it can be increased without leading to more unemployment, but make those earning the minimum wage better off, then that points strongly in favor of a raise. If, however, many people will lose their jobs from even a small increase in the minimum wage, then such a raise will hurt the very category of people it is meant to be helping.

This policy question requires an understanding of the *causal* effect of a rise in the minimum wage on employment. Looking merely at the unemployment rates in places with high minimum wages and comparing those rates to places with low minimum wages is not helpful, because whatever correlation exists there could be the result of any number of other factors.

Of course, economists have realized the importance of causal evidence on this matter for a long time, but it was not until the early 1990s that statistical techniques and research strategies were developed to help understand the causal effect of policies like minimum wages on unemployment. This revolution in applied microeconomics has come to be known as the *identification revolution* (because it led to the "identification" of causal effects) or the *credibility revolution* (because it made research designs and policy conclusions "credible").[12]

The classic academic paper on this issue was published in 1994 by economists David Card and (the late) Alan Krueger. To this day it is cited in policy circles and by commentators discussing the impacts of minimum wage rises on employment.[13] Card and Krueger examined an increase in New Jersey minimum wage from $4.25 to $5.05 an hour in 1992 and found that it did not lead to an increase in unemployment, contrary to the standard prediction of standard economic theory. They described their research design to isolate the causal effect of the New Jersey minimum wage change as follows:

> On April 1, 1992 New Jersey's minimum wage increased from $4.25 to $5.05 per hour. To evaluate the impact of the law we surveyed 410 fast food restaurants in New Jersey and Pennsylvania before and after the rise in the minimum. Comparisons of the changes in wages, employment, and prices at stores in New Jersey relative to stores in Pennsylvania (where the minimum wage remained fixed at $4.25 per hour) yield simple estimates of the effect of the higher minimum wage.

This technique has become known as "difference-in-differences" estimation. In the Card–Krueger setting, it allows them to identify the causal effect of the New Jersey minimum wage increase by factoring out the before-and-after effect in Pennsylvania, which is in the same metropolitan area and thus makes for a good comparator.

One commonly pointed out wrinkle in the Card–Krueger study is that the New Jersey law mandating the increase was enacted back in early 1990, giving restaurants a good deal of time to get ready for the actual minimum wage increase. Rather than do nothing for two years and then suddenly lay off a number of workers, it could well be that employers modified their employment choices in the period after the announcement of the policy but before its enactment. Indeed, the rationale for this type of lag between announcement and implementation of a policy change is to give firms time to adapt.

There has been a huge amount of economic research on minimum wages following Card and Krueger's work. There are two broad types of objections to the finding that increases in the minimum wage have a negligible effect on employment.

First, there is a question about how good a counterfactual Pennsylvania is for assessing changes in policy in New Jersey. If there were "pre-trends" in the period before the study—that is, there were differential things going on in the two states that pertain to employment in fast food restaurants, then the empirical design of the study will not deliver true causal estimates. There has been a long debate about the Card–Krueger study, given its importance. There are legitimate arguments on both sides. A very good, if rather skeptical, summary of this and the broader minimum wage debate is contained in a recent paper by David Neumark.[14]

Second, the specific setting that Card and Kreuger study involves a moderate change in the minimum wage. Moving from $4.25 to $5.05 an hour is an 18.9% increase. This is clearly a lot for people earning the minimum wage, and it is not insignificant for employers—particularly those for whom wages are a large proportion of their cost base. But it is small relative to some of the increases that are now advocated. Moving from $7.25 an hour to $15 an hour is more than a doubling of the minimum wage, and even when moving from $10 or $11—the level of some of the more generous current state minimum wages—to $15 and hour is increase of between one-third and one-half.

There is no reason to believe that the employment effects of a 19% increase in the minimum wage are the same as those for an increase of double, triple, or a five-fold percentage increase (as in the case of more than doubling the minimum wage from $7.25 to $15 an hour). Indeed, the very thing that makes credible the empirical strategy that Card and Krueger use in identifying the causal estimate of a policy change means that its conclusions are limited to small changes. In the language of economics, they identify a "local average treatment effect," and one needs to be cautious in extrapolating that effect to large-scale (or "global") changes.[15]

We agree, and it is a central plank of democratic liberalism, that a dignified social minimum needs to be afforded to everyone; and this means guaranteeing a minimum wage that allows for a dignified life for full-time workers. But raising the minimum wage needs to be done openly and based on evidence and debate, not via the backdoor of a large increase in the minimum wage for public sector rather than private sector workers. It also needs to be done with a view to avoiding a harsh tradeoff between decent wages and access to employment.

Many advocates of a jobs guarantee implicitly claim that there is no tradeoff between minimum wages and employment, but this begs the question of why they need a jobs guarantee at all. Why not simply require the private sector to pay $25 an hour plus benefits? Or $30. Or $40.

As a matter of logic, the answer is that the private sector would not provide a sufficient number of jobs at those rates of pay. But even if one believes that there is no tradeoff between minimum wages and unemployment, the forces of automation and globalization would leave a significant "jobs gap." Our jobs guarantee seeks to fill that gap, but not in a way that makes the gap larger by reducing private sector employment.

The key point to understand is that there are two problems to be solved: (i) there are not enough private sector jobs; and (ii) at the current minimum wage in the United States, many of those jobs that do exist do not provide a sufficient social minimum. And, solving those problems requires two different instruments—a jobs guarantee that provides work to those who need it, and a boost to private sector conditions through the universal leave and other programs discussed earlier.

Trying to use a jobs guarantee with generous terms and conditions to solve both the amount and nature of work problems is a mistake. It makes the jobs gap larger, and it puts the government in direct competition with the private sector not out of necessity (in employing people to provide essential government services) but by design (as a way of forcing the hand of the private sector).

This may be justified in some circumstances: for instance, in India there is a national "workfare" or jobs guarantee program that is deliberately designed to put competitive pressure on private sector employers to adhere to the law and actually pay the minimum wage to private sector workers.[16] But absent this kind of compliance or rule of law concern, democratic liberalism favors a more direct approach to raising both the minimum wage and guaranteeing residual public sector employment for those who need it.

B. Historical Precedents and Australia as Model?

As we noted earlier, there is some historical precedent for a jobs guarantee of this kind. For instance, US President Franklin Roosevelt's New Deal established the WPA, which employed a staggering 13 million workers (more than 11% of the entire, not just working-age, US population at the time) building infrastructure and environmental projects such as national parks. Argentina's "Plan Jefres" began in 2001 and hired 13% of the workforce in a manner similar in spirit to the WPA, at a time where unemployment exceeded 20% in Argentina. As the Argentine economy recovered, the plan was gradually wound back.

In India, the National Rural Employment Guarantee Act is a large and self-targeted "workfare" program that guarantees citizens 100 days of paid work at minimum wage. Nobel Laureates Esther Duflo and Abhijit Banerjee have also suggested might be a model for a US federal jobs guarantee. As they describe it:[17]

> Every rural family is entitled to a hundred days of work per year at the official minimum wage, which is higher in most places than the actual wage. There is no official screening, but there is the requirement to work, usually on construction sites,

which screens out anybody with something better to do than stand in the sun for eight hours a day.

And, as Pavlina Tcherneva documents, there have been smaller, more local-ized jobs programs in a range of other countries including France, Belgium, and the United States in the late 1970s.[18]

The specific democratic liberal jobs guarantee proposal, however, has especially strong parallels with the modern Australian model of unemployment benefits, and the general Australian emphasis on democratic liberal over democratic socialist policy approaches. In the United States, unemployment benefits are determined in large part at the state level, although there are federal programs with which the state programs interact. In general, benefits are based on an insurance model, where workers make contributions (i.e., premium payments) through payroll taxes while they are employed.[19]

The state-based nature of unemployment benefits schemes in the United States—an artifact of history given their development in the New Deal era—means that in practice, there is significant variation in how generous benefits are depending on the state. For instance, benefits range from $235 per week in Mississippi to as much as $1,113 in Massachusetts, and the average duration of benefits is 26 weeks but ranges from 12 weeks in Florida and 13 weeks in North Carolina, to 30 weeks in Massachusetts.[20]

Countries like Italy and Japan are more generous than the United States in terms of the duration of unemployment benefits, but like the United States, they rely on a contributions-based model. For instance, in Italy, under the *Assicurazione Sociale per l'Impiego,* or ASPI, workers receive up to the 75% of their previous wages for up to 16 months when they become unemployed.[21] In Japan, the system is explicitly labeled "unemployment insurance," with contributions coming from both employers and employees. The duration of benefits depends on the age of the employee and the amount of contributions they have made during their employment.[22]

Canada, the United Kingdom, and Germany also all have an insurance-based system where workers make contributions while employed. In Germany the baseline payments are quite low at €374 per month, but "reasonable" ac-commodation is also funded.[23] The Canadian system is run at a provincial level and is more complicated still. Canadians are eligible only if they have paid the 1.58% contributions tax during employment.[24] They can then receive benefits when unemployed, calculated at 55% of insurable income up to ap-proximately C$500 per week. But the duration of the benefits depends on the rate of unemployment in their province.

By contrast, Australia has benefits that are not particularly generous but are neither based on a contributions/insurance model, nor do they have a fixed expiry date. To be eligible one must be at least 22 years old (but not old enough to be eligible for the aged pension), looking for work, and be under an income and asset test limit. A single person meeting the eligibility requirements receives around $275 per week, with single parents and others with various caring responsibilities receiving more, as do people with disabilities.[25] The "looking for work" requirement involves fairly rigorous monitoring by the relevant government agency, Centrelink, to ensure that recipients are making a genuine attempt to find a job and move off benefits.

And, there is a supplemental "work for the dole" program, which begins after six months of unemployment and offers modest additional payments in return for job seekers engaging in between 10 and 50 hours of "gardening and maintenance works, conservation or environmental activities, retail work, hospitality services, office administration or warehouse duties" aimed at building an individual's skills and experience and making a broader contribution to the community.[26]

The model of jobs guarantee we propose has much in common with the Australian model of unemployment benefits. To provide adequate safety-net benefits must not be time-limited or based on prior work history or insurance-based forms of contribution. Indeed, it recognizes that unemployment benefits must be a true social insurance scheme, not a quasi-privatized scheme based on individual contributions but administered by government agencies.

At the same time, it aims to *encourage* individuals to look for private sector work, so that people do not receive the benefits indefinitely if they are able to work and receive decent wages and benefits elsewhere. The payment level is thus set at a low enough rate to make it unappealing as a long-term solution, but high enough to ensure a level of dignity and the ability to actually look for work (though the pre-Covid-19 level in Australia clearly fell short of this ideal). People with disabilities or substantial caring responsibilities are also either provided for under different programs or receive additional unemployment benefits.

This is also what distinguishes our proposed model from a jobs guarantee that is democratic socialist in design. Where one seeks to provide a last-resort but dignified option for those unable to find work in the world of free trade and automation, the other looks a lot like a backdoor attempt to raise the minimum wage and create universal access to health care. And while these goals may be laudable objectives in themselves, this conflates two quite different objectives: fixing private sector work and benefits, and providing work to those who simply cannot find it in the private sector. It also ensures that a federal jobs guarantee would likely be extremely (and unnecessarily) expensive.

A democratically liberal jobs guarantee, by contrast, would aim to ensure a living wage for all citizens (and most likely permanent residents) and access to basic benefits, but at levels below what the private sector provides—and in ways that continue to give workers incentives to rely on private sector jobs wherever possible. This also makes such a jobs guarantee much closer to a guarantee, or measure of last resort, than its policy twin—a Green Manhattan Project.

C. Substitutes

One of the hottest topics in attempting to address the pre–Covid-19 crisis in work and wages has been the concept of a universal basic income, or UBI. A UBI would provide some baseline level of income, perhaps $20,000 per annum in a country like the United States, to all people regardless of their means, other income, or activities. Or, to use the useful definition offered by Philippe Van Parijs and Yannick Vanderborght in their recent book *Basic Income*: "a regular income paid in cash to every individual member of a society, irrespective of income from other sources and with no strings attached."[27] It is paid to individuals (perhaps just adults, perhaps children, too) rather than households. It is paid in cash, not in kind.

The idea of a UBI has gained traction in part due to tech luminaries such as Mark Zuckerberg and Elon Musk making approving noises about the possibility of it combating mass unemployment due to automation.

Zuckerberg, in his Harvard Commencement address put it this way:[28]

> Let's face it: There is something wrong with our system when I can leave [Harvard] and make billions of dollars in 10 years, while millions of students can't afford to pay off their loans, let alone start a business. Now it's our time to define a new social contract for our generation. We should explore ideas like universal basic income to give everyone a cushion to try new things.

Musk spoke in somewhat more apocalyptic tones when he said in a tweet[29] in June 2018: *"Universal income will be necessary over time if AI takes over most human jobs."*

A slew of authors have written books advocating one or another version of the UBI.[30] And there have been several trials of some version of a basic income in certain communities around the world.

Silicon Valley acceleration Y-Combinator ran a pilot study of a basic income in Oakland, California, and plan to conduct an evaluation involving a group of 1,000 people who will receive $1,000 per month for five years.[31] The Ontario government in Canada began a three-year pilot in April 2018 involving a treatment group of 4,000 people and a control group of 2,000.[32] And there have been a range of studies in low-income countries: one of the most wide-ranging and carefully designed trials is by GiveDirectly in Kenya, which aims to give 21,000 people in rural Kenya a basic income over a 12-year period. By providing for different amounts of money over different time horizons (different "treatments"), the GiveDirectly trial hopes to isolate the most effective form of basic income. The GiveDirectly researchers are quite explicit that the existing negative income tax or other trials of versions of the basic income are inadequate for evaluating the effectiveness of a pure UBI because they were insufficiently universal, too short-term in nature, or were not part of a properly randomized controlled trial.

It will take time to learn the outcome of these trials, but they will provide gold-standard evidence on the range of impacts the researchers are focusing on, including income and assets, use of time (such as work, education, leisure, community involvement), business creation, female empowerment, and outlook on life. There is also good reason to think that some kind of basic income could be promising in very poor communities in developing countries, especially as a form of international assistance and foreign aid. There are obvious advantages to a UBI as a means of addressing severe poverty in the developing world—especially if it is funded by wealthy countries and individuals.

There is persuasive evidence that cash transfers to very poor households can provide an effective and reliable means of boosting their economic welfare. It would be a means of providing international aid or development assistance. And a UBI of this kind would be a complement, not a substitute, for work. It thus has the potential to be a practical and effective means of addressing current forms of poverty and economic deprivation.

We suggest, however, that a UBI is exactly the wrong response to the current threat to work in developed economies—because of its impact on both economic security and stability of liberal democratic citizens and governments, and its tendency to displace, rather than complement, work as a source of dignity, meaning, and community.

(i) Economic Cost and Sustainability

As for fiscal sustainability, a UBI may be economically viable in parts of the developing world or Global South, especially if it is underwritten by wealthier nations: roughly 1.3 billion people in the world survive on less than $US1.25 a day. Giving those people a basic income that (say) doubled that amount would thus be both economically transformative and feasible. And while a $600 billion price tag sounds high for an aid/development program of this kind, recall that in 2018 the total global gross domestic product (GDP) was $135.2 trillion.

But imagine trying to achieve something of a similar scale in OECD countries where the average annual income is closer to $33,000 per year. The fiscal arithmetic of a true UBI in a country such as the United States is extremely daunting, if not prohibitive. A $20,000 per annum UBI for every American 18 years and older would cost approximately $4.7 trillion—substantially more than the entire federal budget outlays of $3.8 trillion and more than double Social Security, unemployment benefits, Medicare, and education combined. Worse still, the shortfall would need to be made up by taxing others more, creating distortions throughout the economy that further shrink the tax base.

The cost of a truly universal basic income in advanced economies is thus prohibitive. Indeed, the Ontario government announced, just four months after announcing the trial of a UBI in 2018, that it was shutting down the trial due to the expense of running it even on a limited scale.

One potential response to this comes from the way in which Democratic presidential hopeful Andrew Yang has explained and advocated for his "Freedom Dividend," which was arguably the defining feature of his bid for the Democratic Party's 2020 nomination.

Yang's freedom dividend is instructive in highlighting how one might pay for a UBI and what one would need to believe about its benefits for it to make fiscal sense. Yang's plan[33] would provide every American over 18 years old with $1000 a month, regardless of their other income or wealth. In that sense it is, indeed, truly universal. Part of the way that Yang sees this being funded is by replacing certain existing expenditures including the Supplemental Nutritional Assistance Program (SNAP/food stamps), disability, and some other welfare payments. As Yang himself sometimes points out, in this sense it looks much like a negative income tax, whose proponents included no lesser (neo)liberal than Milton Friedman.

Another thing Yang has frequently pointed out is that he "likes math," but even if certain welfare programs could be removed with his freedom dividend, the math is daunting. Start with the cost, which the UBI Center (a think tank that provides open-source tools that allow one to assess various UBI proposals) calculates as being $2.8 trillion per annum based on the 236 million adult citizens in the United States.[34] The Tax Foundation used their fiscal model to estimate what tax increases, of the five that Yang's plan points to, would raise to offset this cost.[35] The largest of these proposed taxes is a value added tax, along the lines of which many other countries have (although usually replacing a sales tax of the kind that most US states levy). The Tax Foundation finds that a 10% VAT in the United States (which, for instance, is the rate in Australia on non-exempt goods and services) would raise $952 billion a year. Add to that Yang's other tax proposal: removing the current cap on the Social Security payroll tax ($133 billion), a $40 per metric ton carbon tax ($123 billion), and a financial transactions tax ($78 billion), along with taxing capital gains and dividends at ordinary-income rates ($14 billion), comes to a total of $1.3 trillion in tax offsets.

Yang's plan involves an "opt-in" whereby retaining access to certain existing welfare programs while accessing the freedom dividend is reduced. As his website puts it: "We currently spend between $500 and $600 billion a year on welfare programs, food stamps, disability and the like. This reduces the cost of the freedom dividend because people already receiving benefits would have a choice but would be ineligible to receive the full $1,000 in addition to current benefits." The Tax Foundation and the UBI Center estimate that the net benefit of this opt-in—the federal government saving money from those who decline the freedom dividend in favor of their current benefits, and from those who give up their current benefits by electing to receive the freedom dividend—saves $151 billion per annum.

What remains to bridge the gap is a boost in economic activity from the freedom dividend. Yang's campaign website claims that this will amount to between $800 and $900 billion per annum, stating, "the Roosevelt Institute projected that the economy would grow by approximately $2.5 trillion and create 4.6 million new jobs. This would generate approximately $800–900 billion in new revenue from economic growth and activity." This is based on a suite of optimistic and highly questionable assumptions by the Roosevelt Institute,[36] including but not limited to: zero distortion from the increased taxes involved in the plan despite these being a 120% increase on the existing total tax base; that there are no supply constraints in the economy; that all firms in the economy can be captured by a representative firm; and that the marginal propensity to consume across the economy will increase significantly as a result of the policy.

The Yang plan highlights the stark difficulty of the UBI fiscal math. Even at the relatively modest level of $1,000 per month, limiting it to adult US citizens (however one might do that, given the prevalence of undocumented workers), and include two significant and no-doubt controversial new taxes (a VAT and a carbon tax), one needs to rely on heroic assumptions about increased productivity and labor supply just to break even.

And, as the Tax Foundation points out, it is important to factor in the reduction in economic activity due to the increased taxes required to pay for the freedom dividend. Their model suggests that the implied increase of 8.6 percentage points in taxes on labor income would reduce the total hours worked in the US economy by 3%, leading to a reduction in income tax revenues of $124 billion per annum.

Furthermore, there is good reason to believe that the negative labor supply effects from a UBI of the magnitude of the freedom dividend could be larger than this. As the University of Chicago economist Luigi Zingales has argued, a change of the magnitude of a UBI can affect social norms, particularly around the importance of work. Zingales points to the experience of countries like Iran, where there has been a shift in attitudes of young people about work after large cash transfers have become part of the welfare state. This can lead to permanent, negative, irreversible effects on labor supply.

In light of all of this it is hard, then, to see how a UBI can be a meaningful solution to a general crisis in work and wages. Moreover, those advocates of a UBI who seek to address the fiscal arithmetic problems by arguing for a more modest level of payment, for instance a few hundred dollars a month per adult, are essentially ducking the question of how a UBI can address the problems stemming from automation. If literally tens of millions of (net) jobs are going to vanish from the US economy, a $500 monthly basic income is not going to address that level of social and economic dislocation in any meaningful way.

But in many ways, a "partial UBI" is more dangerous than that. One of the animating ideas behind Milton Friedman's concept of a negative income tax (where people below a certain level of income would receive payments from the government, unlike an unconditional UBI) was that it would justify the removal of a range of welfare programs. A UBI that is not enough to live on, but which justifies the removal of targeted welfare payments, is dangerous, as it provides a basis for society absolving itself of the responsibility to take care of its most vulnerable members. And, as the analysis of Yang's freedom dividend shows, even at that partial and insufficient level, it is a budget buster.

Later in this book we will return to other ideas for funding a UBI, along with other programs like universal childcare and Medicare for all. These ideas include a wealth tax, value added tax, taxing capital income more heavily, selling off natural resources, and even printing money. The fiscal arithmetic of all of these ideas, as well as the negative incentive effects that come with many of them, are daunting. But that is not to say that no more revenue can be raised, as we discuss in Chapter 8.

(ii) Beyond Fiscal Arithmetic

There are also other reasons, other than fiscal sustainability, to value work in a liberal democratic context. It affords a sense of dignity and purpose, it develops skills, and it provides community and an avenue for a broad range of social interactions.

Work affords people dignity. Work provides people with community. Work gives people purpose. And the absence of work robs people of these things. And, as we mentioned earlier, there is a well-established link between work and mental health—particularly in terms of depression and addiction. While the opioid crisis in the United States surely has multiple causes, dislocation in the labor market has clearly played a role, as is evidenced by the geographic concentration of both job losses and the prevalence of addiction.

There is also a basic philosophical point that connects to the fiscal arithmetic we have discussed. That is, the absence of a work requirement that is central to a UBI implies that *by design*, some people will free-ride on the labor and toil of others. Or, as Jon Elster has put it, a UBI "goes against a widely accepted notion of justice: it is unfair for able-bodied people to live off the labor of others."[37]

There is one other philosophical aspect of a UBI that is worthy of note. The work of those who have caring roles that are not part of paid employment— such as stay-at-home parents, or people caring for their (elderly) parents— does not show up in official statistics such as GDP. According to Andrew Yang (for example) people in these roles receiving a UBI provides them with acknowledgment that their work is valued.

There are two problems with this argument. This first is that a UBI, by its very nature, is universal. It is therefore unclear how a UBI would provide acknowledgment to people not working outside the home, when everyone else would be receiving the same payment from the government. The second problem is that a UBI is the wrong tool to use in addressing the underlying issue.

It is certainly the case that official economic figures like GDP can be misleading because they do not capture the value added by people in all sectors of the economy. The case of women caring for children is a perhaps the quintessential example of this. The appropriate way to address this issue is to ensure that unpaid work—such as that inside the home—can be properly measured, and a shadow price for the good or service be established.

Indeed, we have suggested that one promising way to do this might be to allow families to make tax-deductible contributions toward the retirement savings of members of the household engaged in this kind of unpaid work. In many countries, doing so would go a long way toward addressing the current gender imbalance in retirement income. And by definition, it would provide a way to capture the economic value of that work.[38]

Finally, proponents of the UBI like Andrew Yang believe that a $1000 monthly UBI will lead to a new era of entrepreneurship and human flourishing. As he put it in an interview with the *New York Times* podcast *The Daily*, "if we had an economy that was based on making us happy, then we would do this yesterday, clearly. Let's imagine I'm president in 2021, the freedom dividend goes out, there's a town of 10,000 people in Missouri, so that means there's another $10 million in spending power every month, and one person there decides to open a bakery, which might have been a really dumb idea before the freedom dividend, but now it's a good idea. They open a bakery, it sells muffins, people like the muffins. Were there cheaper ways to get those muffins to those people? Probably yes. Is the new bakery, like, somewhat economically inefficient? Perhaps, but does it make the community happy, does it make the bakers happy, does it make everyone's life better despite its economic imperfections? Yes. That is the vision of the economy we have to move towards."[39]

That vision of the economy, one based on an esoteric notion of happiness and communitarianism that is explicitly disconnected from, and indeed directly at odds with, efficiency is a very different vision of the economy than most liberal democracies currently have. And it remains far from clear to many observers, us among them, that an unconditional UBI will lead to town after town of "happy bakers" making their "freedom muffins" rather than a generation of people with video-game addictions and substance-abuse problems who never come to know the sense of purpose and dignity gained through work.

D. Complements

Finally, it is useful to consider how the adoption of a jobs guarantee could be combined with other measures—in addition to a decent minimum wage—that could boost the earnings of those workers who remain wholly or predominantly in the private sector.

A fair markets approach suggests that governments should seek to boost wages for private sector workers in a range of ways: through a decent and in many cases higher minimum wage, but also through newer and more innovative approaches—such as a generous EITC, encouragement for universal access to wage-earner equity as well as salary payments, and place-based policies that include some form of wage subsidy.

This has the advantage of boosting worker wages in the short run, but also encouraging ordinary workers to share in the increasing returns to capital, which currently seems to drive much of the inequality in wealth and income worldwide. We also see efforts to guarantee decent work and wages as complementary: if private sector wages are too low, a public jobs program will become much more attractive for hundreds of thousands if not millions of workers in ways that inevitably strain its financial sustainability. A commitment to protecting unions and rights to collective bargaining is likewise an important and complementary step to ensuring that workers receive a greater share of the returns from their labor, or the overall economic surplus.

(i) An Expanded EITC

One policy that encourages and subsidizes work as a means of providing the social minimum is the EITC, a policy that has been around in the United States since 1975. Despite beginning as a very modest program, it was expanded in 1986, 1990, 1993, 2001, and 2009.

The EITC is a refundable tax credit for lower-income working Americans, which encourages employment. The amount received depends on family structure and the number of eligible children the recipient has. In 2018 these amounts ranged from $519 for a single person without children to $6,431 for those with three or more children.

The EITC currently provides assistance to 28 million Americans and has the effect of lifting 9 million people above the federal poverty line.[40] It is the third-largest welfare program in the United States after Medicaid and the Supplemental Nutritional Assistance Program ("food stamps"), with a headline cost of around $60 billion per annum. But because it encourages work and hence makes fewer people dependent on other forms of welfare, as well as boosting income tax revenue, it is estimated that the true cost is around 13% of the headline figure.[41] One additional benefit of the EITC that has been emphasized in recently published work is the gender impacts, with the EITC accounting for an increase in maternal employment of 6% in the United States.[42]

A program that lifts nearly 10 million people out of poverty, encourages work and the attendant social benefits that come with it, and that directly returns seven dollars for every eight that is spent on it seems ripe for expansion. The fact that it indeed has been expanded a number of times lends further weight to this view.

A starting point is that singles without children are only eligible for benefits if they earn less than $15,270 a year. That is basically the federal minimum wage, and insufficient for most people to live on. This threshold rises to $40,320 for a single parent with one child—which seems much more reasonable. A starting point for reform would be to raise the single-person threshold significantly and enlarge the tax credit substantially.

More broadly, when thinking about how one might expand the EITC it is also vital to consider the *effective marginal tax rate* paid by workers. This is the amount of tax they pay for an extra dollar earned, taking account of any benefits or tax credits that are phased out or lost due to eligibility rules in the design of those schemes. It is the effective marginal tax rate which not only determines the incentive for individuals to work more, but also what share of the income generated by that additional work they are able to keep.

Notwithstanding the eligibility thresholds for the EITC, there are "phase-in" and "phase-out" provisions of the EITC to smooth out the effective marginal tax rate and avoid perverse incentive effects around the thresholds. Figure 4.1 shows the relatively smooth nature of the effective marginal rates as income increases.[43]

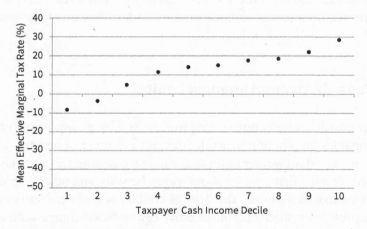

Figure 4.1 Average Effective Marginal Tax Rates, 2010

This means that the greatest incentive effect exists for the lowest income earnings, and that the tax system remains strongly progressive. This is also reflected in *average* tax rates by income level.[44]

Taken together, these facts demonstrate that it is possible to construct the EITC in a way that provides incentives for low-income people to seek employment and that compensates them for doing so.

The non-financial benefits of employment are significant. Work plays an important role in providing people with purpose and dignity; it provides a positive role model for children, and it helps develop skills and human capital that make future employment both more likely and more remunerative. Thus, the overall structure of the EITC in the United States is quite workable—it is the levels that need to be adjusted. Other countries, however, could benefit from the introduction of a similar scheme. Although countries like the United Kingdom, Australia, and a number of Western European nations have schemes that support low-income households and provide a variety of child tax credits, these typically do not have the same work-incentive properties as the EITC.

Canada's "Working Income Tax Benefit" (WITB) is a refundable tax credit that is fairly similar to the US EITC. Andrew Jackson provided evidence that for those who qualify, the program is relatively effective, but that its design could be improved to ensure that more working poor qualify for the WITB.[45]

The Biden administration's "Families Plan" announced in April 2021 sought to make permanent the EITC expansion for workers without children, as introduced in the American Rescue Plan earlier in 2021. That plan nearly tripled the EITC for childless workers, helping 17 million low-wage workers.[46] It expanded the EITC for these workers from $534 to $1,502 and relaxed the eligibility requirements to include workers under 25 years of age and those over 65.

(ii) Wage-Earner and Shadow Equity

Another possibility for compensating workers is through ownership stakes in the companies for whom they work. This has a number of benefits. It better aligns the interests of workers with senior management and also shareholders. It can reduce intra-firm conflict about wages, benefits, and other employment terms. One manifestation of this type of conflict is when executives receive large payouts from stock options or other equity-based compensation while "ordinary workers" are facing redundancies, pay cuts, or cuts in benefits.

Giving workers a slice of the same type—if not the same level—of compensation enjoyed by senior executives helps reduce this conflict.

It also has the potential to help compress the huge difference in compensation inequality that has developed over the last several decades between managers and workers. An oft-quoted statistic is that in recent years, the average CEO of a top-350 US firm earns roughly 300 times what an average worker does. In 1978 that ratio was 30:1.[47] Some of this is due to a handful of extremely highly paid CEOs (earning over $100 million in a given year), but the massive disparity between CEOs and workers is hard to deny, as is the fact that it has exploded in the last 40 years.

The pressures that have led to the crisis in work and wages that we currently face—from automation to globalization—have put significant downward pressure on the returns to human capital for a wide range of workers, and hence put downward pressure on their labor income. At the same time, many of the changes to the global economy that have reduced the returns to labor have also been associated with increasing returns to capital. And as the famous French economist Thomas Piketty has pointed out, and as we discussed in Chapter 2, when returns to capital exceed the rate of economic growth in the economy, there is upward pressure on income inequality.[48]

Of course, there is very little stopping firms from issuing equity to their employees at the moment—but there are steps that can be taken to make it more attractive to both firms and workers. Some of these involve making it more financially beneficial to the firm, and others involve ameliorating a number of the existing downsides to equity-based compensation.

In other words, it's not the case that firms can't provide equity-based compensation to workers; rather, there is a social benefit to it, in addition to whatever benefits accrue to the firms themselves through worker recruitment, retention, and productivity, that is not being factored into the calculus of compensation. It is a classic example of a *positive externality*.

In general, when there are positive externalities from certain activities undertaken by firms, it is quite common for governments to subsidize them through tax credits or stepped-up tax deductibility for the activities.

A leading example of this is the tax treatment of research and development (R&D) expenditures. The OECD reported in 2017 that 29 of the 35 OECD countries offer preferential tax treatment for R&D expenditures, as do 22 of 28 members of the European Union.[49] Although these schemes are sometimes complex in their design, and differ across countries, it is not uncommon for the headline rate of tax subsidy to be around 20%.[50]

One can imagine a similar approach to equity-based compensation for employees—that is, an additional 20% tax deductibility from (federal) company taxes for eligible equity-compensation payments. Under this approach, up to 10% of any employee's total compensation would be eligible for "stepped-up" tax deductibility at the rate of 120% (compared to the existing 100%).

An alternative to federal corporate tax deductibility is for state or provincial governments, who typically levy payroll taxes in most jurisdictions, to offer an exemption for the cost of making payments of this kind. This has the potential to be less comprehensive unless all state/provincial governments adopted it. In this case, it would impose a cost on states that would generate a spillover benefit to other states, and therefore raise concerns about a "free-riding" problem where states may not find it in their own interest to implement the deduction unless other states also do it. On the other hand, there would clearly be an offsetting effect whereby states that do adopt such a policy become more attractive places to do business.

On the positive side, this approach would be a way for the scheme to gain a foothold and momentum without requiring national legislation. The same is true for other measures states could take to promote the idea, including measures designed to encourage newly privatized entities to offer employees equity as part of the initial public offering process. In the United States, for instance, this is a step that the Securities and Exchange Commission could take.

Interestingly, China instituted preferential individual income tax treatment for equity awards by both listed and unlisted companies to encourage the use of equity awards as a form of compensation in China.[51]

The key benefit to expanding equity-based compensation beyond executives to a wide range of employees is its capacity to redress the current decline in real wages—and increase the long-term compensation growth enjoyed by average wage earners.

Figure 4.2 shows the real wage index in Australia—a jurisdiction that has seen some real wage growth over the last four decades—as well as the real return on Australian equities (the All Ordinaries Accumulation Index) and US equities (the S&P 500 Accumulation Index).[52] These indices are a measure of the real returns to capital on a broad basket of (around 300 in Australia and 500 in the United States) publicly traded stocks. As such, it is a useful measure of the return on wage-earner equity discussed here.

To give a sense of the impact this can have, consider the impact on the earnings of an employee who received 90% of her income in wages and 10% in wage-earner equity. Using the Australian figures—since at least in Australia there has been some real wages growth—if the wage-earned equity earned the same average return as the broad index on average for the last 25 years, then over a 10-year period the employee's earnings growth rate would be 1.8%

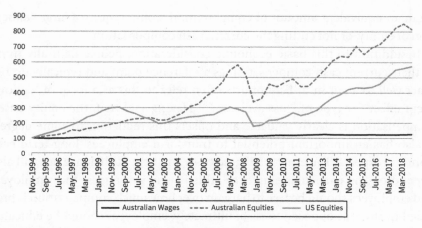

Figure 4.2 Returns to Labor versus Returns to Capital

compared to the 0.9% in wages alone over that period—or roughly double for the same 10-year period.[53]

For the average full-time income earner, this translates into an annual average income one decade out that is 20% higher than their current income. This is equivalent to an increase in real terms from A\$86,640 per annum to A\$103,800 per annum, compared to A\$94,980 under wage-only compensation.[54] This represents a 9.3% difference between the income under wage-earned equity and wage-only compensation.

The key issue with equity-based compensation is that it is risky—it depends on the market value of the company in which it is earned. By contrast, wages are risk-free. And employees generally do not like risk, because they have fixed payments like a mortgage, rent, car, or education loan payments, school fees, and so on.

Consider the trends set out in Figure 4.2. There are two things to note from that chart. The first, as we already noted, is that the real rate of return on capital is substantially greater than the increase in real wages. But the second is that it is also more volatile. Stock prices—even whole indices—can move up or down by double-digit percentage points in a given year, whereas wages are much more stable, for very natural reasons, both in terms of increases and decreases. These two basic facts are reflected in the difference in annualized returns between wages and stocks (9.1% versus 0.9% per annum), and also the standard deviation of those returns (9.4% and 1.1%, respectively).

An immediate implication of this is that simply replacing some proportion of employees' current cash compensation with an equivalent amount of equity-based compensation will make them worse off in expectation. To give them an equivalent amount of compensation would require a larger allocation of equity, or not cutting the current cash compensation.

In addition to this basic economic consideration, people naturally think of their current cash compensation as a reference point and typically do not react well to a cut in it. Economists often refer to this as a form of "endowment effect" or type of "loss aversion."[55] Having said that, the equity-based compensation is clearly valuable and offsets this reduction to some degree. It also has an important potential to transform employees' long-term economic prospects. The exact way these costs and benefits balance out will also depend on the particular employee. This is why we suggest that employers and employees should be free to bargain over how much compensation is provided in stock as opposed to cash: ultimately, employees should be educated about the long-term benefits of compensation via stock but given maximum choice in the mix of stock versus cash compensation they receive.

Employees should likewise be encouraged to *retain* equity in a firm for as long as possible, but not required to do so. In other words, we do not propose that wage-earner equity schemes should be subject to the same "lock in" or vesting periods that often apply to CEO compensation.

In the context of bargaining between employers and employees (perhaps in the context of union negotiations), this approach also means that wage-earner equity should be treated as an "additional" payment. It may be included in a workplace-level or "enterprise" bargain, as one option open to employees as part of a package of above-safety-net-level remuneration. But it could not be used to replace cash compensation at that safety-net level.

Rather than mandating any specific percentage of compensation in stock, for ordinary employees, this subsidy approach simply encourages employers to expand the range of options it offers employees as part of a process of bargaining over employment terms and conditions.

One important issue about implementation of this plan is how the equity-based component of compensation would be issued and held. For publicly traded companies this would be easy to execute, and the equity-based compensation would be liquid and easily valued. For private companies, which could be both small in size and highly illiquid, this would be much more challenging. It would be hard—perhaps impossible—for workers to monetize their equity-based compensation in a small private company.

There are, however, at least two solutions to this difficulty: one possibility is that for non-publicly traded companies, equity-based compensation could come in the form of equity in an exchange-traded fund purchasing the broad-based public equity market. This would address the liquidity issue, though it means a further disconnect between the relationship between the effort and actions of workers and the equity they receive.

The other possibility would be to harness new developments in blockchain technology that allow firms to raise money for blockchain investments, via Initial Coin Offerings (ICOs) or so-called tokens or coins.[56] Tokenization means that one can use tokens to invest or bet on specific components of a company; and this means that it is possible to have publicly traded securities that are tied to a much more granular level of performance within an organization. It obviously doesn't mean that it's possible to have equity securities in the impact of single worker—but it is conceivable to have such securities for divisions of companies or even teams within divisions.

It will take time for these new technological developments to play out, but there are also affirmative steps that can be taken. An obvious candidate for this is increased tax deductibility of equity-based compensation to employees. This form of tax relief could be tied to the level of employees receiving it, ensuring that it is targeted to the type of workers most at risk from the challenges to work and wages.

(iii) Place-Based Policies

Finally, governments could seek to boost private sector wages in certain areas hit especially hard by globalization or automation by adopting place-based policies that target particular geographic areas and that include scope for wage subsidies for workers hired in these areas.

There is a long history of place-based policies of various kinds, even extending back to the Roman Empire. But as Patrick Kline and Enrico Moretti—two of the leading social scientists who have analyzed place-based policies—point out, national governments began to focus on these policies in the 20th century.[57] Indeed, the US federal government spent more than $15 billion on such policies in 2012, while state and local governments spend a further $80 billion. To put this in context, that is more than triple what is spent on unemployment assistance in the United States in a typical year.[58]

One of the largest and most famous examples in the US context is the Tennessee Valley Authority, which was designed to modernize the economy of the region through investment in public infrastructure, specifically roads and electricity.[59] The TVA helped modernize the local economy and brought manufacturing to a largely agricultural area. Kline and Moretti find that the program achieved a significant increase in manufacturing employment, which continued to grow after the program's end, and an increase in the average wage which remained long after the program ceased.

Place-based policies have also been used in a number of other countries, again with a clear positive impact on employment and wages. In the United Kingdom, the "Local Enterprise Growth Initiative" (LEGI) targeted economically deprived areas from 2006–2011. The results of this program show the need for careful design. Elias Einio and Henry Overman from the London School of Economics evaluated[60] the LEGI and showed that while there was increased employment on the LEGI side of the "treatment area boundary," there were employment losses on the other side of the boundary (i.e., in areas not receiving the LEGI). The positive and negative effects were of similar magnitudes. In addition, the positive effects were not sustained after the program ended.

In Japan, a place-based job creation plan was designed to support municipal job creation policies. Local authorities design a plan and compete for subsidies from the Ministry of Health, Labor and Welfare. Rather than being a tax credit, it was subsidy for the individual job creation plan. Sachiko Kazekami (2017) provides evidence that the plan increased employment, particularly in the agricultural, retail trade, and service sectors.[61]

Using data on China's "Special Economic Zone" (SEZ) program, Yi Lu, Jian Wang, and Lianming Zhu found evidence that SEZs have a positive effect on capital, employment, and output, and increase the number of firms as well as having positive effects on wages.[62]

Of course, there is the natural question of why one particular place should be privileged for historical reasons. Put another way: why put resources into saving a beleaguered community rather than spending those resources on new communities or supporting and expanding those areas that are doing well?

One important reason is that many people have a natural and understandable attachment to their existing community and are sometimes unwilling to move even with fairly significant inducements to do so. This leads to a situation where there are—almost literally—dying towns from which people are unwilling or unable to move. The extremely negative health effects and other social costs of communities in decline have been extensively documented.[63] This leaves us with the question of how to rejuvenate some, or perhaps most, of these towns.

For a town or city to flourish requires solving what amounts to a difficult coordination problem. A business is not going to set up in a particular place unless it believes that enough people are going to live and work in that place, and have decent incomes to act as customers for their business. Similarly, people aren't willing, if they have a choice, to live in a place that has very few amenities. This coordination problem can lead to a situation where, even though it would make economic sense to do so, businesses don't invest in a community. That makes it unattractive for workers to live there, which rationalizes and confirms businesses' decision not to invest there. It's a self-fulfilling prophecy driven by a cycle of negative beliefs about what other people are going to do.

In 2016, one of the authors (Holden) published a paper with Robert Akerlof showing how well-connected economic agents (that Akerlof and Holden call "Movers and Shakers") can solve this coordination problem and turn a potential cycle of negative beliefs into a virtuous cycle of positive beliefs.[64] This "moving and shaking" phenomenon is particularly important when it comes to cities and towns, and the role played by government in this respect can be made significantly easier by focusing its energies and resources on an existing place. Central to the virtuous cycle of beliefs that is required for a particular place to flourish is people believing that other people believe that it will flourish. The very fact that a particular place *has flourished* in the past helps make credible the belief that, with appropriate support, it can do so again.

This argument only goes so far. A town that sprang up because of a complete accident of history, which has no real reason to exist as a community other than it once did, may not be possible to sustain and may make for a poor use of government resources. Gold mining towns that thrived while the gold was there are not typically good candidates for sensible, place-based policies once the gold is gone, for example. But the coordination possibilities and "focal" aspect that once-great cities or towns offer is a powerful force that government can harness through the astute use of place-based policies.

It would be naïve to think that place-based policies are some kind of panacea for all the downsides, dislocations, and disruptions that globalization has caused. For one thing, although industries that are highly exposed to trade tend to be highly concentrated geographically, there are plenty of people who have lost their jobs to trade that are more dispersed, and these people need to be helped, too. Place-based policies are, by construction, not going to be particularly effective in helping these folks.

But the adverse effects of globalization and trade tend to hit particular industries, and because of economic geography and agglomeration economies, industries are often highly geographically concentrated. This basic fact suggests that place-based policies may be more effective at mitigating the negative consequences of globalization than policies which target individuals based solely on income or even employment status.

5

Baseline Benefits: Universal Healthcare (Australian Style) and Beyond

A key component of a fair markets approach is the provision of a generous social minimum. This involves ensuring that all individuals have access to a range of core goods, including a minimum level of (1) food, (2) clothing, (3) clean water, (4), electricity, (5) housing, (6) healthcare, (7) education, (8) rest and leisure, including as a worker and a senior, and (9) time with family, including as a parent.

Perhaps the most important way in which liberal societies guarantee access to these core goods is through decent-paying work and wages. With access to decent-paying jobs, most adults can afford to purchase access to these goods in the market. Or so, at least, is the classical and neoliberal assumption.

The difficulty with this assumption, however, is twofold. First, not all adults are in a position to undertake paid employment: they may have a disability, a medical condition, or caring responsibilities that prevent it. Second, not all core goods are affordable for ordinary workers absent government support.

One of the challenges for a fair markets approach is that the cost of core goods that constitute the heart of a generous social minimum have often risen faster than wages in recent decades. Healthcare, housing, and energy costs certainly fall into this category in most advanced economies. This is an example of the famous Yale University economist William Baumol's "cost disease," whereby productivity rises in one sector drive up wages in other sectors that have not experienced those productivity increases.[1] Thus, the boom in the technology sector makes housing and even healthcare more expensive. In health, one must add to this the advent of new, but expensive, life-saving drugs and procedures.

This leads to a significant challenge for a liberal society—how to pay for a generous social minimum when costs are rising potentially much faster than wages.

There are essentially three possible policy responses to this. The first is pure public provision of core goods through a government-run single-payer system that democratic socialists tend to favor. The second is a slightly softer "public option" approach whereby a government-run healthcare (or education, childcare, and so on) alternative competes with the private sector, and there are potentially incentives to use the public option through subsidies. The third alternative, and our preferred one, is a *public baseline*. Under this alternative the government guarantees a baseline level of benefits meeting the dignified social minimum (in the relevant category) to all citizens, but those citizens can purchase additional benefits from private sector firms on top of this.

Healthcare, where there is universal coverage to a dignified level—as is the case in Australia—but where private insurance allows additional benefits such as a private hospital room is a good example of this. This ensures a generous social minimum but still permits individual choice, through private insurance, for a level of care or comfort above that minimum.

Of course, the nature of a public baseline will inevitably vary by the type of benefit—in healthcare it will need to be fairly comprehensive, while with various forms of leave it will be relatively basic. And the private top-up will sometimes come from employers and sometimes from individuals. Both employer-provided and individually funded top-ups will, in some areas, receive tax incentives from the government.

But the basic principle is the same: The challenge in all of these benefits systems is how to provide universal access to benefits that are necessary to guarantee the social minimum, but ensure that they are paid for by those who can afford to, paid for by government for those that cannot, and all done with an array of taxes and subsidies that imposes the fewest possible distortions on incentives to work. In general, we suggest, the best way to do this will also be via a public baseline plus private top-up approach.

In the remainder of the chapter, we begin in part A by outlining the general arguments in favor of this kind of public baseline plus private top-up approach. In parts B–D we then explore how this approach could inform the design of new approaches to healthcare, childcare, and paid leave—including universal basic leave for self-employed and gig workers. Finally, in part E, we explore the differences and similarities between these different benefits, and their relationship to commitments to adequacy versus equality of access explored in Chapter 3, as well as economic concepts such as "asymmetric information" and "adverse selection."

A. Fair Markets and a General Social Minimum: Guiding Principles

If a dignified social minimum requires universal access to a particular benefit, then it is tempting to think that this benefit should not just be paid for by the government but that the government should be the *only* entity that should pay for the benefit. In reality, however, there are three broad options for achieving universal access to core goods: a public system, a public option, and public baseline.

The government can be the sole funder and provider of a good, or operate a truly public system for its provision. This is, for example, the nature of the healthcare system in Canada, the United Kingdom, and much of continental Europe.

A system may allow private provision with a combination of taxes and subsidies to achieve universality and affordability for the government. The healthcare system in the United States (for those under the age of 65 and who are not military veterans) after the passage of the Affordable Care Act is an example of such a system. There are subsidies to buy healthcare based on income, and combined with the individual mandate this amounts to a carrot-and-stick system to ensure universal coverage.

A third approach to benefits is for the government to provide a public baseline to all citizens and allow for there to be a private market in which "top-ups" of higher quality or additional services can be purchased. Importantly, the public baseline is designed to be sufficient to ensure a dignified social minimum, and the private market is for top-ups to, rather than a replacement for, the public baseline. And while the public baseline is provided by and paid for by government, that does not preclude the use of the tax system to ensure a combination of carrots and sticks that make the government funding of the public baseline sustainable. A good example of how this type of benefits system works is the Australian healthcare system, which we describe below.

Which of these approaches is most consistent with a fair markets approach? Both the public option and public baseline approaches have advantages. There are certain advantages to a public option—especially in the fraught political environment surrounding reforms to the US healthcare system. Universal coverage and maintaining existing private insurance is, perhaps, more politically feasible in the United States if there is also a public option that competes with private providers in a truly national healthcare market. It may also be easier to sustain in a context where the United States maintains relatively open borders, and thus where even free basic public healthcare may serve as an additional reason for non-citizens to seek entry.

A public option can also help exert an important form of competitive pressure on private providers and give the government useful information about how much to pay for or subsidize private providers, where this is part of the overall policy scheme. This is a variant of what has become known as *yardstick competition* for its pioneer, Andrei Shleifer. In his words:[2]

For any given firm, the regulator uses the costs of comparable firms to infer the firm's attainable cost level. Borrowing the term that describes the comparison of private and state-controlled firms, we call this regulatory scheme "yardstick competition."

This allows for the use of the relative performance of different providers as a means of ensuring appropriately low costs. Similarly, it can be used to ensure the appropriate balance of cost reduction and quality of service. Where the government has limited visibility into the cost and quality structure of private providers, as is typically the case for complex markets like healthcare, the government actually being a provider in that market—through a public option—provides valuable information about how to regulate private providers in that same market.

Like all regulation, this is somewhat imperfect. But an important goal of any regulatory scheme is that it not be information-intensive, and that it be relatively robust to *gaming* by the firms involved. The type of scheme we just outlined performs relatively well compared to those goals.

A drawback of the public option approach, however, is that for private and public insurance to coexist requires what antitrust lawyers call *competitive neutrality*. Democratic liberalism holds that government should intervene in markets in order to provide a core good that the market fails to provide, but that intervention should not be designed to drive private sector firms out of the market by undercutting them and using the unique advantages of the state to create a government monopoly. And government, therefore, must not use its inbuilt advantages from scale, cost of capital, or regulation to give it a competitive advantage over the private sector firms with which it is competing.

Achieving competitive neutrality in practice is also hard. Even a slight edge can cause consumers to shift from private providers to the public option, leading to an unraveling of the private part of the market. Put another way, it is all too easy for a public option to morph into a *Corleone Option*: people are made an offer they can't refuse. Rather than seeing this as a drawback, democratic socialists tend see this as a desirable design feature of Medicare for All—sometimes describing it as "a feature not a bug."

A public baseline approach, in contrast, avoids the tricky question of how to ensure competitive neutrality that arises with a public option approach, and provides truly universal coverage. It also does so in a way that addresses the challenges of quality noted in Chapter 3.

Its potential drawback, however, is its greater cost. The public baseline, being costless at the margin for citizens, implies that there will be essentially universal uptake and use. This certainly comes at a cost to the government's budget bottom line, but it instantly solves the sometimes vexing problem of ensuring universality of coverage. It also means that all citizens experience the benefits of the system which, if adequately funded, increases political buy-in.

B. Fair Markets and Access to Healthcare

To see how this plays out in practice, consider ongoing debates in the United States about the reform of healthcare. A number of candidates for the Democratic Party's 2020 presidential nomination advocated a system of "Medicare for All," which is either a single-payer system with immediate effect or a transition path to a single-payer system over, say, 10 years. For instance, Elizabeth Warren and Bernie Sanders support a single-payer system that would do away with the private insurance market as soon as practically possible. Others, like then Senator Kamala Harris, wanted to enroll every newborn American into a government plan and seek to move others into that plan, so that over a period of 10 years private insurance would no longer exist, and what would remain is a single-payer plan.

Still others supported a "public option" whereby people have the right to buy into Medicare at a certain price.[3] In principle this could coexist with a private insurance system, but as we discuss above, the challenge is setting the price in a way that does not undercut private providers and lead to them being squeezed out of the market. Some advocates of the public option (in healthcare) in fact claim that this eventual squeezing out of private provision is the ultimate goal of establishing the public option.

As mentioned, the Biden administration plans to expand the Affordable Care Act (ACA) rather than moving toward a single-payer system like Medicare for All. As we write, the initial Covid-19 relief plan (the "American Rescue Plan") expands insurance subsidies in the ACA, and Biden's proposed "American Families Plan" seeks to make that expansion permanent. The public option on which he campaigned has not been part of any legislation as of this writing.

This debate about healthcare in America also highlights the pros and cons of different types of benefits systems, and also the ideological clash involved. On one side are democratic socialists who believe in Medicare for All, as implemented by expanding the existing Medicare program into a universal, single-payer system that either undercuts private insurance on price so much that it kills it, or perhaps private insurance is simply made illegal. Those are just two different paths to the same government-run single-payer health system.

On the other side are those who want to use the ACA as a starting point toward more universal coverage. For this side, the abolition or effective abolition of the market for private health insurance—a market that serves around 170 million Americans at present—is a nonstarter, and an approach likely to be met with fierce political resistance.

Part of the difficulty in reconciling these two approaches to healthcare is a deep difference in how much markets should be trusted. To Medicare for All proponents, health insurance companies are bad actors that profit from the suffering of their policyholders while busily trying to deny their claims. For supporters of the ACA, private insurance is an essential part of the path to universal coverage. The prospect of wiping out private insurance led Michael Bloomberg to observe in January that Medicare for All would "bankrupt us for a very long time."[4]

The creation of a public baseline combined with private insurance, however, would offer one way of cutting through this ideological divide. John Delaney, who was a candidate for the Democratic Party's 2020 presidential nomination, proposed such a plan—although his candidacy and his policies failed to gain much traction. His plan would have created a new universal public system for all Americans under the age of 65 while maintaining a private insurance system so that "Individuals and employers will be able to purchase and negotiate supplemental coverage from private insurers to cover additional health needs." He also proposed using the government's bargaining power to negotiate drug prices, which he estimates would save $850 billion a year.[5]

Take the Australian healthcare system as an example. The Australian healthcare system involves a free baseline plan that covers all Australians which is, confusingly perhaps, called Medicare. This provides all Australians with a baseline level of medical coverage for all needs, ranging from seeing a primary care physician, to hospital coverage. Australian Medicare also includes coverage for prescription drugs, through a scheme known as the Pharmaceutical Benefits Scheme. That is the public baseline.

The system also involves a mix of carrots and sticks designed to encourage higher-income earners to take up private insurance, which can both top up their own level of non-essential benefits and help cross-subsidize the cost of the essential baseline for all. The carrots or top-up benefits include access to private hospital rooms and beds, priority elective surgery and a range of ancillary benefits. The sticks involve a tax penalty of an additional 1% on one's marginal tax rate for not purchasing private health insurance if family income is above A$180,000, scaling up to 1.5% for family incomes above A$280,000. The purchase of private insurance, however, again involves some benefits or carrots for those who choose to take it up: it covers access to private hospital rooms and beds, priority elective surgery, and a range of ancillary benefits.

Notice that nothing about the Australian system is "neoliberal." Contrast the Australian system with the pre-1965 situation in the United States. That was the archetypical neoliberal approach to healthcare. Some Americans, by implicitly sacrificing some of their wages, received healthcare through their employer. The rest of Americans were left to fend for themselves—which essentially meant they did not have healthcare (the exception being veterans, with Veterans Administration [VA] healthcare established by President Herbert Hoover in 1930).

This neoliberal approach of "private insurance for some" has become further complicated over the years with a combination of VA, Medicare, Medicaid, and, since the passage of the ACA, government subsidies for individuals to purchase private insurance. Yet at its core, it requires the majority of Americans to buy their own insurance in the market, or do without.

The Australian model offers something different. Rather than "private insurance for some" it offers a mixture of private and public insurance that achieves universal coverage, consistent with the view that healthcare is a right. In other words, the Australian model is more of a *public baseline* than a *public option*—although it gives people the option not to buy private insurance yet still have coverage.

The operation of the model also demonstrates the strengths of this kind of baseline model. This system of carrots and sticks ensures universal access to healthcare, provides individuals with choice, and shares the cost of providing healthcare between individuals and the government. And it helps keep total healthcare costs down—total healthcare expenditures (public and private) in Australia are around 10% of GDP, compared to 18% for the United States. And the Australian system works well, contributing to a life expectancy of 82.8 years, the fourth highest in the world.

C. Childcare and Paid Leave

Similar principles apply to the provision of childcare as a core good necessary for a dignified life, including access to the employment opportunities needed for economic dignity.

There are many different approaches to making childcare affordable in different countries, and they range from essentially purely public provision to a private system, sometimes involving tax credits or tax deductibility.[6] For instance, in France there are government-run crèches that are funded by local authorities but are partially means tested, with higher-income families paying a fee. Children as young as three months are eligible to attend, and crèches are typically open 11 hours a day (although closed on public holidays and for the month of August).

A number of other western European countries have similar state-run systems in whole or in part. One example is Finland, where local authorities are required to provide childcare services but can provide them directly, in combination with other localities, or contract with private providers to do so.[7]

Other countries rely at least in part on tax incentives. In Belgium, the costs of communal crèches are tax deductible, while care in publicly accredited crèches (as well as by accredited child-minders) is also subsidized.[8] In Germany, up to two-thirds of childcare costs for children under 14 are tax deductible (up to a maximum of 4,000 Euros), in addition to childcare subsidies.[9]

Childcare expenses for children aged 11 or under are also deductible in Norway (up to a maximum of NOK 25,000 for one child, and an additional NOK 15,000 for each additional child), with subsidies also available.[10] In Austria, childcare costs are deductible (up to a maximum of 2,300 Euros per child) for children up to the age of 10, in private or public institutions, alongside subsidies.[11] And in Canada, childcare tax deductions are available for parents with children aged under 16, with subsidies also provided by provinces. The deductible amount is limited to $8,000 for children six and under, and $5,000 for children between seven and 15, and with the total deduction generally limited to two-thirds of the lower-income partner's earned income.[12]

Meanwhile, a small number of countries provide a tax credit system for childcare costs. For example, although the United States initially introduced a tax deduction for childcare costs in 1954, in 1976 this was changed to a tax credit. At present, the Child and Dependent Care Tax Credit provides a non-refundable tax credit covering 20% to 35% of childcare costs, depending on family income.[13] France also provides a 50% tax credit for childcare expenses for children under six years of age, in addition to subsidized care in a government-run creche and nanny subsidies.[14]

All of these models have strengths and weaknesses. But much like for healthcare, a fair markets approach suggests that a "public baseline" model is again the best way to balance fiscal sustainability with market-based competition and choice.

The core component of a public baseline for childcare involves ensuring that all families have access to a certain level and amount of childcare. This can be achieved in a number of different ways, and some of those variants will be more or less appealing in different jurisdictions depending on local norms and preferences, and other economic arrangements.

The first and perhaps most important component of a public baseline for childcare is to ensure that all families have affordable access. A straightforward way to do this is by giving all parents of eligible children a voucher that gives them the ability to purchase childcare from, say, 8:30am to 5:30pm, five days per week, 50 weeks a year (excluding public holidays) for each child. Who is an eligible child? That may well vary by jurisdiction. A country like France has already taken the position that a child who is two-and-a-half months old is eligible. In other countries it might be a child who is one or two years old. That is largely a sociopolitical question.

But a key design element in such a program is how to ensure that the voucher allows parents to purchase sufficiently good quality childcare, while keeping costs of provision under control and not leading to windfall profits for private providers.

One approach to doing this is to have state-run childcare centers as at least some component of the market. On the plus side, this gives government clear visibility into costs of provision and hence the ability to set the value of the voucher to a level that ensures the amount of childcare in the public baseline. On the minus side, there is a large body of evidence that highlights the inefficiency of public providers compared to private providers, and thus the higher costs that would likely flow from pure public provision.[15]

Private providers, on the other hand, might come with increased efficiency compared to higher-cost public operators, but the government tends to have less visibility into those costs. Moreover, if there is not sufficient competition in the childcare market, the prices charged by private providers may be well above (marginal) costs, leading to windfall profits or what economists call "rents."

One might think that, with a large number of childcare centers, there is a lot of competition and hence windfall profits are not much of an issue. But it is important to remember that having childcare close to one's home or work (or perhaps both) is a highly desirable attribute of a center. It is, indeed, one aspect of "quality." This type of economic geography means that childcare centers might not have a lot of "local" competition and that they can, in fact, end up being borderline local monopolies.

This, in turn, suggests the benefit of having at least some form of public provision of the baseline level of care—both as an additional source of competition for these local providers, and as a useful source of information about the actual costs incurred by providers.

The remaining—and very important—design question is how to ensure fiscal sustainability of the program by ensuring that parents make some contribution to the cost of childcare, while maintaining the access and affordability that are core to a public baseline.

This scheme could be implemented by (a) allowing any households who want to use the voucher to do so, and (b) allowing any household to opt to forego the voucher and instead receive a rebate equal to some fraction (call it R%) of the voucher amount and a tax deduction for childcare expenditures up to an annual cap (call that amount $C per annum). Under this proposal, in two-parent households, *each* parent would qualify for 50% (of their marginal tax rate) deductibility. The choice of the rebate amount as a fraction of the voucher amount (R) and the tax deductibility cap (C) could be chosen by policymakers based on the specific details of the income tax system in their jurisdiction. For instance, setting R equal to 0 would be equivalent to completely foregoing the voucher and simply taking tax deductibility (up to the annual cap) for childcare expenses.

The point of these two policy-design variables is that they have different distributional implications depending on household income. They also affect how generous and hence how fiscally sustainable the scheme is, as well as how large is the incentive generated for increased labor supply.

The Biden administration's proposed "American Families Plan" allocates $225 billion over 10 years to help make childcare for children under 5 years of age more accessible and affordable. Households with incomes below 1.5 times the median income in their state would receive free childcare under Biden's plan, and those above that level would have their childcare payments capped at 7% of annual income.[16]

This is very similar to Senator Warren's "Universal Child Care Plan"—on which she campaigned during the 2020 Democratic presidential primary. Her plan sought to make childcare free for any households whose income is below 200% of the federal poverty line, and would cap fees at 7% of income for households over that level.[17]

It is unclear, as we write, what the outcome of legislative negotiations on the American Families Plan will be, but it is fair to say that Biden has proposed what is effectively a democratic socialist childcare plan. This contrasts to a degree with our democratic liberal proposal—most notably the Biden-Warren plan contemplates price caps, and it is unclear how negative effects on quality or availability of childcare stemming from such caps will be avoided. Yet there are shared objectives, both in terms of access and choice for families as well as labor productivity. But again, this highlights the policy continuum along which these two policy approaches are located.

D. Basic Leave

There has been fierce backlash in many countries against the rise of casual-ization, and especially the gig economy. Some on the left, including the UK Labour Party, have promised to ban certain parts of the gig economy—such as Uber and AirBnB—outright.[18] And several jurisdictions have imposed a levy on ridesharing services like Uber and Lyft. For instance, New York City imposed a $2.75 fee per ride for all such trips in Manhattan.[19]

Some of these measures are also inconsistent with democratic liberalism and a commitment to markets—for instance, those aimed at deterring ridesharing. A tax that is specifically imposed on ridesharing services, but not on taxis, makes ridesharing relatively less attractive compared to taxis and thus tilts the playing field in favor of taxis. A tax with this purpose is illib-eral in the sense that it reduces the benefit that comes from ridesharing. The sole basis for such a tax is to please a certain constituency—taxi owners and drivers—that have political clout. In assessing the appropriate intervention, be it a tax or other policy, it is important to treat all people who are in the same economic situation the same way, regardless of the particular part of a given sector they are in. If job security and lack of access to leave and other benefits is a problem for one set of workers in the point-to-point transporta-tion market that warrants intervention, then that intervention should apply equally to all workers in the point-to-point transportation market.

Other measures, however, reflect a concern to protect existing businesses, including taxi medallion holders who have experienced a sharp decline in the value of their medallion as a result of the introduction of ridesharing serv-ices.[20] Compensation for medallion owners disadvantaged by ridesharing services is also consistent with democratic liberalism. Although technological progress almost always produces winners and losers, and compensation is not always warranted, some medallion owners constitute a particularly sympa-thetic case.[21]

Taxi drivers who once enjoyed being part of a point-to-point transporta-tion market with high barriers to entry have seen their position, and earnings, come under significant pressure. Sometimes this has had tragic consequences. These economic pressures, along with predatory practices from unscrupulous lenders facilitated by shady medallion brokers,[22] have led to a spate of suicides among New York taxi drivers, as the *New York Times* reported in 2018.[23]

And some levies reflect a commitment to worker protection and the pro-vision of benefits: for instance, a per-trip tax is used to fund the kind of leave entitlements that workers in the gig economy typically do not receive, such as annual, sick, or parental leave. As has been widely commented upon, these people are classified by the platform companies that power the gig economy as independent contractors rather than employees. This means that, in particular, they do not receive benefits such as healthcare and overtime pay (or even social security contributions); they are unable to unionize; and they are not even required to be paid the minimum wage.

Of course, this is in dispute, both legally and politically. The classification of such workers as independent contractors was the subject of a lawsuit, *Dynamex Operations West v. Superior Court,* where the California Supreme Court decided in favor of the workers bringing the suit in mid-2018. But the *Dynamex* case did not address other aspects of the workers' compensation such as rest and meal breaks, leave entitlements such as parental leave, or other benefits more broadly, and a related case, a class-action suit about worker classification called *O'Connor v. Uber* has been pending since 2013.[24]

How this issue is ultimately resolved in the courts thus remains to be seen. California has introduced legislation, Assembly Bill 5 or "AB 5," which essentially seeks to codify the court's approach in *Dynamex,* but the debate in most states and countries worldwide remains ongoing.

Another way in which democratic governments could achieve this same objective, however, would be to introduce a true public baseline for all benefits—including basic leave benefits. As the European Union Social Affairs Commissioner Marianne Thyssen puts it: "We need rules adapted to new forms of work, with adequate protection[s] for workers across the economy."[25] And this means rethinking the nexus between work and basic benefits—such as healthcare, sick leave, maternity leave, and holiday pay—and moving toward a model of *universal basic benefits.*

There are fewer existing models of baseline leave than of public baselines for healthcare and childcare—in part perhaps because most countries are only beginning to grapple with the realities of the gig economy. But the same principles involving a public baseline could be usefully applied. For instance, payroll taxes for all traditional employees, along with proceeds from taxes like a "per-trip" ridesharing levy, could be used specifically to fund (say) two weeks of annual leave for all workers in the economy at the minimum wage.

This would be very much a baseline rather than an expectation of what many employees would receive. Employers could easily top up this baseline annual leave entitlement both in terms of duration and the rate of pay. Many employers already provide more generous annual leave than two weeks at the minimum wage, presumably based on their views about how to attract the best talent. A baseline universal leave scheme would not change that, other than to provide public funding for the two-week at minimum wage baseline leave component.

For employers already offering more generous leave, this would simply serve as a tax credit making providing employment more attractive. But for workers in the gig economy and outside the traditional employment model, it would provide a basic level of leave entitlement. Furthermore, because the levies that help fund this entitlement would be raised from all providers in a given sector, it would ensure a level playing field between gig economy firms and traditional providers in those sectors.

Take the point-to-point transportation market as an example. A per-trip levy used to fund the baseline annual leave entitlement would apply equally to traditional taxi operators, black car operators, and ridesharing platforms like Uber and Lyft. This would mean that none of those operators would be at a particular disadvantage relative to other operators, so that traditional taxi operators would not need to be concerned about ridesharing platforms not offering annual leave and hence putting them at a competitive disadvantage. Similarly, drivers on ridesharing platforms would receive a baseline annual leave entitlement that is often missing under existing arrangements and which those firms are often disinclined to offer.

Both the funding structure and application of this kind a baseline universal benefit could usefully be applied beyond annual leave—although annual leave itself is clearly an important component of a dignified social minimum. But sick leave and parental leave are other leading examples of benefits that are an important part of the social minimum, and which are under threat from the changing structure of work and employment in the modern economy.

It is instructive to compare this approach with a simple government mandate of various forms of leave entitlements. These mandates are often part of broader wage-entitlement systems that specify not just a minimum wage across all sectors (as in the United States) but terms and conditions across all sectors, and sometime sector-specific employment conditions (as in Australia and parts of Europe). Consider a mandate that all employees receive two weeks annual leave, "paid for" by the employer. This amounts to a given employer getting 50 weeks of work from an employee but paying for 52.

This is completely consistent with democratic liberalism, and in an economy where there was plentiful work in traditional employment relationships this would be a perfectly satisfactory way to guarantee the social minimum. But in an economy where the lines between traditional employment and independent contracting are blurry at best, maintaining a level playing field while ensuring that the social minimum is met is crucial. If this form of neutrality is violated, then the independent contractor form of arrangement becomes more attractive to employers, as this lowers their costs relative to traditional employers in the same sector and gives them a competitive advantage.[26]

E. Differences and Similarities Among Benefits

A dignified social minimum—which is at the heart of a fair markets approach—requires universal access to certain benefits. Benefits like annual, parental, and sick leave, and perhaps the most important benefit of all, healthcare, are at the core of providing people with a dignified social minimum and are central to a democratic liberal approach to work.

Given this, it might be tempting to think that it means the benefit should not just be paid for by the government, but that the government should be the only entity that should pay for the benefit. But as we have shown in this chapter, there are in fact three broad options for achieving universal access to core goods: a public system, a public option, and a public baseline. The government can be also the sole funder and provider of a good, or operate a truly public system for its provision. How these benefits are provided will depend on the type of benefit and the political context (and history) of the jurisdiction in question.

In general, however, we have argued that the public baseline approach is the most compelling. Among the competing options, it most satisfactorily balances the provision of a dignified social minimum with an efficient and market-based approach that respects individual choice where appropriate.

It is also important to recognize, however, that there will be important differences between benefits that affect the desirability of these different approaches and what they entail.

The market for healthcare, for example, is characterized by significant "adverse selection" problems.[27] Economists define this problem as one that occurs where people have hidden information that is not observable by another party (here, about their health), or there is significant "asymmetric information" between parties to a transaction.[28] Informational asymmetries of this kind can lead to significant downward or upward pressure on the price at which goods or services are traded—because the party buying a good, or selling a service such as insurance, is not sure if they are purchasing or selling something of high or low value or cost. This, in turn, can lead to higher value, or lower cost, parties no longer benefiting from a transaction and exiting the market. The classic example of this is the secondhand car market. As George Akerlof famously showed, a secondhand car market without regulation or a system of private inspections to check quality quickly unravels: no one wants to buy a lemon, and yet lemons are the only cars offered, once the chance of a lemon is built into the overall price for used cars.[29]

In healthcare, these problems also mean that unregulated health insurance markets often have prices that encourage healthy people to opt out of private insurance, and hence the risk in the insured pool gets larger, driving more people out of the market. This is why universality in healthcare coverage is not just an issue of dignity but also key to ensuring that these markets don't unravel.

The childcare market, in contrast, has no inbuilt reason to unravel, and there is therefore less need for governments to encourage the universal purchase of paid childcare. Indeed, there are good reasons in a liberal society for governments not to nudge parents strongly toward or away from paid as opposed to parental forms of childcare.

Similarly, for some benefits, simply ensuring that everyone has access to a dignified minimum is sufficient, even if some people enjoy a much higher level of that benefit in either quality or quantity. Annual leave is a good example of this. While inequality is always an issue to some degree, it is a much less pressing concern with respect to annual leave. It is far more important that everyone have access to at least two weeks leave, even if some people get six, than it is to ensure than everyone has a very similar amount of annual leave. There is no real expressive harm of somebody else getting more annual leave than I do, provided that I get a reasonable amount of leave—the baseline or dignified minimum.

But for some core goods, there is an inherently rivalrous dimension to enjoyment of the goods. And as we note in the next section, this may demand a quite different approach to the level or quality of the public baseline, and its relationship to private alternatives.

F. Toward Equal Relative Goods: Childcare and Education

This suggests two possible policy interventions that are not mutually exclusive. The first is to ensure that the baseline is set at a sufficiently high level to reduce the amount of inequality between those who access the baseline, and those who are able to purchase the relative good in the market to access outcomes above the baseline. One might call this *leveling up*. The obvious tradeoff here is that increasing the quality of the public baseline is costly and, all else equal, requires additional distorting taxation to fund it.

The second response is what one might call *leveling down*. That is, either preventing or reducing the ability of those with more wealth from accessing superior outcomes. A familiar policy in healthcare that takes a relatively light-touch approach to this is the so-called Cadillac Tax whereby expensive private health insurance that provides access to superior health outcomes is taxed. As in all things, taxing something makes it less attractive. This does not ban such insurance plans, it merely makes them less attractive. It also generates tax revenue that can be used to help level-up the public baseline, so it has a direct and an indirect effect on inequality. Such a Cadillac Tax could easily be applied to other markets, such as education.

A more radical approach is to mandate equal access to certain relative goods like education—essentially banning differential access and the use of wealth to acquire it.

In general, we suggest that the most "fair" or democratic liberal approach will be to combine private provision and a public baseline, and one that varies in its "generosity" based on the degree to which it is important to achieve adequacy versus actual equality among individuals in the enjoyment of the relevant good or benefit.

To see how this might work, take primary and secondary education as a concrete example. In most countries there is a mixture of public and private education. Public provision of education is seen as essential for a number of reasons. First, a baseline level of education is required to be a fully participating member of society—as the capabilities approach emphasizes. This should not be denied to certain children and afforded to others due to an accident of birth. Second, there are positive externalities to education. Both the economy and society generally function better when everyone has a certain level of education.

It is also generally believed that parents should have the right, at their own expense, to provide a high-quality education for their children that imparts certain values, emphasizes certain educational objectives, or is simply superior in terms of vertical quality than that provided by the public system.

From a liberal perspective it makes sense that parents should be able to make this choice. But it raises the question of whether such choices negatively affect children of other parents.

It is generally accepted by most economists that, in the long run, the primary driver of what workers earn is determined by their level of skill and what the market demand for those skills is. Moreover, market demand for, and labor supply of, certain skills can adjust over time. If there are very few talented software engineers, then they will be paid highly, thus making it more attractive to become a software engineer. This drives up the labor supply of software engineers, and the market wage falls. Similarly, if there is a strong supply of such engineers, then firms employing such workers can expand, leading to more job opportunities for software engineers.

The wrinkle in all of this is that it can often take time for firms to expand in order to take advantage of the supply of skilled workers. In the short run, demand for workers—especially high-skilled workers—is relatively fixed. This means that would-be workers—namely students—are competing for a basically fixed number of "slots" in well-paid jobs.

This turns education into a kind of "rank-order tournament" with a fixed number of high-placed winners. Moreover, because getting a good job gives one good opportunities to improve one's skills and develop networks, there is a path dependence to early-career success. So being near the "top of the class," broadly defined, is really important. And when one parent spends a lot of money educating their child to improve her chances of getting a place near the top of the tournament, that makes it harder for kids from less advantaged backgrounds.

As we discussed above, a democratic liberal approach to this conundrum involves a combination of "leveling up" public education and "leveling down" private education.

In the United States in 2019, the average spending in public schools was $13,187 per student. Of the 100 largest public school districts, the three that spent the most were New York City ($28,004), Boston ($25,653), and schools in the District of Columbia ($22,406).[30]

And, while average tuition for private schools is $11,645 a year ($10,645 for private elementary school and $15,112 for private high school) and is comparable, elite schools charge dramatically more.[31] For instance, tuition alone at New York's most expensive elementary school—the Quad Preparatory School—is $79,250.[32] And many elite private schools have sizeable endowments along with significant "voluntary" contributions that provide additional resources.

Leveling up public schools would involve all schools receiving a generous level of government funding—regardless of the property taxes collected in the school district. This level of funding should recognize the additional challenges—and costs—involved in educating children from less advantaged socioeconomic backgrounds.

Leveling down private schools could be achieved through a progressive Cadillac Tax on private school tuition. This could kick in at a high-enough threshold that private schools charging tuition at or just above the public level would not attract any tax. But as tuition—and hence school resources per student—increased, the tax *rate* would also increase. This revenue could be used to help fund public schools. In addition to this, the tax deductibility of gifts to private schools should also be reconsidered.

This would not provide equal resources for public and private schools. But in countries like the United States, Britain, Australia, and others it would mean a considerably more level playing field than at present—both by helping fund a leveling up approach and by discouraging elite schools from seeking to become even more elite, and unequal, compared to other public and private schools.

Of course, some on the left understandably believe that since any private education has a negative impact on less socioeconomically advantaged children, and thus think it should be banned outright. For instance, the American Institute for Progressive Democracy has suggested this.[33] And in 2019, the British Labour Party's conference voted to "integrate" private schools into the public system with measures to include seizing the assets of private schools, removing the charitable status and tax exemptions of such schools, and prohibiting universities from admitting more than 7% of students from private schools.[34]

As democratic liberals we see this as too great a prioritization of equality over freedom, and one that is not likely to achieve full equality in any event. Parents provide all sorts of intellectual and emotional support for their children that might help them in the "tournament of life"—yet it would clearly not be compatible with liberal ideals to tax or ban helping children with their homework or reading them bedtime stories. Good public policy must acknowledge the negative effects of private education on the children of the less privileged, but strike a balance between eliminating such effects and respecting the individual autonomy that is at the core of liberalism.

The appropriate way to strike this balance is through a combination of leveling up public education through increased resources for public schools, paid for in part by leveling down private schools through a Cadillac Tax.

6
Regulating Market Power

There is a long tradition in economics of being critical of monopolies. It dates to at least Adam Smith, who pointed out in *The Wealth of Nations* that monopolists will tend to reduce the amount they supply to increase their profit:

> ... monopolists, by keeping the market constantly understocked by never fully supplying the effectual demand, sell their commodities much above the natural price, and raise their emoluments.

Furthermore, the effect of this is to increase price. In fact, the pure monopoly price for a good is the highest possible price that consumers are willing to pay, whereas in a perfectly competitive market, prices are set at the lowest cost that producers can bear and still make a profit. Because demand curves slope downward—consumers tend to buy more at lower prices—monopolists have an incentive to reduce the amount supplied in the market, and this has the effect of driving up market prices. This is good for producers but bad for consumers.

One might think that these two effects wash out, but in fact the harm to consumers is almost always larger than the benefit to producers. Economists call this *deadweight loss*. Thus, economists have long advocated what has become known as *antitrust* regulation whereby monopolists either have their prices regulated or, in extreme cases like that of J.D. Rockefeller's Standard Oil, are broken up into smaller pieces that compete with each other.

Though this is basic economics, and a viewpoint with which democratic liberalism is completely comfortable, neoliberalism has found excuses for monopoly. While the democratic liberal approach is *pro-market*, by tilting the playing field in favor of producers, the neoliberal view is more *pro-business*.

In the rest of this chapter we present three case studies. The first, in part A, concerns banking and financial regulation, which illustrates the basic tradeoff just discussed. The second, in part B, relates to technology or "new economy" firms and offers an important cautionary tale for regulation. Many platform markets exhibit *network externalities* where one consumer buying more increases the value to other consumers. In these markets, very high market shares may not be a good measure of monopoly power, and regulation—either in the form of price regulation or breakup—may not be warranted. The third case, outlined in part C, concerns international trade and considers the extent to which unfettered trade is good for overall welfare, and examines the case for strategic manufacturing of certain core goods by nation states.

A. Banks and Financial Regulation

There can be little doubt that the US banking industry is dominated by a relatively small number of very large institutions. The five largest banks control 45.6% of all assets, up from 28.1% at the turn of the millennium.[1] This concentration, while not as extreme as in some technology markets with network externalities (e.g., the Internet search market or point-to-point transportation market), raises natural concerns about the ability of these large banks to charge high prices and as a result harm customers. This pricing power might manifest itself through high credit card interest rates, low deposit rates, or significant account-keeping fees and other charges. It could also involve "bundling" of different products, or so-called tie-in sales where, in order to purchase a certain product, a customer is required to buy a second product.

A neoliberal response to these concerns might be along the lines of what Richard Posner has described as "The Chicago School of Antitrust Analysis."[2] The Chicago School line of argument is that unilateral action by firms—such as tie-in sales or resale-price maintenance—cannot boost monopoly power because consumers require some form of compensation for entering into arrangements and contracts that make them worse off. This narrows the focus of antitrust efforts to, as Posner put it, "(1) cartels and (2) horizontal mergers large enough either to create monopoly directly, as in the classic trust cases, or facilitate cartelization by drastically reducing the number of significant sellers in the market." This type of neoliberal argument is certainly consistent with the classically liberal or libertarian arguments of the 19th century.

Of course, Posner's point about horizontal mergers might have purchase in making further consolidation and concentration in the US banking sector possible. But the current situation in terms of both concentration and consumer treatment doesn't raise immediate neoliberal red flags.

Democratic liberals take a more skeptical view of concentration and market power in the banking industry. Healthy competition in any sector of the economy requires the ability for new firms to readily enter the market (what economists call "free entry") and for small firms to be able to compete relatively effectively with large firms. There is good reason to question both of these cornerstones of competitive markets when it comes to the banking industry.

First, it is hard to simply start a "new bank." Quite apart from the regulatory approvals that are required in most jurisdictions (and that appropriately protect consumers from risky or unscrupulous banks), reputation is a significant barrier to entry. Most people are loath to move their finances to a little-known bank, even if they are protected by deposit-insurance schemes like the FDIC in the United States.

Second, there are significant switching costs that make it hard to move from one's existing financial institution. New credit and debit cards need to be obtained, direct debits and other recurring payments have to be transferred over, and mortgage holders typically need to go through substantial amounts of paperwork to change their lender. Banks, of course, know this and understand that customers will put up with some real degree of dissatisfaction before taking the time and effort to switch banks. This gives existing banks a degree of market power.

Finally, large banks can typically borrow money themselves at lower cost than smaller banks due to their perceived risk profile. This "cost of capital advantage" provides big and existing banks with another edge over potential entrants, thus deterring entry.

All of this gives democratic liberals concern about the competitiveness of the banking sector, and it suggests that there is a role for government regulation in increasing competition. Democratic socialists see even greater problems with the market power of large US financial institutions or need for state intervention in the sector.

Senator Elizabeth Warren, for instance, has been critical of the financial industry broadly—not just banks—since she became a law professor. While a professor at Harvard Law School in 2007, Warren proposed the establishment of the Consumer Financial Protection Bureau (CFPB), and in 2010 President Obama appointed her Assistant to the President and Special Advisor to the Secretary of the Treasury on the Consumer Financial Protection Bureau. Despite her role in creating the CFPB, she was opposed by Republicans as its first head and never served in the role.[3] That said, Warren clearly left her mark on the Bureau and its mission to "make markets for consumer financial products and services work for Americans—whether they are applying for a mortgage, choosing among credit cards, or using any number of other consumer financial products." Since 2011 it has delivered more than $12 billion in relief to more than 31 million consumers.[4]

This consumer protection role is consistent with the approach of other democratic socialists like Bernie Sanders and Alexandria Ocasio-Cortez, who both introduced legislation in May 2019 to cap interest rates on credit cards at 15%.[5] According to Sanders, "Wall Street today makes tens of billions from people at outrageous interest rates," with Ocasio-Cortez putting it this way: "There is no reason a person should pay more than 15% interest in the United States. It's common sense—in fact, we had these usury laws until the 70s . . . It's a debt trap for working people and it has to end."[6]

Warren has also proposed making private equity firms legally responsible for the debts owed by their portfolio companies, and change bankruptcy and tax provisions to end what she calls "legalized looting."[7] But she also has plans to shake up the core business of commercial banking through "postal banking," which would involve the US Postal Service (USPS) partnering "with local community banks and credit unions to provide access to low-cost, basic banking services." And she wants the Federal Reserve Board of Governors to implement "real-time payment technology" that will make it cheaper and easier to make routine, small-dollar transfers.

Democratic liberalism shares some, but not all of these prescriptions about how to respond to the current market power of banks. One relatively simple way of increasing competition in banking would be the introduction of so-called open banking, which gives customers control of their financial services data in a format that can be shared with other potential financial services providers. In Australia, for instance, legislation providing consumers with such data ownership was passed in August 2019, with implementation being progressively rolled out through mid to late 2020.[8] Such a system makes it easier for customers to switch from one bank to another and thereby reduce barriers to entry in banking.

This is also typical of the kind of intervention favored by democratic liberals and resisted by neoliberals. It is an intervention that takes market power seriously and tries to reduce barriers to markets operating efficiently. It draws a very clear line between what is *pro-market* and what is *pro-business*. The former is about overall economic surplus and efficiency; the latter is simply about corporate profits.

Unlike the neoliberal position, democratic liberalism also acknowledges the possibility that consumers are not fully rational but are subject to a range of well-documented behavioral biases.[9] As such, they can certainly be exploited by firms, and consumer protections may well have a useful role. This lack of "hyper-rationality" also implies that what Posner calls "unilateral actions" can lead the firms garnering monopoly power, which implies that antitrust law has a role to play in curbing these practices, contra the Chicago School view.

Democratic liberalism's commitment to well-functioning markets likewise means that it would be in favor of requirements involving product disclosures and information about the true cost (and risk) of financial products. Informational asymmetries can lead markets to break down, and mandates for information provision can help prevent this unraveling. But that same logic causes democratic liberalism to stop short of favoring interest rate caps so long as adequate information about the true cost of credit card and other loan products have been provided to consumers.

Indeed, interest rate caps can easily be counterproductive and hurt the least well-off consumers the most. If banks cannot earn an appropriate risk-adjusted return on loans, they will deny credit to the riskiest borrowers. This forces those borrowers into the illegal loan market or to be unable to access credit altogether. And although the average credit card interest rate of 17.68% sounds and is high,[10] that number needs to be seen in the context of unsecured borrowing where, if the borrower defaults, the lender has no collateral to seize. In bad economic times, lenders certainly can and do lose significant sums of money.

Rather than make credit card markets work better, interest rate caps could easily make them less functional and harm precisely the people that they are intended to help. It is almost as if proponents of such measures have a zero-sum view: that what is bad for banks must be good for their consumers. But this is not always the case; in fact, it is more often the exception rather than the rule. Democratic liberalism, by contrast, views well-functioning markets has having the ability to help both borrowers and lenders, rather than being zero-sum.

Finally, in assessing the market power of banks, democratic liberalism would look to measures like the return on equity (ROE) as a way of gauging potential "supra-normal" returns, or economic rents, to stockholders. In the post 2008-world, US banks have generally earned ROEs of around 10%–12%, and many smaller banks have earned ROEs of 8% or below.[11] These are not indicative of supra-normal returns.

B. Big Tech

In response to the size and influence of America's largest corporations, a number of people from a range of different backgrounds and perspectives have proposed breaking up big technology companies or regulating them in various ways. These calls have come from democratic socialist senators like Elizabeth Warren and Bernie Sanders, leading technology commentators such as Kara Swisher, a number of legal scholars including Scott Hemphill and Tim Wu,[12] and even a Facebook co-founder in Chris Hughes.[13]

Indeed, the so-called New Brandeis Movement—arguing that big companies are *per se* problematic—has been motivated in large part by tech companies such as Amazon.[14]

Warren has made it clear that this rationale for breakup goes beyond any possible consumer harm, with her plan emphasizing: "America has a long tradition of breaking up companies when they have become too big and dominant—even if they are generally providing good service at a reasonable price." Warren, and certain progressive antitrust scholars such as Ganesh Sitaraman and Sabeel Rahmann, see this as part of a long history of American antitrust enforcement, comparing technology companies to railroads and telephone companies.[15]

The clear implication of this is that the core businesses of various major technology companies would be broken apart. As Warren herself says: "Amazon Marketplace, Google's ad exchange, and Google Search would be platform utilities under this law. Therefore, Amazon Marketplace and Basics, and Google's ad exchange and businesses on the exchange would be split apart. Google Search would have to be spun off as well." It also seems clear that not only would Facebook's acquisitions of WhatsApp and Instagram be reversed (something we discuss below) but also that Facebook.com, at least as it is currently constituted, would be broken up as well.

These advocates of breakup also make a number of arguments about the dangers posed by large technology companies like Facebook, Amazon, Google/Alphabet, and others.

One is the standard antitrust argument that these companies, along with Uber in ridesharing, have very high market shares, and this gives them a lot of pricing power that can be used to extract high prices from consumers and force extremely low prices on suppliers[16] including workers. This cross-industry concern was nicely captured by Elizabeth Warren's campaign website, where it said:

In industry after industry—airlines, banking, health care, agriculture, tech—a handful of corporate giants control more and more. The big guys are locking out smaller, newer competitors. They are crushing innovation. Even if you don't see the gears turning, this massive concentration means prices go up and quality goes down for everything from air travel to internet service.[17]

Related to this are concerns that with very high market shares, these companies can serve their own interests in related markets. Perhaps the leading illustration of this issue relates to search results. Google has been accused of favoring its own search ads over those of competitors.

An investigation by the *Wall Street Journal* in late 2016 and reported in January of the following year involved "analysis, run by search-ad-data firm SEMrush, examined 1,000 searches each on 25 terms, from 'laptops' to 'speakers' to 'carbon monoxide detectors.' SEMrush ran the searches Dec. 1 on a desktop computer, blocking past web-surfing history that could influence results." They found that advertisements for products sold by Google or other related-party companies were in the top search spot in 91% of searches, and in 43% of searches such ads were in both the top and second-top spot. The *Journal* suggested that Google's search algorithm was designed to achieve this outcome, arguing that Google searches for phones favor Google's own Pixel phones, searches for laptops brought up ads for Google's Chrome browser, and those for smoke detectors favored Alphabet's Nest Internet-connected alarms.[18]

A second argument made by those who advocate breaking up technology companies concerns the regulation of content and speech on platforms.[19] This argument applies much more to companies like Facebook than, say, Uber or Amazon. In calling for the breakup of the company he co-founded with Mark Zuckerberg, Chris Hughes wrote in the *New York Times* that:[20]

> Mark's influence is staggering, far beyond that of anyone else in the private sector or in government. He controls three core communications platforms—Facebook, Instagram and WhatsApp—that billions of people use every day. Facebook's board works more like an advisory committee than an overseer, because Mark controls around 60 percent of voting shares. Mark alone can decide how to configure Facebook's algorithms to determine what people see in their News Feeds, what privacy settings they can use and even which messages get delivered. He sets the rules for how to distinguish violent and incendiary speech from the merely offensive, and he can choose to shut down a competitor by acquiring, blocking or copying it.

The third main argument against "mega-corporations" is that they corrupt the political process through lobbying efforts and campaign contributions, particularly in the United States in a post-*Citizens United* environment where there is essentially no regulation of money in politics. This extends far beyond the technology sector, but is often especially pronounced in this context given their additional role in relation to the regulation of speech on their own platforms.

Part of a democratic liberal approach also involves taking both these political and market power concerns seriously, and taking a number of different steps to impose stricter antitrust regulation. One important first step would be to impose stricter controls on competition-reducing mergers among technology firms, especially those with the capacity to reduce innovation. The large market shares garnered by many successful firms give them both the ability and incentive quickly buy up startups in their sector; and this may be harmful to innovation. This also suggests that particular scrutiny should be applied to acquisitions like those that Facebook undertook with WhatsApp and Instagram. It may be too late to disentangle those assets from Facebook, given the integration that has taken place since the time of acquisition and the economic damage it would entail, but preventing innovation-reducing acquisitions in the future is certainly possible.

There are also a range of other measures that could make antitrust regulation more effective in the digital era. One leading proposal, by the Stigler Center at the University of Chicago Booth School of Business, is to create a specific digital regulator or "digital authority" empowered to collect data from platform companies regarding market transactions, including the kind of customer-level details currently used by companies to target product offerings to those customers.[21] This kind of "platform-eye view" would provide regulators with an unprecedented look into the practices of platforms, but also a richer understanding of their use and potential abuse of market power and informational advantage, and thus also how the exercise of that power should be regulated.

Other proposals that aim to reduce the market power of big tech firms include proposals to prevent the automatic renewal of technology contracts and strengthening "data ownership." If consumers aren't paying very close attention, they can automatically be renewed into another year of service for products ranging from cellular telephone plans to magazine and digital music or streaming subscriptions. This is inherently anti-competitive since it deters comparison shopping. One action a digital authority could consider, therefore, is banning or circumscribing such automatic renewals.

Similarly, strengthening individuals' data ownership, or "data control" (which might specify the nature and extent of access rights of other parties to one's own data) have been widely discussed and could be appealing from a privacy and also competition perspective. Such rights, either control or ownership, could lower so-called switching costs, making it easier for consumers to move from one service provider to another. This can lead to lower prices and possibly also reduce entry barriers for new firms wishing to enter the market. "Number portability" in telecommunications and "open banking" (discussed above) are examples of where this kind of portability exists in other parts of the economy.

A final area that a digital authority might naturally focus on is the establishment of "interoperability standards" that all competitors can use. This would facilitate and promote competition by removing what would otherwise be barriers to entry. The Stigler authors point out that electronic devices in the home would be a natural area where lack of interoperability can be harmful for competition. A useful remedy might be to require adherence to an open standard so that, for example, an Apple thermostat would easily function with a Google home assistant. Such standards might slow down innovation, but they definitely reduce "lock in" and the market power that stems from it. This, in turn, provides a greater incentive to innovate in the first place.

What is less consistent with democratic liberalism, however, is the idea of breaking up existing technology firms. In most of these markets, the power of large technology firms stems from network externalities. Unlike traditional markets, when the source of market power is also the source of consumer harm, in these markets the source of market power is also what consumers (and producers, in the case of two-sided platforms) value—being connected with other consumers and producers.

The key driver of the value that these firms create is precisely the *network externalities* that they bring about. Facebook is valuable to users because lots of other users are on Facebook. Uber is a desirable ridesharing platform for users because there are lots of drivers on it, so wait times are short. And it is desirable for drivers because there are lots of riders to service. The same argument applies to Amazon as a marketplace in terms of buyers and sellers (as analogs to riders and drivers). Google is a superior search engine because in performing so many searches, machine learning allows its algorithm to get better and better, making it a more desirable search engine.

Network externalities are the driving force that tends to lead to these markets having one player with large market share in equilibrium, but it is also the force that creates economic value. Breaking up the large players will stop there being just a few large players, but it will also stop there being nearly as much economic value created.

Moreover, recent work by Akerlof, Holden, and Rayo[22] on these markets provides a clearer picture of why markets with network externalities tend to exhibit three features: (i) "winning" firms serve a disproportionate share of their markets; (ii) it is difficult to become a winning firm (Microsoft has tried very hard with Bing but had limited success), but success is fragile (for example, Netscape was once dominant in the browser market); and (iii) winners are not "asleep"—they constantly innovate and seek to raise quality.[23]

This suggests that there is a qualitative difference between markets with network externalities—like the technology platform markets in social media, e-commerce, ridesharing, and Internet search— and markets like oil, or even railroads. In particular, the fragility of the winning position implies that these firms, even if they have 80%-plus market share, may have very limited pricing power and charge consumers very low prices. This is certainly consistent with a large amount of free provision (with money earned from advertising), and with companies like Amazon losing money, essentially, until the advent of a different business in Amazon Web Services, and Uber losing large amounts of money to this day.

And therein lies the regulatory dilemma. Breaking these companies up does immediate harm. Imagine a "regional Facebook" where users on the east coast of the United States could not be friends with users on the west coast or those in the midwest. Similarly, an Uber that could only connect riders aged 18–25 with drivers aged 30–35 would be smaller, have less market power, but be far less useful for both riders and drivers.

C. From Free Trade to Fair Trade and Strategic Manufacturing

As Chapter 3 notes, one of the most powerful forces in improving living standards around the world in the last three decades—especially in poorer countries—has been the increase in international trade. Free trade, however, also has clear downsides. As Chapter 2 notes, it has had a large impact on the work and wages of certain workers. And, it arguably carries risks for markets themselves.

During Covid-19, many businesses have come to better appreciate the risks associated with supply chains that span the globe and that have few if any redundancies built into them. The failure of one supplier to be able to produce one component of a product in a timely manner can lead to significant delays in the production of entire products. As companies have embraced the efficiency that comes from specializing the production of components to sometimes a single supplier for each component, and in utilizing "just in time" delivery of components and products rather than holding significant inventories of them, they have exposed themselves to shocks that, when they shatter one part of the supply chain, effectively shatter the entire supply chain.

Covid-19 has also highlighted the extent to which many advanced economies rely on other countries for supplies of critical pharmaceuticals. For instance, China and India are responsible for the manufacture of a significant proportion of important drugs sold in the United States.[24] This is another example of where globalization has lowered costs of important goods and has, on the whole, been extremely beneficial. Lowering the costs of drugs in the United States means that Medicare Part D can cover a larger range of drugs, and private insurance that covers pharmaceuticals can be broader and cheaper relative to what it would otherwise be. On the other hand, the stretching of supply chains means that a disruption like Covid-19 can put Americans at risk of having an inadequate supply of essential and life-saving medications. The same, of course, is true for many other countries in Europe and around the world.

One natural and instinctive response to this is to basically hold more inventory in the United States. If there is a six-months' supply, say, of these critical medications, then even a modest sized supply chain disruption can be managed. There are two issues with this. The first is that there are technological limits to how large a "supply buffer" can be held due to the shelf life of medications. These products cannot be held indefinitely, and there is considerable uncertainty about how long many drugs retain their efficacy.[25] In addition, if refrigerated storage is required, the costs of storing manufactured, consumer-ready pharmaceuticals can be significant.

But there is a larger, more complicated and more sinister issue than shelf life and storage. Having critical infrastructure, goods, or services controlled by *contract* rather than by *ownership* gives rise to the possibility of opportunism by one or other of the contracting parties when contracts are incomplete or not completely enforceable. Economists refer to this as the "hold-up problem"—and it has a range of consequences and implications. Indeed, the implications of the hold-up problem have given rise to three Nobel prizes in Economic Sciences: to Ronald Coase, Oliver Williamson, and to Oliver Hart.

This theory has had powerful implications for the boundary of the firm—what economic activity takes place in markets (via contract) and what takes place in firms. In particular, the body of work developed by Oliver Hart and co-authors that has become known as *property rights theory* emphasizes the role that asset ownership can play in alleviating the hold-up problem. If I own the assets necessary for production, then if I have a contractual dispute with my supplier I can simply refuse to allow production to happen. In the language of property rights theory, I have *residual rights of control*. This is powerful, and it puts the asset owner in a superior bargaining position. This means the asset owner has a larger incentive to invest in the relationship. Consequently, the party whose investment is relatively more important to the value of the relationship should own the assets.

Now consider the same logic as it applies to, say, medical equipment or generic pharmaceuticals, and consider the perspective of the United States—although one could replace the United States with the UK, Germany, Australia, or any other advanced economy. Now, instead of "private" ownership, think of it as "foreign" ownership. As in the prisons example, having medical equipment produced overseas (for example, in China) will likely lead it to being produced at lower cost. But it will also give the Chinese government hold-up power. If, when equipment is in particularly acute demand—such as during a pandemic—all the United States has to rely on is a contract or international diplomacy, then they are in a very weak position.

Having such equipment produced in the United States avoids the hold-up problem, but brings with it the loss of efficiency that comes from low-cost manufacturing in a country like China. In short, the United States would have to pay more for such equipment in order to have greater security of supply. This is the fundamental tradeoff in moving toward strategic domestic manufacturing.

In light of this, it is understandable that early in the pandemic there were calls for greater domestic production of critical supplies in a number of countries. French President Emmanuel Macron said in March 2020 that by the end of the year, France would produce both N95 masks and respirators. And US trade adviser Peter Navarro began a push for the federal government to focus its purchases of such equipment, and pharmaceuticals, on domestic producers.[26]

The optimal way to balance the tradeoff between efficiency and certainty of supply likely involves a graduated approach. That could involve stockpiling equipment and pharmaceuticals that have a relatively long shelf life and refreshing them on a rolling basis, combined with building domestic manufacturing capacity along a continuum from "always manufactured" to "can be manufactured."

For instance, it might be that critical supplies like insulin or antibiotics have a constant amount of domestic manufacturing capacity that could be further ramped up in a crisis. Other supplies—hand sanitizer is one example—might have zero constant capacity, but the ability to ramp up quickly (say in a matter of days) in a crisis. This involves having a plan to convert existing manufacturing capacity on short notice in the event of a crisis. The Covid-19 experience has shown that, to choose one example, distilleries can be quickly converted to producing hand sanitizer provided that there are sufficient bottles available. In the next crisis there could be a clear roadmap for making this transition, rather than having to do it for the first time.

The provision of vaccines against Covid-19 has also underlined the importance of strategic manufacturing. For instance, in late January 2021 the European Union imposed a ban on exports of Covid-19 vaccines produced within the EU. Given that a significant portion of the world-leading Pfizer vaccine was produced at a factory in Belgium, this put the supply of vaccines for the United Kingdom, Australia, and even the United States under pressure—if only relatively briefly. Australia is an example of a country that had recognized the importance of local manufacturing to protect against this kind of "vaccine nationalism" and had ensured that local company CSL could produce the Astra-Zeneca vaccine within Australia under license.

D. Conclusion

Market power can be a serious threat to fair markets, and pre- (and post-) neoliberal economics took, and continues to take, market power as something that needs to be reined in for markets to function efficiently. Sometimes, as in many financial markets, this involves mandated disclosures to help ensure that consumers and financial firms have the same information. Moreover, the well-documented behavioral biases that many individuals exhibit provide grounds for somewhat more aggressive intervention in these markets, including "sophisticated investor" requirements for certain financial products.

In markets with network externalities, in which some of the world's largest "platform" companies like Amazon, Facebook, Google, and Uber are key players, traditional antitrust approaches are less appropriate. In these markets, large market shares for the best firms are both natural and common, but also benefit consumers precisely because of those network externalities. Concentration or market share *per se* does not confer pricing or monopoly power upon large firms, and as such, traditional antitrust approaches are not well suited to the situation. That said, preventing mergers with start-up competitors remains a concern even within this framework and should be pursued more aggressively than it has been.

7

Internalizing Externalities: Toward a Carbon Dividend

Climate change has been described by leaders worldwide as the greatest moral and political challenge of our time.[1] As a recent Intergovernmental Panel on Climate Change (IPCC) report noted,[2] human activities have caused 1.0°C of global warming above pre-industrial levels. Worse still, at the current rate, that number is likely to reach between 1.5°C and 2°C between 2030 and 2052.

The consequences of these changes are severe for both the planet and human health and security. Temperature rises of this kind are likely to lead to further and significant rises in sea levels due to melting of polar ice caps, extreme temperatures in inhabited regions, heavy precipitation in some regions, and severe droughts and wildfires in others. The flow-on effects of this include species extinction, risks to marine biodiversity, destruction of fisheries, lack of food security, and threats to the water supply.

With its orientation of being pro-business rather than pro-market, neoliberalism has also manifestly failed to respond to these challenges. Worse still, the neoliberal hostility toward both taxes and regulation have meant that those subscribing to this philosophy have an inbuilt bias against taking any meaningful action on climate change.

We are, however, moving toward greater consensus on the need to take action, and to define targets. As part of the Paris Agreement, nearly 200 nations committed to each doing their part to limit global warming to below 2°C, and preferably 1.5°C, compared to pre-industrial levels, consistent with the warnings of the IPCC. For instance, both the United States and Australia agreed to cut emissions by 26%–28% from 2005 levels by 2030; European Union countries committed to a 40% domestic reduction in emissions by 2030 compared to 1990 levels, Canada a 26% reduction in emissions compared to 2013 levels by 2030, Japan a 26% cut on 2013 levels by 2030, and South Korea a 37% reduction to business-as-usual emissions by 2030, to name some of the targets of OECD economies.[3]

While President Donald Trump withdrew the United States from the Paris Agreement, President Joe Biden made it one of his first orders of business to rejoin the agreement by executive order. Moreover, Biden has announced ambitious plans for "a clean energy revolution and environmental justice" including investing US$1.7 trillion over the next decade in "green energy" and achieving net-zero greenhouse gas emissions by 2050.[4] Notwithstanding challenges to this from within his own party—such as from West Virginia Senator Joe Manchin—the commitment of the Biden administration is clear. And the United States is not alone in announcing serious targets. Even before COP26 in Glasgow, the European Union, Japan, and South Korea had committed to net-zero emissions by 2050. China's net-zero target is 2060.

The real question is how to achieve these targets or goals. One option is for government regulation of emissions, another is increased green investment, and another still is for governments to adopt a form of cap and trade system.

The Obama administration, for example, adopted a range of environmental policies that angered many in the environmental lobby, as they included continued domestic oil and gas development, ethanol subsidies, support for so-called clean coal technology, and an expansion of nuclear energy. But those policies also included a cap and trade system, increasing fuel efficiency (CAFE) standards from 27.5 to 35.5 miles per gallon by 2016, and allocating $90 billion of the $800 billion Recovery Act for clean energy initiatives including the ARPA-E energy research program.[5]

The Trump administration took a very skeptical view of climate change as an issue and rolled back many existing regulations. The Biden administration, by contrast, has said that it will pursue large-scale investments in green energy to both boost jobs and reduce emissions, and has also announced updated CAFE standards.[6]

The European Union and Britain began exploring a price on carbon matched with a "carbon border tax" in 2020 and 2021, respectively.[7] China has also made large investments in green energy technology, such as solar power.[8]

Each approach has certain advantages as well as disadvantages. But a democratic liberal approach suggests that by far the most effective and equitable response will be one that involves a universal price or tax on carbon—which is then directly returned to citizens (or residents) in the form of a carbon "dividend."[9] An approach of this kind ensures that polluters pay for the full social cost of their actions rather than gain subsidies or exemptions in doing so. And it creates the right incentives for a rapid transition from fossil fuels to renewable sources of energy: it encourages investment in new, renewable sources of energy and technologies and puts those technologies on a level playing field in the market.

At the same time, by redistributing the proceeds of this tax to citizens, a carbon dividend-based approach addresses the other great failings in current neoliberal policies: it recognizes that food, transport, and electricity are all necessary parts of a dignified life, and are markets in which there are increasing cost pressures. It likewise recognizes that economic inequality is a pervasive and growing problem in many advanced economies, and one that can often undermine the actual and perceived legitimacy of both the economic and political system. While the carbon dividend itself is a flat dividend, paid equally to all households regardless of income or wealth, its actual effect is progressive in nature: in percentage terms, it is a far more meaningful amount of money and degree of compensation for low income and low spending households as opposed to high income and high spending households.

A carbon dividend approach also reflects the more general logic of a fair markets–based approach: it seeks to recognize that markets often fail and to harness the power of both the state and market forces to address problems of social cost, dignity, and inequality.

In the remainder of the chapter, we outline the arguments for and against alternative regulatory approaches, including various forms of emissions regulation or "direct action," state investment in green technology, and cap and trade style systems. In part B, we make the case for an approach that involves a price or tax on carbon as the simplest and most effective way of responding to the current climate crisis—in ways that both encourage a rapid transition to carbon neutrality and recognize the need to make tradeoffs around reliability and affordability of energy and other carbon-emitting products along the way. At the same time, in part C, we acknowledge the impact of a price on carbon on the affordability of certain goods for low-income earners, and show how rebating the proceeds of a tax directly to citizens can substantially overcome that problem and provide a valuable political incentive for voters in democracies to support the introduction of a democratic liberal response to climate change. Finally, in part D, we show how this kind of "dividend"-based approach can be adapted to the realities of an open economy where not all trading partners have taken similar steps to address the climate crisis, and to other areas in which there are negative externalities that could usefully be addressed by some form of Pigouvian tax, as well as note the degree to which democratic liberalism entails a broader set of responses to externalities.

A. Addressing Climate Change Without a Price on Carbon

(i) Regulation

One approach is for the government simply to regulate the level of emissions that can occur in certain industries, for instance by banning fossil fuels or mandating the progressive closure of coal mines and coal-fired power plants. This can also involve what is sometimes called "direct action," where firms are essentially paid not to pollute above a certain level. This was, for instance, the policy of the Australian government under former Prime Minister Tony Abbott.

Although this policy is easy to understand and is better than outright climate denialism, the key drawback of this kind of approach is that it involves the government balancing the social benefits and social costs of emissions rather than letting the market do it once the social cost of carbon is internalized into the price mechanism. This is reminiscent of the so-called Lange-Lerner-Taylor-Hayek debate of the mid-20th century about whether governments could mimic the market by a central planner doing the same kind of calculation done by dispersed individuals with local information. It became increasingly clear over the course of the 20th century that this required too much information, and that market-based mechanisms were preferable.[10]

That is not to say that mileage efficiency standards for vehicles, or energy efficiency standards for appliances, do not have a role to play. Regulations such as CAFE mileage standards and energy efficiency requirements for home appliances are a sensible means of contributing to reductions in emissions. There is a severe coordination problem for manufacturers of motor vehicles or appliances, whereby if one producer unilaterally moves to higher standards at higher cost, they lose a significant amount of market share. This deters any producer from acting unilaterally lest they be reduced to serving a relatively niche market of consumers who are (and can afford to be) environmentally conscious. But by imposing a standard on an entire industry, no individual producer is uniquely harmed, and the regulation internalizes the environmental externality from having fuel-inefficient cars or energy-inefficient appliances.

In the United States, these standards have also had a major impact in reducing carbon emissions. The CAFE standards introduced by Obama were estimated to reduce greenhouse gas emissions by more than 900 million metric tons over the lifetime the new vehicles. As Obama himself put it, this was "the equivalent of shutting down 194 coal-fired power plants."[11] And the administration's increased standards for appliances, overseen by energy secretary Stephen Chu, delivered another 210 million metric-ton reduction in greenhouse gas emissions.[12] The Trump administration reversed these and many other Obama-era regulations, notably reducing fuel efficiency standards from a 5% reduction to a 1.5% reduction in April 2020.[13]

But such standards are also not adequate to address economy-wide emissions problems and are much harder to calibrate on an economy-wide basis. First, they only cover certain parts of the economy and, by their very nature, would be hard to apply to others such as industrial production or agriculture.

Furthermore, they do not involve compensation. Cars with higher fuel efficiency and more efficient appliances are typically more expensive, and this burden hits consumers without compensation.

The "direct action" policies that Australia pursued beginning in July 2014 are even more problematic. As we have said elsewhere, this raises "significant questions about how to measure and monitor the purported emissions reductions, what this would cost, and the economic distortion from raising tax revenue to fund the payments. This approach is inefficient on multiple levels. It involves government winner-picking of worthy projects based on limited or no information and, rather than generating revenue, it uses government funds to essentially bribe organizations to reduce carbon emissions. This comes at the usual cost of distortionary taxation, as well as the informational inefficiency from winner picking."[14]

(ii) Green Government Investment

Another potential approach is for government to invest in or subsidize renewable energy in order to lower emissions. On the downside, this is economically costly because it requires taxpayer dollars funded from distortionary taxation (e.g., reducing labor supply).

On the plus side, there is good reason to believe that there is market failure in the clean energy sector. As the experience with solar panels has shown, clean energy technology starts out being more expensive than fossil fuels, but these costs decline over time as the technology improves, economies of scale are realized, and input markets become more developed. This is what economists call the "experience curve." Given the nature of this curve and the short-termism that is pervasive in public equity markets, a completely free market will tend to underprovide investment in clean energy technology.

Venture capital funds are a partial fix for this—they tend to have a longer investment horizon and greater appetite for risk than public equities markets.

Yet, given the size of investments that are required, the length of the investment horizon often stretching beyond a decade, and the risk profile of many of these investments, venture capital is at most a partial solution to the inherent market failure. Public funding of or subsidies for investments in clean energy technology is therefore often necessary in order to encourage the development of new, green technologies.

That said, it does involve a form of government winner-picking with all its attendant drawbacks. It is very hard for the government to discern which are the promising technologies and which are unlikely to work out. By contrast, private investors and venture capitalists have strong financial incentives to try and overcome such informational problems.

Moreover, government investments are often subject to intense lobbying efforts by the potential beneficiaries, potentially leading to inferior technologies being funded for political rather than scientific and commercial reasons.

President Obama's support of green energy certainly ended with a range of failures, as well as successes. Numerous clean energy companies that received federal loan guarantees filed for bankruptcy, including Solyndra, Abound Solar, Beacon Power, Ener1, and electric car battery maker A123.[15] And there is good reason to think this is an inevitable part of any large-scale public green investment strategy—not any lack of due diligence or care on the part of the administration.

(iii) Cap and Trade

Another longstanding proposal to address climate change involves some form of emissions trading scheme or so-called cap and trade system (as in Waxman-Markey), where permits that grant firms a right to pollute a certain amount are distributed, and they can be traded in a secondary market for such permits. This ensures that firms that can most effectively use the right to pollute buy the permits from those who can do so less effectively. Just like a carbon tax, this ensures that the marginal benefit of pollution (through economic development) is matched to the marginal cost of pollution (though environmental harm).

This provides an incentive for firms to reduce the amount they pollute, so that they can sell part of their allocation to other firms who want to pollute more, thereby earning revenue on the sale of those rights/permits.

While cap and trade is vastly preferable to inaction, and as a market-based mechanism is more consistent with democratic liberalism than direct regulation or a green new deal, it does have two important drawbacks. First, determining the total amount of pollution that should be allowed is complex. It is certainly more complicated than determining the social cost of carbon, which underpins the rate of a carbon tax. There is a mathematical relationship between the two, but it requires knowledge of how each business would respond to a carbon tax in terms of emissions reduction. This requires a massive amount of information that the government cannot possibly have. The decentralized solution provided by a carbon tax does not require this information.

The second drawback is determining how to allocate permits to businesses. A natural starting point is to allocate permits proportional to the existing emissions of each firm. But this rewards the largest emitters that have contributed the most to the climate change problems we face. It also arguably dulls their incentive to reduce emissions to some degree, although that is ultimately an empirical question that has not yet been satisfactorily answered to our knowledge.

B. Democratic Liberalism and a Price on Carbon

Another approach, however, is for governments to impose a "price" or tax on carbon, which reflects the actual environmental cost of carbon emissions for world health, weather patterns, and changes in sea levels.

The best scientific evidence is that the social cost of carbon is at least $US36 per ton. The testimony of perhaps the world's leading climate economist, University of Chicago professor Michael Greenstone, to the US House Committee on Science, Space and Technology, Subcommittee on Environment, Subcommittee on Oversight in February 2017 emphasized this point.[16] Indeed, recent work by Greenstone and Tamma Carleton suggests that the current social cost of carbon is almost surely above US$50 per ton, and may be as high as $US125 per ton.[17]

There is also recent evidence suggesting that the true social cost of carbon could be substantially higher, particularly once mortality costs are factored in.[18] As the IPCC have pointed out forcefully, if we continue to fail to take meaningful action on climate change, the social cost of carbon will rise—potentially dramatically.

The advantage of a carbon tax, as previously stated, is also that it "internalizes" the externality caused by pollution into the price mechanism, so that the market then balances the social benefit of economic activity that causes pollution with the social cost that stems from that pollution.

This is not purely a matter of theory. Recent evidence from Sweden demonstrates that the effect of a carbon tax on consumer behavior can be significant. By comparing Sweden to a weighted average of other OECD countries (the so-called synthetic control method), economist Julius Andersson showed that CO_2 emissions in the transportation sector fell 11% after Sweden introduced its carbon tax, and that most of this was in fact due to the carbon tax. Moreover, he showed that the "carbon tax elasticity of demand for gasoline is three times larger than the price elasticity" of demand for gasoline. In other words, the carbon tax has a very significant impact on consumer behavior at the margin.[19]

A Pigouvian tax also puts different forms of energy—from fossil fuels to renewables—on a level playing field. This provides the appropriate incentives for the private sector to invest in clean energy technology at the same time as providing consumers with the right incentives to adopt energy produced from these technologies.

The growth in scale of renewable energy like wind and solar has led to a dramatic reduction in the cost of generation. Over the last decade, the cost of wind has fallen 70% and solar 89%, according to 2019 analysis by investment bank Lazard.[20]

This now puts unsubsidized wind power as costing between $28 and $54 per megawatt hour (MWh) and unsubsidized solar at $32 to $42 per MWh. This compares to $66 to $152 per MWh for coal and $44 to $68 for gas. Even focusing on the marginal cost (taking the cost of existing generating capacity as sunk), coal costs between $26 and $41 per MWh. Even nuclear energy, which entails very expensive plants that take many years to bring online, has a marginal cost of between $27 and $31 per MWh. In short, clean energy has now become (more than) cost competitive with existing fossil fuel sources, and for new generation capacity it is clearly the dominant option from a cost perspective.[21]

That said, reliability remains an issue with green energy such as wind and solar. There are real examples of blackouts in jurisdictions with essentially complete reliance on renewable energy, such as the Australian state of South Australia in 2016.

But improvements in battery technology are making storage of large amounts of renewably generated energy more and more a reality. In addition, improvements to the electrical grid are making it possible to transmit energy over larger distances without significant leakage, thus allowing for transmission of energy generated in different geographic areas with different weather patterns and reducing the chance of power outages.

In addition, so-called reliability markets can help address variability in green energy supply. These involve physical energy capacity coupled with an option to supply energy above a certain strike price. Capacity is priced through bids in an auction, and performance incentives are provided through a "load-following obligation" to supply energy above the option's strike price. As economists Peter Cramton and Steven Stoft have pointed out, this both hedges against high spot prices and reduces supplier risk. Furthermore, it reduces market power in the spot market.[22] Such markets have been implemented in the United States (first in New England) and also in Colombia.[23]

C. Taking Economic Inequality Seriously: Toward a Carbon Dividend Approach

The most obvious downside of putting a price on carbon is that it acts as a tax on consumers as businesses pass through their increased input costs in the form of higher prices for final goods and services. Worse still, this increase in prices is proportionally higher for lower-income households, since they spend a larger percentage share of their income on goods that are made more expensive by a price on carbon—such as energy, fuel, and transportation. In this sense, any price on carbon is essentially a regressive tax.

A natural response to this is to exempt certain people or certain goods from any carbon tax, but of course this unravels the incentives that the tax is there to provide. If people don't pay the marginal social cost of their carbon emissions, they will not reduce them to the efficient level. So, for instance, when the Gillard government in Australia exempted tradespeople (electricians, plumbers, etc.) from the price on carbon they had established, it was a clear mistake that undercut the very policy they had introduced.

A second approach is to provide compensation to certain groups. If this compensation is "lump sum" in the sense that it does not depend on the amount of carbon emissions from a given individual, then it does not distort their incentives to reduce emissions. They get a certain amount of compensation no matter what, so they still have every incentive to reduce their carbon footprint to avoid paying the carbon tax.

That said, such "targeted" compensation schemes are extremely difficult to implement as a practical matter. First, there is intense political lobbying from different groups who all claim to have a legitimate rationale for compensation. Second, it is almost certainly the case that compensation will be either over- or under-inclusive.

A better approach is to compensate every citizen equally. Notice that in doing that—paying every citizen the same dollar amount—is inherently progressive. Why? Because lower-income earners spend less money in general, and as such are less affected by a carbon tax. But if they get the same dollar amount of compensation as high-income earners, they are better off on a net basis.

This leads quite naturally to the idea of imposing a carbon tax and using all of the funds generated from it to pay a dividend back to all citizens on an equal (*pari pasu*) basis. This is the key idea behind the carbon dividend approach to which we now turn.

We have suggested elsewhere that the best way politically to take meaningful action on climate change is to couple a carbon tax with a plan that distributes the proceeds of that tax as a dividend to all citizens of the country in question.[24] This has political appeal to both conservatives and progressives.

This "climate dividend" plan would make sure that alternative energy sources are put on an even footing with coal and gas, and therefore encourage new investments in renewable energy. But it would do so in a market-based way, which would ensure that energy reliability is retained—and fossil fuels such as coal-fired power remain part of the mix, so long as it is necessary to ensure reliable energy supply. Rather than mandating a certain proportion of renewables, energy choices would be determined by market forces.

Most importantly, it would address the affordability problem in new and important ways: instead of providing *ad hoc* forms of compensation to different groups, as many countries that have introduced even modest carbon taxes have done (Australia in 2011 is a notable example), it would provide universal compensation to all citizens in the form of a carbon dividend—an equal slice of the revenue raised from the carbon tax. This could leave, for instance, around 70% of American households better off financially under a carbon dividend plan, and as many as three-quarters of Australian households.

This is also before making any behavioral changes to reduce their carbon footprint. If they did make such changes, they would be even better off. For businesses, it would not provide compensation but assumes that increases in cost could be passed on to consumers (who are receiving compensation).

In some ways, the plan is quite radical: it openly embraces the idea of a price or tax on carbon. And it suggests that this tax should apply to all key carbon emissions—that is, to energy, transport, and agriculture. Ultimately, any meaningful climate policy puts an implicit price on carbon—the only difference is that we do so openly, in a clear and transparent way that members of the public can understand. Clarity of this kind also helps give businesses the certainty they need for major investments in the economy more generally.

In other ways, the proposal is also highly centrist: it seeks to transcend left–right divides and create a policy that can command support from all sides of the political spectrum. It is market-based and focused on maintaining the economic competitiveness of a nation that implements it in ways that reflect conservative traditions. Yet it takes climate change and economic inequality seriously in ways that give effect to a range of progressive demands.

A concrete proposal for carbon dividends of this kind was developed in the United States by the *Climate Leadership Council* (CLC), a Washington-based think tank, and has begun to gain traction as a way to address the social cost of carbon emissions but provide compensation to citizens and preserve the competitiveness of domestic industries.[25] For instance, it is backed by a large number of companies, including as founding members major fossil fuel companies like BP, ExxonMobil, and Shell. It has been backed by 27 Nobel Laureates in Economics, 15 former Chairs of the Council of Economic Advisors, and four former Chairs of the US Federal Reserve. We built on this to develop a related proposal for Australia, the *Australian Carbon Dividend Plan*.

The basic idea of the CLC proposal is to institute a carbon tax (at US$40 a ton) and return the proceeds from that tax as a dividend to every American on an equal basis. The plan has two core features. First, the plan involves instituting a US$40 per ton tax on carbon dioxide emissions in the United States (in Australia this would be A$50 per ton, to be equivalent). This would be implemented at the point where carbon enters the economy—such as a mine, a well, or a port. The CLC plan envisages the rate of the tax increasing over time, but a fixed US$40 per ton rate is a sensible starting point.

Second, the plan involves returning all of the (at least net) proceeds of the tax to all citizens of voting age on an equal basis (this could include lawful permanent residents as well, or be broader, such as everyone with a social security number). This would occur via direct deposit, dividend checks, or even contributions to retirement savings accounts. The Internal Revenue Service would administer this, and the dividend would go to any eligible person.[26]

The dividend component of the plan is attractive for two reasons. First, it is a means of compensating those individuals who will pay more for goods and services as a consequence of the carbon tax. The tax will increase input costs for firms, resulting in some of those increased costs being passed on to consumers. But because the compensation is lump sum in nature, it does not diminish the incentive for individuals and households to reduce their carbon footprint. It is thus superior to compensation that targets high users of carbon.

The fact that the dividend is allocated equally across all individuals means that the carbon tax is not regressive. Indeed, the US Treasury estimated that the bottom 70% of US households would be *better off* as a result of the carbon tax–dividend combination.[27]

Second, the carbon dividend makes the tax more politically viable. In effect, a dividend-based approach harnesses the power of economic incentives both to change behavior *and* promote political support for regulatory change. Of course, citizens also bear a cost, through a Pigouvian tax addressing the externality, but the scheme affords them the opportunity to modify their behavior to minimize their payment while still receiving the dividend.

The payments to households under a carbon dividend plan are substantial. The CLC has estimated that in the United States, the plan would lead to a dividend of approximately US$2,000 a year for a family of four. This would leave seven of the 10 income deciles better off overall, with the lower-income households in the United States receiving the largest gain as a proportion of their income—more than 8% for the lowest income quintile—as the Figure 7.1 illustrates.

In Australia, our variant of this plan, the Australian Carbon Dividend Plan, also generates substantial income flows to households from the dividend payments. We have estimated that a typical household of two adults and two children under 18 would receive approximately A$2,600 per annum in tax-free payments. Rewards of this kind have the capacity to offset a significant amount of increased energy costs and create a major shift in the perception of the relative winners and losers arising from addressing carbon emissions.

Of Australia's overall carbon emissions, 466 million metric tons of CO_2 equivalent would be taxed, from electricity, direct combustion, transport, fugitive emissions, and industrial processes. This excludes agriculture (79 MMT CO_2e), waste (16 MMT CO_2e), and land use/forestry (66 MMT CO_2e). These are excluded because of the difficulty in capturing such emissions at the point

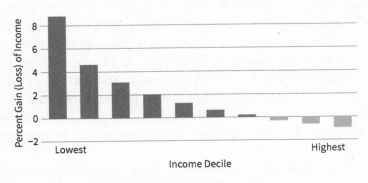

Figure 7.1 Impact of Carbon Dividends on US Family Incomes

source. In the case of agriculture, it also avoids some challenging questions about compensation.

Given the A\$50 per ton carbon tax, the plan generates A\$23.3B in revenue. A proportion of this is generated by government carbon emissions and, to make the impact on government revenue neutral, we deduct this from the available proceeds of the plan. Using an assumption of 10% of total revenues to cover government usage and administration costs of the plan, the available funds for the dividend to Australians is A\$21.0B.

In addition, the specific version of a carbon dividend approach we advocate aims to ensure that citizens of a particular country play a fair role in addressing the costs of climate change, but not a greater share than is fair or appropriate—and to ensure that it does not unjustifiably damage the competitiveness of (say) US exports, or US-made goods relative to imported alternatives.

The fees charged based on the carbon component of goods exported to the United States from other countries that do not have a carbon tax make those exporting countries less competitive on carbon-intensive goods. This gives them an incentive to produce and export less carbon-intensive goods. Moreover, it gives them an incentive to adopt a carbon tax themselves and avoid all such fees regardless of the carbon component of their exported goods. The other part of the border adjustment—that US exporters to countries without a carbon tax get a rebate for taxes paid—means that such exporters are not disadvantaged by the carbon tax. An important implication of this is that other countries do not have an incentive *not* to adopt their own carbon tax as a way of securing a competitive trade advantage.

This border-adjustment component of the plan could be subject to a challenge before the World Trade Organization, but we also believe that this is a challenge the country instituting the carbon dividend plan could successfully defend.[28]

The carbon dividend plan thus (i) internalizes an important negative externality—carbon dioxide emissions—through a Pigouvian tax; (ii) allows a well-functioning market to partially substitute for government regulation; (iii) returns the proceeds of that tax equally to all citizens, thus avoiding regressivity and improving political buy-in; and (iv) provides incentives for other countries to adopt a similar approach.

The key feature of the plan is that it provides direct financial rewards to citizens when their government effects positive change. This, in turn, provides incentives for citizens to support such efforts. This can also create new forms of democratic coalitions in support of measures to address global challenges—namely, a new coalition of politically motivated citizens and politically supportive "citizen-shareholders" who see a combination of philosophical and economic rewards to regulatory change.

A coalition of this kind can also provide governments, who may themselves support change, with a receptive domestic political environment. This can be particularly important for challenging issues such as climate change. For example, studies show mixed support for a carbon tax: in Australia, around 40% of Australians support an emissions trading scheme or price on carbon;[29] in the United States, studies suggest between 35% and 50% are strongly or somewhat supportive of a carbon tax;[30] while in Canada, just under 60% support carbon taxation.[31]

D. Beyond Carbon

The same logic that underpins carbon dividend plans could also be readily applied to so-called congestion taxes. These taxes, commonly used in many major cities to deal with traffic flows and congestion during peak hours in inner cities and business districts, can be very effective in reducing the social cost of congestion. For instance, London, Stockholm, Singapore, and New York City all have congestion charges of one form or another.

In London there is fee of £11.50 per day for vehicles to enter or travel within a designated "congestion charge zone" between certain hours (currently 7 a.m. and 6 p.m. on weekdays). Residents who live within the congestion charging zone are eligible to apply for a 90% discount on (one) primary vehicle of theirs, and there are a variety of discounts and exemptions for commercial vehicles like taxis.

This has led to a reduction in congestion, with one study[32] reporting that before there was a congestion charge, London had average traffic speeds slower than eight miles per hour and lost £2–4 million per week in time due to congestion. The congestion charge helped contribute to a 15% reduction in traffic in central London, with travel delays reduced by 30% and excess waiting time on buses falling by one-third.

The same report found that in Stockholm, there was a 20% drop in traffic in the congestion-zone area as a result of its congestion tax.

Congestion taxes—much like a carbon tax—are uncontroversial among economists. They internalize a negative externality that is not captured by the market's price mechanism, thereby allowing the market to allocate resources more efficiently. But, as with a carbon tax, there are broader political considerations that make implementing congestion taxes more vexed.

The first is that they impose a cost that is not related to people's income, thereby hitting lower-income earners the hardest for a given amount of use. The second is that they generate revenue for the government, which can be seen as a good thing but for fiscal conservatives is viewed as a drawback.

One way to address both of these issues is to ensure that the revenue raised from a congestion tax is spent on a dedicated area related to the externality that generates it. In this instance the obvious candidate is public transportation. Doing so means that the size of government isn't expanded *per se*, and also that lower-income individuals have a way of avoiding paying the congestion tax by using public transport rather than, say, driving.

The obvious analogy here is the use of revenues from a carbon tax to invest in green energy initiatives. And that is not a bad thing to do by any means, but it does leave open the question of compensation as well as whether the investments made by the government are done in the most efficient way.

By contrast, paying the proceeds of a congestion tax back to citizens as an evenly distributed dividend deals with the compensation issue, preserves the economic incentives to avoid creating congestion, and leaves the important question of the most efficient way to invest in public transportation as an issue to be addressed in its own right rather than being seen as somehow "free" or not involving opportunity cost.

Of course, this principle of distributing dividends back to citizens based on revenues generated by taxing negative externalities can be extended beyond carbon and congestion taxes—although they are perhaps the two leading examples. For instance, the use of common property resources such as fisheries is often governed by licensing regimes that generate revenues; so-called sin taxes on tobacco, alcohol, or gambling can also generate significant revenues. Fines for traffic violations and parking infringements arguably fall into this category as well. The list goes on.

In all of these instances, there is an argument for distributing the proceeds of taxes, fines, and license fees that internalize these externalities back to the public in general. In part this provides the government with an incentive to think more carefully about the optimal level of those taxes and fines, rather than seeing them as simply a means of revenue generation that can be used—in the more cynical view of the world—for pork barrel spending to improve the reelection prospects of particular political actors.

It is also worth stressing that the externalities to which democratic liberalism seeks to respond are not limited to environmental harms. They include a wide range of other social costs and benefits not borne or enjoyed by parties to a market-based transaction. A good example of this kind of non-environmental externality is the that associated with one person contracting

Covid-19 and failing to socially isolate: their illness risks imposing large-scale adverse health and economic effects on others in their community.

Another example, which lives large in the minds of many critics of neoliberalism, is the way in which certain risky individual financial transactions can pose systemic risks to the stability of a nation's entire financial system.

Take the risky financial instruments—such as mortgage-backed securities (MBSs), credit default swaps (CDSs), and derivative securities such as collateralized loan obligations (CLOs)—that were at the heart of the 2008 financial crisis. The neoliberal view of these instruments is simple: government regulation of such instruments in an unwarranted intrusion in the private affairs of sophisticated contracting parties. Perhaps, neoliberals might concede, there is some role for consumer protection laws to ensure that "mom and pop" investors don't enter into risky financial dealings. They might even view disclosure requirements for financial (and other) firms with some skepticism, wondering why there isn't sufficient incentive for market participants to unearth price-sensitive information, since they could be handsomely rewarded for so doing. Even insider trading is sometimes defended by neoliberals as being an efficient way to compensate entrepreneurs or to accelerate the incorporation of information into securities prices.[33]

Democratic liberalism, in contrast, focuses on the capacity of these instruments to pose systemic risks of financial contagion, and on the externalities that one firm's actions in trading in such instruments can have on the financial system as a whole.

For instance, in the lead-up to 2008 the imprudent creation of, and trading in, mortgage-backed securities arguably fueled a massive housing bubble. At the same time, many non–deposit taking institutions like Lehman Brothers were incredibly highly leveraged (around 30 dollars of debt for every one dollar of equity) and provided high-powered incentives to their traders, leading them to take massive bets on the US housing market. And when those bets went south, the interconnectedness of these firms with otherwise sound institutions like Goldman Sachs led to mass financial contagion and a modern-day bank run on *all* of these firms, sound or not.

A fair markets approach thus supports measures such as the Dodd–Frank Wall Street Reform and Consumer Protection Act (2010) that required credit default swaps and other formerly "over-the-counter" transactions to be settled on an exchange or through a clearing house, and gave the Federal Reserve the power to regulate systematically important (i.e., network-connected) institutions. The expanded capital adequacy requirements put in place in many jurisdictions after 2008, requiring banks to hold more equity capital to buffer themselves against potential losses, are also squarely consistent with democratic liberalism's emphasis on preventing externalities—including in the form of the risk of financial contagion.

This is also in clear contrast to the democratic socialist view that financial products like CDSs, CLOs, and perhaps even some forms of MBSs are, to use Warren Buffett's famous term, "financial weapons of mass destruction" and should be banned outright.[34] A fair markets approach takes the risk these securities pose seriously to the financial system as a whole, and seeks to regulate them in an effective manner, but in a way that does not destroy the market for them. It takes the perspective that mortgage-backed securities, for instance, helped expand the mortgage market and extend credit to a greater number of lower-income but creditworthy borrowers. It was fraudulent loans, chronically lax underwriting standards, excess leverage, and moral hazard–fueled speculation—that is, a failure of market regulation, not MBSs themselves—that that led to the 2008 financial crisis.

PART III
REALIZING FAIR MARKETS
IN PRACTICE

8

Paying for Government's Role in Democratic Liberalism

The ideas we proposed in earlier chapters are deliberately designed to be more affordable—or economically sustainable—than leading proposals for a UBI. But some of the ideas we propose still come at a significant cost.

The Jobs Corps is the largest of those, but guaranteeing a generous social minimum and funding universal basic benefits are also a real draw on the public purse. Some of our proposals, like place-based policies and wage-earner equity, also involve tax breaks that reduce government revenue. We have outlined earlier in this book how parts of our plan can be funded by consumer taxes, such as those on point-to-point transportation. And sometimes internalizing externalities will generate revenues. But that still leaves additional revenue that needs to be raised, and one needs to grapple with how to do so in democratically liberal way.

The first thing to note is that the sustainable level of government debt may well be higher than has previously been thought possible. Former US Treasury Secretary Larry Summers has forcefully argued[1] that the so-called equilibrium real interest rate—the real interest rate consistent with a stable macro-economy for countries like those in the OECD—has fallen substantially in recent decades and is now probably negative. If one accepts this *secular stagnation hypothesis*, then governments like that in the United States will be able to issue government debt at very low real interest rates. That is certainly the case now, where the US government can borrow for 30 years at around 1.5% per annum in nominal terms, and inflation is running at around 1.8% a year. This implies that some of the additional expenditure required for a jobs guarantee and a generous social minimum—most notably subsidized universal healthcare—could be paid for, in part, out of additional government borrowing.

But as we will discuss in more detail below, this does not mean that governments can borrow unlimited amounts, and it certainly does not mean that they can simply "print money" without inflationary consequences. And it makes it important for government accounting to distinguish between what one of the authors has previously called "good debt" versus "bad debt"—that is, debt that essentially funds investments in a strong and greener economy, versus debt that is simply used to fund ongoing expenditure like social welfare programs.

Beyond borrowing more, there are also four potential sources of revenue to which governments can usefully look: (i) personal income taxes, (ii) taxes on capital, (iii) value added taxes, and (iv) stepped-up compliance efforts and loophole/tax-shelter crackdowns. Our rough estimates (along with those outlined by Natasha Sarin and Larry Summers on some of the measures)[2] suggest that they could also lead to a meaningful amount of new revenue. In the United States context, between an increase in capital taxes to three-quarters of the rate on ordinary income (generating around $24 billion a year), a progressive value added tax (VAT) with a 15% rate but $7,500 per adult exemption replacing state and local sales taxes ($85 billion per year), devoting more resources to tax compliance ($30–$40 billion per year), cracking down on personal loopholes ($40 billion per year), corporate tax shelters ($30 billion per year), and eliminating the stepped-up basis ($25 billion per year), one arrives at more than $230 billion a year in additional revenue. If the relatively modest but more speculative "black economy" revenue benefits that come from a movement toward cashless transactions as part of the progressive VAT came to fruition, the new revenue would be closer to $300 billion a year.

This would not be sufficient to fund every government program or "wish list scheme." It would take *all* of this money to fund the expansive Medicare for All scheme of a Bernie Sanders, Elizabeth Warren, or Kamala Harris. And even all of these revenues would be insufficient to fund an unconditional universal basic income. But it would certainly provide the fiscal room to achieve the dignified social minimum at the heart of a democratically liberal approach post-Covid-19. And these potential sources are both more consistent with the principled foundations of democratic liberalism and likely actually to raise revenue than a range of other current proposals—including wealth taxes, estate taxes, and natural resource taxes.

The rest of the chapter explores these ideas in more detail. Part A considers the idea of safe and unsafe levels, or "good" versus "bad" forms of debt, and the degree to which increased borrowing by governments could shoulder the fiscal load that democratic liberalism requires. Part B explores potential sources of tax revenue that are consistent with a democratic liberal approach, and the idea of effective and efficient taxation. Finally, part C explores a range of alternative proposals from democratic socialists and proponents of "modern monetary theory" (MMT) and highlights the dangers they pose to a fair markets agenda.

A. Beyond Austerity and (Consistent) Balanced Budgets

One of the most frequent concerns raised about government's role in guaranteeing a generous social minimum is that it involves governments taking on an unmanageable fiscal burden—and therefore also level of government debt—or debt levels that impose a large fiscal burden on future generations.

This argument has some merit. All governments, including democratic liberal ones, should be concerned to maintain *manageable* or sustainable debt levels and minimize the fiscal burden they place on future generations of voters and taxpayers. This is one reason, in part B, that we suggest democratic liberalism should be understood to entail a commitment to increasing tax revenue.

The argument, however, is often made in a way that fails to distinguish between different levels and forms of debt—or between sustainable and unsustainable levels of government debt, or what might be called "good" or productive forms of government debt and "bad" debt.

Debt is not necessarily, by itself, a bad thing for an economy. Just as businesses often borrow in order to fund investment and expansion, governments can also use debt to finance new economically and socially productive investments. Borrowing in order to fund investments of this kind can be seen as a form of "good debt": it helps underpin socially and economically productive forms of public investment and economic growth.

Other forms of debt, however, raise greater questions about whether the government should be balancing the budget—or finding ways to fund current expenditures out of current revenue. Some government programs, for example, may be extremely important to maintaining a generous social minimum but involve what are largely *recurrent* forms of expenditure.

Take certain forms of cash welfare payments. They are often extremely important to ensuring the dignity of citizens. But they have little chance of reducing future government spending or increasing future economic growth. Hence, there is a strong argument that they should be funded out of current not future tax revenue.

Countries also have different starting points when it comes to taking on new debt, in ways that affect the degree to which new forms of government borrowing should be viewed as *sustainable* or *unsustainable* in nature.

Most importantly, countries vary in the level of net government debt as a proportion of GDP.

Figure 8.1 shows net government debt as a proportion of GDP for selected advanced economies before the Covid-19 crisis.[3]

The proportion of net debt to GDP ranges from zero for Singapore (in fact, since Singapore government assets outweigh gross debt, the net debt number is actually negative) to 151% for Japan. It is important to notice that Italy—hit very hard by Covid-19—has net debt to GDP of 119%, and Spain (also hit very hard) has a ratio above 80%.

This is important for one key reason—it affects a government's ability to service its debt or make interest payments on it. In the final analysis, holders of government debt have a claim on the ability of that government to levy taxes in order to pay the debtholders. As long as there continue to be counterparties willing to hold government debt, the actual face value (the amount borrowed) of the debt does not need to be paid back, only the interest on it. If there are willing holders of government debt when the existing debt is due to be paid back (it "matures") then the debt can be essentially "rolled over" from one set of debtholders to another.

Indeed, if the dollar amount of net debt grows at a slower rate than GDP does, then the ratio of net debt to GDP will decline over time—it will be "grown away" rather than paid back. As Luigi Zingales, a professor of finance at the University of Chicago Booth School of Business has framed the matter: "the crucial question that we need to figure out, is not whether we can repay the existing debt but whether we can sustain the payment of interest on a regular basis."[4]

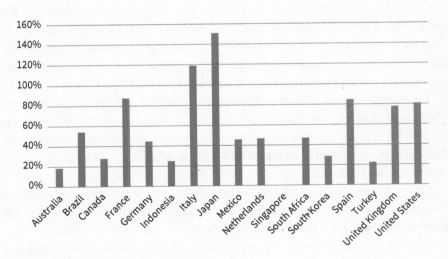

Figure 8.1 Net Debt/GDP Selected Countries, 2020
Source: IMF World Economic Outlook.

There is no hard and fast rule about what level of debt makes it hard or materially more expensive to issue government debt. But as the Zingales quote makes clear, that level depends on what investors think is a sustainable amount of tax collection. And, since income and other types of taxes used by the government to raise money are typically distorting, and this shrinks economic activity and hence GDP, there are definitely limits.[5]

But for many countries—the United States, the United Kingdom and Australia are leading, but far from the only examples—long-term government debt can be issued at around or below 1% interest rates. That it is long-dated means that it won't need to be rolled over for many years, and the very low interest rates mean that it is relatively cheap to service.

There are also good arguments for government spending—and borrowing as a means of financing that spending—as a means of combating what, even before Covid-19, was a fast-emerging problem of declining real interest rates. Even before 2020, it was also clear that many advanced economies were suffering from what Former US Treasury Secretary Larry Summers—picking up on an old idea from Alvin Hansen—has termed *secular stagnation*.[6]

Summers has forcefully argued that the so-called equilibrium real interest rate—the real interest rate consistent with a stable macro-economy for countries like those in the OECD—has fallen substantially in recent decades and is now probably negative.[7] This also poses a very real challenge for policymakers seeking to encourage economic growth: if interest rates are negative, "desired levels of saving exceed desired levels of investment, leading to shortfalls in demand and stunted growth."[8]

If one accepts this *secular stagnation hypothesis*—and there is strong evidence in support of it—then even pre-Covid-19 growth rates in advanced economies were structurally lower than historically. And because of the causes of secular stagnation, this is a problem with demand, not supply. Hence, the logical response is to address these demand-side deficiencies via expansionary fiscal policies or levels of government spending that can "reduce national savings, raise neutral real interest rates, and stimulate growth."[9]

Furthermore, all of the demand-side problems that secular stagnation highlights will be exacerbated post-Covid-19. So, on top of the government spending required to address secular stagnation—as Summers has emphasized—we will need more government spending to solve the aggregate demand problems caused by the Covid-19 crisis.

All of this suggests that whatever the limits of government borrowing capacity, they are relatively high. For countries entering the Covid-19 crisis with net debt to GDP of around 40% or below, there is therefore the capacity to borrow significantly to help manage the economic effects of the crisis and establish a more democratic liberal state after it is over.

B. Fair Markets and Taxation: Maintaining Our Current Tax Base

Part of how we pay for a fair markets approach is by maintaining existing taxes—such as progressive income taxes and corporate taxes. But fair markets principles also suggest that concerns about individual economic behavior and global competitiveness may place limits on the capacity further to rely on these as sources of additional revenue.

For the additional revenue needed to fund policies such as a jobs guarantee or universal baseline healthcare, greater innovation in tax policy will likely be required. And in this part we propose two promising potential areas of innovation: new forms of value added taxes, which carve out a threshold free from tax, and increased capital taxes. Both these taxes have the capacity to raise significant additional revenue without imposing massive distortions or downsides for economic equality. In fact, modest but meaningful capital taxes may actually go a long way to addressing current sources of economic inequality.

(i) Personal Income Taxes and Corporate Taxes

A large source of government revenue in most advanced economies is personal income tax, which makes it a natural place to turn for additional revenues to fund the social minimum. In addition to this purely practical consideration, there is an ethical justification for those who earn higher incomes paying taxes to fund a dignified social minimum for those whose incomes are insufficient to sustain that minimum. This is, of course, the essential premise behind progressive income taxation, which has existed in the United States since Abraham Lincoln, strapped for cash during the Civil War, signed into law the Revenue Act of 1861, which imposed a federal income tax of 3% on incomes over $800 a year.

If this redistributionist or "fairness" logic were the only consideration in levying income taxes, then the calculus involved would be fairly simple. But there are also efficiency consequences from raising income taxes. As we mentioned briefly earlier in this book, economists have long understood that income taxes reduce the marginal benefit of people going to work, while the marginal cost of working remains unchanged. Or, put another way, the opportunity cost of leisure is lower. This effect causes people facing higher income taxes to rationally substitute their time away from work and into leisure, and it is thus known as the *substitution effect*. There is a second effect that goes in the other direction, however. An increased tax rate, all else being equal, reduces income, which causes people to rationally want to consume less leisure and work more. This is known as the *income effect*. Which of these two effects dominates is an empirical question—it depends on the preferences of workers, their starting incomes and tax rates, and the size of the tax changes. Ultimately, one is interested in the percentage change in hours worked (labor supply) for a percentage change in after-tax income. This is known as the *labor supply elasticity*.

The reason this object is so important from a policy perspective is that if this elasticity is negative (which it is almost always estimated to be), then an increase in income taxes reduces the amount that people work, and thus reduces overall output in the economy. In other words, income taxes shrink the economic pie. If this number is negative and *large*, then these efficiency consequences are also large. The ultimate policy question is how to balance the positive effects of income taxes (the ability to redistribute to the less well-off) and the negative effects of income taxes (the reduction in overall wealth because of labor supply distortions).

Given the importance of the question, it is not surprising that there is a vast economic literature using different data sets and different statistical methods to estimate labor supply elasticities. We briefly mentioned previously an authoritative survey by Michael Keane, which provides an encyclopedic treatment of this literature. His findings can be roughly summarized as follows.

Estimates of labor supply elasticities for men range from fairly small to quite large, with the average of credible estimates still implying a significant distortion from income taxes.[10] For women, labor supply elasticities are estimated to be large, and taxes can often lead women to not participate in the workforce. This highlights the role of fertility decisions, how care responsibilities are allocated within households, and how the combination of income taxes and childcare costs can impact female labor force participation.

The starting level of taxes is crucial in determining how large a distortion an increase will have, so discussion of how to balance the positive and negative effects of income taxation cannot be sensibly had absent that context. It is fair to say, however, that a large increase in the rate of personal income tax in, say, the United States, United Kingdom, Australia, or Canada would have serious efficiency consequences. These could well be amplified given the increasing ability of high income earners to relocate internationally. This phenomenon of *human capital mobility* is not unlike (if surely smaller in magnitude) the mobility of financial capital around the world that has been associated with a general lowering of corporate tax rates in OECD countries in order to retain tax competitiveness and not see domestic companies move their operations (or at least tax domicile) overseas.

Of course, not every US worker is suddenly going to up and move to Ireland or Singapore, like some companies have, because of income tax rates. But some very high-earning and thus potentially high-tax-paying individuals, whose human capital lies essentially in their heads or their hands, are very mobile. This constitutes another limitation on overly high personal income tax rates, in addition to the standard issue of labor supply.

Perhaps recognizing this, some recent proposals to increase personal income tax rates have focused on the very highest income earners. A notable example is Representative Alexandria Ocasio-Cortez's idea to institute a 70% marginal income tax rate on incomes over $10 million a year. Yet there are so few people in this category that even at that extremely high rate of taxation, and assuming no distorting effects of the tax, it would raise very little income. As Bill Gates put it: "In terms of revenue collection, you wouldn't want to just focus on the ordinary income rate, because people who are wealthy have a rounding error of ordinary income . . . They have income that just is the value of their stock, which if they don't sell it, it doesn't show up as income at all, or if it shows up, it shows over in the capital gains side. So, the ability of hedge fund people, various people—they aren't paying that ordinary income rate."[11]

This is surely correct, and it suggests that focusing on capital taxes is a more fruitful idea. Before moving on to capital taxes, we pause briefly to discuss corporate income taxes.

Corporate income taxes are a longstanding source of revenue in advanced economies. For instance, in the United States the corporate income tax still represents 6.6% of total receipts to the Treasury, and has been as high as 30.5% in the postwar era.

But Figure 8.2 also shows a secular decline in the share of total revenues contributed by the corporate income tax. This decline reflects, in no small part, increased international tax competition combined with highly mobile capital. As countries compete for large companies to locate in their jurisdiction, they are often willing to offer low company tax rates to achieve this. Ireland is a classic example, with its 12.5% company tax rate attracting technology companies like Apple to "locate" there (at least in corporate form, if somewhat less so in terms of physical presence and employment).

Figure 8.2 US Corporate Income Tax Share of Total Receipts
Source: https://www.whitehouse.gov/omb/historical-tables/.

In fact, 15 countries have no corporate income tax at all. With the exception of the United Arab Emirates, these are small island nations such as the Cayman Islands, Bermuda, or the British Virgin Islands.[12]

While the corporate income tax, just like the personal income tax, is part of economic orthodoxy it also has a downside in addition to its revenue-raising upside. Corporate income taxes tend to reduce investment by companies, since it reduces the post-tax returns flowing from those investments. This, all else being equal, reduces investment. The flow-on effects of this are reduced rates of employment and economic growth.

Increasing recognition of this fact, combined with the greater mobility of capital in the digital age, has put downward pressure on corporate income tax rates around the world. In 1980, the global average corporate tax rate was 40.1%, while in 2020 that rate had fallen to 23.9%. On a GDP-weighted basis the drop is even starker: from 46.5% in 1980 to 25.9% in 2020.[13]

Merely protecting the existing revenue flowing from corporate income tax is a daunting challenge—let alone hoping to increase revenue from this source.

Recently, US Treasury Secretary Janet Yellen floated a plan to try and mitigate international tax competition through a global minimum corporate tax rate. In a speech to the Chicago Council on Global Affairs, Yellen said: "It's important to work with other countries to end the pressures of tax competition. We're working with G-20 nations to agree to a global minimum corporate tax rate that can stop the race to the bottom."[14] Indeed, in October 2021, 130 countries agreed to set a global minimum tax rate of 15%.

By contrast, and due to "double-taxation" concerns we discuss below, the prevailing view for decades has been that capital taxes should be at or relatively close to zero. This view has begun to be called into question, and with that reconsideration comes to possibility of increased revenues without particularly harmful incentive effects.

C. Growing the Tax Base for Fair Markets Policies

(i) Capital Taxes

It has been fairly widely suggested in recent years that capital income should be taxed more heavily than it typically is at present. In many jurisdictions, taxes on capital income, like dividends or capital gains from stocks, real estate, and other assets, received preferential tax treatment relative to labor income. For instance, in the United States, capital gains on assets held for more than a year are generally taxed at 15% or 20% (for those with income above $434,500).

Raising the rate of capital tax to the same level as that on ordinary income (35% for household incomes over $400,000 and 37% for incomes over $600,000) would seem to both potentially raise a lot of additional revenue and also treat capital and labor income equally—on a level playing field. Unfortunately, this is not the case. The main reason that capital income is taxed at a concessional rate relative to labor income is that capital income comes from money that is invested (capital), and that capital first had to be earned, and in earning it though labor income, taxes had to be paid on it. To tax capital income at the same rate as labor income would, in fact, create an uneven playing field where capital income is essentially double taxed. If we tax the investment earnings generated from saving at the same rate as ordinary income, then people balancing the decision between consuming and investing will be much likelier to consume: the tax system would tilt the playing field in favor of consumption and away from investment.

Now, there is a legitimate argument about how large the tax discount on capital gains relative to ordinary income should be. An old position in economics—emanating from work in the 1970s and 1980s—was that the optimal tax rate on capital income was zero.[15] This stark conclusion stems from strong assumptions about the economic environment and the preferences of individuals and is best viewed as a benchmark result rather than a sound policy prescription. A more mainstream modern position—even from some of those whose work formed the basis for the originally "zero capital taxation results" such as Joseph Stiglitz—is that optimal capital taxes are not zero, but are still lower than the rate on ordinary income.[16] One catchy way to summarize this position was offered by Larry Summers in a podcast with well-known conservative economist Tyler Cowan, where Summers opined that the optimal rate of capital taxation is "closer to the rate on ordinary income than to zero."

Given the current level of personal tax rates and capital taxes in the United States—capital taxes are roughly half the rate on ordinary income[17]—this suggests the additional taxes of capital will raise some incremental revenue but not an overwhelming amount, unless one of two things happen.

First, the capital income tax rate could be raised to, say, three-quarters of the level of the rate on ordinary income. This would see high capital income earners paying 27.75% at present rates. Given that the top current rate is 20% plus the 3.8% "net investment income tax" (the NIIT, from section 1411 of the Internal Revenue code),[18] for a total of 23.8%, this new rate would constitute a (nearly) 4% increase in capital taxes paid by the highest income earners.

Estimating the revenue raised by this increase is a complicated exercise because realized capital gains fluctuate substantially from year to year, and because increased capital taxes may well decrease investment and thus, over time, decrease the tax base for capital gains. But to give a rough sense of the magnitudes involved, recent US Treasury data shows that an average of $600 billion in realized capital gains in a given year is a reasonable estimate of the current capital tax base.[19] Applying the 4% increase to all of these capital gains would yield an increase in revenues of $24 billion a year.

To put this in perspective, this is more than the estate tax has raised in any year during the last decade.[20] Moreover, recent work by Natasha Sarin, Larry Summers, Owen Zidar, and Erick Zwick shows that revenue raised by an increase in taxes on capital gains may be even larger than previously thought, suggesting that the $24 billion mentioned above may in fact be a lower bound on the revenue raised.[21]

President Biden's American Families Plan proposes raising not only the top marginal personal income tax rate from 37% to 39.6%, but also making 39.6% the rate on long-term capital gains for households with total income over $1 million. It is unclear whether this will become law, but it is a more dramatic increase in capital taxes than is consistent with a democratic liberal approach.[22]

(ii) (Progressive?) Value Added Taxes

Another recent proposal to boost tax revenue in the United States involves the idea of introducing a VAT like those in place in much of continental Europe, the United Kingdom, and Australia. Unlike a sales tax, a value added tax levies a charge of a percentage (e.g., 15%) on top of the sale price a business charges for a particular good or service, but provides a tax deduction on the VAT paid for all the inputs used by the business in producing that good or service. The United States is definitely an outlier in not imposing a VAT—all 35 other OECD countries do so.[23]

What is more, a VAT is generally viewed by economists as a relatively efficient tax, in the sense that in creates a small amount of economic distortion per dollar of revenue raised from it. It is thus a promising way for the government to generate revenue.

Moreover, value added taxes typically replace existing, and less economically efficient, sales taxes. Currently in the United States, at the state and local level, general sales taxes raise $377 billion per annum, and selected sales taxes raise a further $182 billion per annum.[24] These would need to be eliminated if a VAT was introduced, meaning that even a 15% broadly based VAT with no exemptions might generate around $370 billion per annum on a net basis[25]— less than one-tenth of what would likely be required for a meaningful unconditional universal basic income.

That said, just because a VAT would not raise sufficient income to fund an unconditional UBI does not mean that it does not have a role to play in the tax mix—as it does in the overwhelming majority of OECD countries. Indeed, the fact that it is less distorting and thus more economically efficient than many other taxes makes it an attractive option to consider as part of a democratic liberal approach.

One important concern, however, is the regressive nature of a VAT (although the same concern also applies to sales taxes). A flat rate of tax on consumption inevitably leads to lower-income households paying a higher share of their income in such taxes because spending on the necessities of life is a large share of their income—sometimes all of their income, or more. This is highlighted by the recent work of Emmanuel Saez and Gabriel Zucman, who have estimated that in 2018 the bottom half of income earners in the United States paid between 12.3% (for the bottom 10% of income earners) and 6.7% (for those in the fifth decile) of their income in consumption taxes, compared to between 3.8% and 2.2% for the top 10% of income earners.[26]

So even if replacing existing sales taxes with a VAT may be economically efficient, and may be a plausible source of additional revenue generation, it has distributive consequences that are less appealing.

In addition to the distributive consequences at the individual level, any federal VAT that replaced state and local sales taxes would need to involve a way of repatriating funds to state and local governments to compensate them for the lost revenue and ensure that their funding base for service provision was not eroded. There are a number of international examples of how this can and has been done, as one would expect with so many advanced economies having implemented a value added tax.

One way to address the distributive consequences of a VAT is to make it "progressive" in the following sense: each adult could be given a "VAT-free threshold" on which they would pay 0% VAT. Once that threshold had been exhausted in a given year, they would pay the stipulated VAT rate.

For the sake of argument, suppose that the annual exemption threshold was set at $7,500 and the VAT rate above that was 15%. How much might such a progressive VAT raise? Obviously, a detailed analysis is beyond the scope of this book, but a back-of-the-envelope calculation is instructive.

The CBO estimate of a 5% VAT on a broad base attempts to include all goods and services, but recognizes that certain of these are difficult to measure. Thus, "financial services without explicit fees, existing housing services, primary and secondary education, and other services provided by government agencies and nonprofit organizations for a small fee or at no cost" are excluded in their calculation. Government reimbursements of healthcare (usually paid by Medicare and Medicaid) are also excluded. After these exclusions, the CBO estimates that around 66% of household consumption would be subject to a VAT.

Starting with a linear extrapolation of the CBO 5% VAT estimate, this implies annual VAT revenue of $930 billion. Deducting the existing sales taxes that would be removed leaves one with approximately $370 billion. One then needs to deduct the amount of VAT foregone by the VAT-free threshold.

Starting with US Census figures[27] of an estimated 2018 total US population of 327 million, and an under-18 share of that population of 22.4%, leaves an adult population of approximately 254 million. Given the $7,500 threshold, this implies $1.9 trillion in exempt expenditure, which at a 15% VAT rate means $286 billion in foregone VAT. Taken together, this leaves $85 billion a year in net new VAT revenue.

Of course, how this VAT exemption would be administered is a very real practical question. There is no way to implement a practical solution that does not go directly through the payment system. Requiring individuals to file paperwork with the Internal Revenue Service would be prohibitively costly and would lead to a significant time gap between when VAT was paid and when it was rebated. This would hit lower-income earners the hardest, and undo much of the design goal of a progressive VAT.

A way that this idea could be practically implemented is via a modern payments system. To ground ideas, imagine that all consumer payments eligible for the VAT exemption had to go through a point-of-sale (POS) network such as those used for credit and debit cards, and for mobile payment and digital wallet services like Apple Pay or Google Pay. And further, imagine that each individual seeking the VAT exemption would enroll any card they wished to use, along with a unique identifying number (like a Social Security number in the United States).

These payments systems already determine availability of funds at POS, and would need to track an additional object linked to each adult—their amount of VAT exemption remaining in a calendar year. At POS the amount of VAT due to be charged would be automatically compared to the remaining exemption for the cardholder, and any remaining amount would be deducted from the payment amount.

The precise details of implementation would vary depending on the POS networks in each country, but one thing to note is that the degree of sophistication of those networks and, particularly, of POS equipment is important to the ability to implement the VAT exemption for most transactions. In countries like Sweden or Australia, where card-based and mobile transactions account for the majority (or even overwhelming majority) of transactions, the existing infrastructure would readily allow for implementation of a progressive VAT. In the United States, the Federal Reserve's FedNow real-time settlement service, due to be in place by 2023 or 2024, would expand the number of transactions that could receive the VAT exemption.[28]

The most glaring set of transactions that would fall outside of the scope of VAT exemptions are those involving cash. Not only would these not receive the VAT exemption, it would arguably be desirable that they do not. The so-called black economy is estimated to be as large as 8%–10% of GDP in the United States,[29] and this is fueled by the relative anonymity of cash as a means of payment. The black economy is not only a lubricant of organized crime and other illicit activity, it is also a major source of tax leakage for governments.

The desire of individual consumers to avail themselves of the VAT exemption as part of a progressive VAT would help stimulate expansion of more traceable forms of payment like debit and credit cards, and mobile payment solutions, that would help bring part of the underground economy out of the shadows. Estimating the size of the tax benefit that might result involves a good deal of speculation, but even if one accepts the lower end of the range of estimates of the size of the underground economy, and if only a quarter of that activity becomes subject to taxation, this would lead to an additional $50 billion in personal income taxes and VAT collection.[30]

(iii) Compliance Efforts

In pushing back on some of proposals discussed above—such as the Ocasio-Cortez 70% personal income tax rate (or the Warren wealth tax discussed below)—Natasha Sarin and Larry Summers have also outlined a number of tax loopholes that could fruitfully be closed and have provided estimates of the amount of revenue that could be raised from those efforts.[31]

Among those, increasing auditing resources for the Internal Revenue Service from the historically low level at present is a particularly important but easy thing to do. As Sarin and Summers point out, the IRS budget has decreased 20% in real terms since 2010, and there are now fewer auditors than at any time since the 1950s. They estimate this could raise $30–$40 billion annually in net terms.

Cracking down on corporate tax shelters could raise a similar amount. As Sarin and Summers put it, "A robust attack on tax shelters—that included, for example, tariffs or penalties on tax havens as well as stricter penalties for lawyers and accountants who sign off on dubious shelters—could raise twice the revenue attainable from a per-country minimum tax, or about 30 billion annually. It would also encourage the location of economic activity in the United States and discourage the vast intellectual ingenuity that currently goes into tax avoidance."

On the personal income tax side, cutting down on loopholes, such as those involving payroll tax, that were proposed during the Obama administration, ending the carried-interest loophole for private equity and hedge fund managers (where carried interest can be treated as a capital gain rather than ordinary income), and eliminating the peculiar and special deal that real estate investors can obtain under so-called 1031 exchanges, would together net around $40 billion a year.

Eliminating what is known as the "stepped-up basis"—as was proposed during the Obama administration—would also generate around $25 billion a year. When earnings in a profitable company are reinvested and not realized, substantial capital gains can accrue. That isn't a problem in and of itself, but the tax code allows the basis for capital gains purposes to be "stepped up" from what was originally paid, to the value of the stock at the time it is inherited by an heir. As Sarin and Summers note, "the gain in value during the investor's life is never taxed."

D. Other Revenue Raising Ideas

(i) Estate and Inheritance Taxes

One source of revenue that is often discussed in the context of funding a UBI is an estate tax or a tax on inheritances. Again, economists have formally analyzed the optimal rate and structure of estate taxes. There have also been calls for repeal of the existing US estate tax by distinguished economists, such as Harvard professor and former Council of Economic Advisors Chair Greg Mankiw.[32] According to Mankiw (and others), apart from reducing capital accumulation, it is also unclear how progressive an estate tax is.[33]

An important question in analyzing optimal estate taxes is how to take account of the benefits that flow to parents versus children or, in the language of economics, what the current "social welfare function" is. One strand of this literature focuses on the leading case where both parents' and children's utilities enter directly into social welfare. That is, society cares about the current and future generation at a given point in time. In this setting—one which was analyzed by (the late) Emmanuel Farhi and Ivan Werning, it can be shown that, in fact, a *negative* bequest/estate tax is optimal.[34] A second feature of the optimal estate tax is that it is progressive—parents with larger estates should face a higher marginal rate of estate tax, but nonetheless it is still negative.

The reason for these two properties of optimal estate taxes in the Farhi–Werning model are as follows. The fact that estate taxes should be negative arises because a subsidy encourages larger bequests to be made rather than more consumption/spending by parents. Greater bequests help children receiving them. As Farhi and Werning put it: "This highlights that, in order to improve the average welfare of newborns, it is efficient to combine a reduction in inequality with an increase in average consumption. In a way, the first generation buys inequality, to improve incentives, from the second generation in exchange for higher average bequests."

The other notable property of optimal estate taxes is that, notwithstanding the level of that tax involving a subsidy, estate taxation should be progressive. That is, parents that are wealthier/more fortunate in terms of their own income, and hence stand to make larger bequests, should optimally face a higher marginal estate tax. This implies that wealthier/more fortunate parents end up with a lower after-tax return on bequests than less fortunate/wealthy parents, and this induces bequests to become more similar, which increases social welfare.

The striking conclusion of this analysis is that far from raising money, estate taxes should actually be subsidized and end up *costing* the government money. The conclusion is that estate taxes can't fund anything, let alone an extremely expensive program like a UBI. Of course, the Farhi–Werning conclusion has not gone unchallenged.

Perhaps the most notable response is from the French economists Thomas Piketty and Emmanuel Saez.[35] Piketty and Saez seek to understand under what assumptions one can justify an estate tax that is strongly progressive and capable of raising substantial revenue.[36] They require fairly stringent conditions to find an optimal estate tax to be positive, let alone large. As they put it: "The optimal tax rate is positive and quantitatively large if elasticity [of bequests] is low, bequests are quantitatively large and highly concentrated, and society cares most about those receiving little inheritance."

In their setup, Piketty and Saez manage to find a role for positive estate taxes but by requiring that inequality be multidimensional and adhering to certain criteria for valuing redistribution as good thing in its own right. As they put it, "Our results on positive inheritance taxation (under specific redistributive social criteria) hinge crucially on the fact that, with inheritances, labor income is no longer a complete measure of lifetime resources, that is, our model has bi-dimensional (labor income, inheritance) inequality."[37]

In sum, there is, at best, dispute about whether estate taxes should even be positive—let alone large enough to raise substantial revenue that could fund a UBI.

(ii) A Wealth Tax

Related to this is a potential *wealth tax*, which was proposed by Elizabeth Warren as part of her 2020 Presidential Bid with advice from none other than the above-mentioned Emmanuel Saez. Warren's version of a wealth tax imposes a 2% percent wealth tax on those with assets (or perhaps net worth) of more than $50 million. Saez and his colleague Gabriel Zucman, from University of California at Berkeley, helped developed the proposal estimate that it would generate as much as $187 billion a year, plus another $25 billion from the so-called billionaire surcharge for a total of $212 billion in the first year of implementation.[38]

That's still not in the ballpark of enough money to fund a meaningful UBI, but it is sometimes seen as part of the revenue-raising puzzle. Even still, substantial doubt has been cast on the Warren proposal, or any wealth tax, to raise a significant amount of revenue. Larry Summers has pointed out that the $187 billion figure is likely unrealistic, suggesting that the actual number might be much closer to $25 billion a year.[39]

A crucial issue in assessing the revenue-raising potential of a wealth tax is the level of avoidance. Saez and Zucman factor in only a modest amount of revenue leakage due to avoidance based on the experience in Denmark and Sweden. They assume a 1% wealth tax (like that which was established in Denmark and Sweden) results in evasion of less than 1%. Yet as Summers and Sarin point out "in both countries, wealth taxation proved so easy to avoid and so difficult to administer that these taxes were repealed. In fact, of the 12 nations in the Organization for Economic Cooperation and Development that had wealth taxes in 1990, only three still have them today."[40]

It is also worth noting that there are legitimate questions about the constitutionality of such a wealth tax. And, even if constitutional, the politics of implementation are extremely challenging. As Summers and Sarin put it in another piece on this topic: "Such a push in the United States would involve forcing the sale of many family-owned businesses and require vast audit resources at a time when the IRS is unable to audit even 10 percent of millionaires. And it will involve placing limits on the ability to be charitable or to establish trusts for the benefits of grandchildren."[41]

In short, even if all the political challenges of introducing a wealth tax could be overcome, it would raise a tiny fraction of the several trillion dollars a year required to fund an unconditional universal basic income. Thus, the only rationale for it is a strong preference for redistribution *per se*, along the lines of the Piketty and Saez argument for inheritance taxes (which, itself, requires an appeal to "multidimensional inequality" as discussed previously).

(iii) Natural Resources Taxes

Others have advocated natural resources as a possible source of tax revenue to fund a UBI.[42] There are multiple variants of the "nature funding" idea. One involves renting out unimproved government-owned land (an idea that goes back to Thomas Paine's proposal for how to fund a pension) or imposing a land tax on privately-owned land. Of course, in many jurisdictions land taxes already exist and fund a range of services including public schools, emergency services, and even trash collection.

A second way that natural resources could be used to generate revenue for a UBI is to sell or lease (and therefore collect royalties from) natural resources such as oil or gas fields that are publicly owned. North Sea oil for Scotland or liquefied natural gas resources in Australia are potential examples of this. The establishment of the *Alaska Permanent Fund* in 1976 is perhaps the most notable and cleanest example of this approach. In the mid-1970s, Alaskan governor Jay Hammond helped Alaska gain ownership of the Prudhoe Bay oil field, which was the largest oil field in North America. In order to ensure that future generations of Alaskans benefited from the oil field, he advocated for the fund to be created and that it distribute an income to Alaskans that was proportional to the number of years of residence in Alaska. It has generated, on average, income of about $1,200 per person per annum, or roughly 2% of gross state product.

As Van Parijs and Vanderborght (2017) observed, Iran's universal subsidy bears some similarity to this approach as well. In Iran's case, an increase in the price of domestically produced oil and the passage in 2010 of an act of parliament known as the "targeted subsidies law" consisted of two steps in doing this. First, it involved raising the then artificially low domestic price of oil gradually up to the prevailing international market price, and thereby doing away with what amounted to a subsidy for domestic oil consumption. The budgetary savings from this were spent in part (about a quarter of them) in subsidizing producers directly affected by the price increase (and concomitant reduction in demand for oil). The rest was slated as going to "compensate the seventy million Iranian citizens for the impact of the general price increase on their standard of living by introducing a monthly cash subsidy. This cash payment was initially intended to start at $20 and to gradually rise to $60 per person per month (about 13 percent of GDP per capita)."[43]

All the different variants of the "natural resource funding" approach raise the same awkward question—why aren't these taxes being levied already? As we noted above, in some cases, such as land tax, they indeed are. In others there are presumably pragmatic reasons why such taxes have not been levied. In any case, the possibility of establishing a UBI does not suddenly make some sources of tax revenue more efficient or more promising as a source of government funds.

D. More Radical Proposals

There are two even more extreme possibilities—not really involving taxation at all—that are sometimes floated to fund a UBI or other large-scale social spending schemes.[44] The first is state ownership of all means of production. In that case, the government can allocate whatever share of economic output it likes to various end uses—and among those could be a UBI.[45]

A second non-taxation option is to simply print money. Proponents of what has become known as modern monetary theory (MMT) argue that (1) countries that control their own currency cannot default on sovereign obligations because they can always print more money; and (2) thus said countries can provide unlimited resources and pay for whatever they want.[46] This could include a UBI.

As one of the authors pointed out, with Chris Edmond and Bruce Preston, the first claim is "neither a new nor a controversial idea. It is well accepted by central bankers, treasury officials, academic economists, and other experts."[47] The problem is that the second claim that the MMT advocates make does not follow from the first. As Edmond, Holden, and Preston emphasize, the key constraint a government faces is not how to cover liabilities that are denominated in its own currency, it is how to pay for actual (or real) goods and services. People only care about currency for what real resources it can buy, and inflation erodes what currency can buy. In this sense, the key constraint is inflation, and mainstream economics has developed a comprehensive framework for analyzing how different monetary and fiscal policies lead to inflation or deflation.

In other words, the only limit on this process is runaway inflation. The cottage industry of "heterodox" economists like Stephanie Kelton, an economic advisor to Bernie Sanders, acknowledge that in principle there is risk of hyperinflation if enough money printing happens, but these heterodox economists argue that's unlikely.

Except that it's not unlikely. It happened in Weimar Germany, and Zimbabwe, and Venezuela. Indeed, it has happened in many emerging-market economies. Even the French tried a similar approach under Francois Mitterand in 1981, as did Germany under Gerhard Schröder in 1998. In both instances they quickly had to reverse course as inflation took hold.

Part of the problem is that in an open economy, financing of large-scale government deficits leads the exchange rate to depreciate, which itself increases inflation. That inflation, in turn, drives up long-term interest rates and capital flight from the country in question. These lead to a vicious cycle where more and more money needs to be printed, simply exacerbating the problem.

The tragedy in Venezuela is instructive. When the crude oil price collapsed in 2014, the government was left with a huge deficit but still needed to pay the salaries of government workers and the military. So, it printed money. With more money in the economy but no increase in the number of things available to buy, the price of goods climbed.

That meant the government had to print still more money for the workers whose incomes bought less, which led to more inflation, more money printing, even higher prices, and pretty quickly to hyperinflation of over 1,200,000%.

9
Conclusion

Fair Markets and Realistic Political Reform?

Democratic liberalism reimagines liberalism in a way that takes more seriously commitments to individual dignity and equality, as well as freedom, within the liberal tradition; and that places the democratic citizen at the center of a liberal approach. It draws heavily on the Capabilities Approach advocated by Amartya Sen and Martha Nussbaum and insists on universal access to economic dignity, or a generous social minimum for all citizens. It likewise insists that *unregulated* markets, in the way some proponents of neoliberalism envisage, do not serve individual freedom, dignity, and equality. Rather, they tend to advance a highly unequal economic system that favors those with market power over both workers and consumers and inflict serious social harms, including economic harms. For liberalism to promote economic dignity, markets must be regulated so as to combat the threats posed by this form of market power and externality. The idea of democratic liberalism is that the democratic state should do just that—and effectively regulate market power and externalities based on the democratic input and views of citizens.

Because of this, it would also be described as a form of liberalism that both insists on the idea of fair over free markets, and one that is *blue, pink,* and *green*.

It is "blue" because it takes seriously the needs and concerns of traditional blue-collar workers (or "ordinary workers") let down by recent more neoliberal versions of liberalism. We argue that in the face of unemployment, the state should create a radical new form of jobs guarantee—not a basic income for everyone, but a more targeted basic jobs program for those who need it most. And, we argue that the state should provide universal access to "basic benefits" including decent healthcare and a universal program of access to basic leave. In most countries, achieving this will likely involve a complex mix of public and private provision and funding. And, as we explain in detail in Chapter 5, this could be achieved in large part following the Australian model when it comes to healthcare. For basic leave, it will require moving beyond the traditional dichotomy between "employees" and "independent contractors" and recognizing a third category of worker, neither employee nor independent contractor but one who demands and needs just the same level of basic leave entitlements as employees. This is the new blue-collar social contract, or the way in which democratic liberalism is blue in nature.

We also argue that for liberalism to be sufficiently democratic and committed to equality and dignity, it must be "pink"—or sensitive to commitments to gender equality. Thus, universal basic benefits should and could extend to childcare, and any form of jobs guarantee needs to be designed in a way that takes seriously the caring responsibilities of those who may need to rely on the program. A jobs guarantee needs to be flexible, part time as well as full time, and allow for people to engage in care as well as market-based forms of work that sustain a dignified social minimum. Childcare must be available and affordable to all families, but in a way that is sustainable both fiscally and in terms of providing good-quality care that it suited to the specific needs of heterogeneous households. The proposals we offer in this context are only part of what a fully pink, gender-equal vision of liberalism would look like. But they are an important start.

Democratic liberalism is also "green" in focus: it insists that a price must be put on carbon and other forms of environmentally damaging activities. It also suggests that, given a commitment to "blue" liberalism, the proceeds of any such tax should be redistributed by government directly to individuals in the form of a "carbon dividend" or other forms of environmental dividend. Liberalism, in this sense, is committed to a form of radical internalization of environmental externalities but also to taking equality seriously. It likewise suggests that a jobs guarantee program should be blue, pink *and* green—that is, focused where there is need on environmental projects.

We further propose six key concrete policy reforms as a means for market-based economies to realize these democratic liberal or fair market ideals:

1. A universal jobs guarantee, which pays decent wages, is flexible, and gives preferences to environmental or "green" projects, but does not crowd out private sector employment and is complemented by measures designed to boost private sector wages;
2. A significant increase in the minimum wage, but accompanied by a meaningful increase in government wage subsidies in the form of a generous earned income tax credit, wage earner equity schemes, and wage subsidies for new industries in towns with high unemployment;
3. Universal healthcare for all citizens based on a two-track model of public and private provision;

4. The expansion of similar approaches to childcare and basic leave benefits, or holiday, sick, and parental leave for all workers, including casual workers, the self-employed, and those in the gig economy, combined with a greater emphasis on actual equality in access to education;

5. A new critical infrastructure policy for nation states to sit alongside a commitment to global free trade, as well as improved trade adjustment assistance for individuals and placed-based policies designed to help the towns and cities left behind by globalization; and

6. Universal pollution taxes but with all (net) proceeds returned directly to citizens by way of a green dividend.

As these proposals demonstrate, democratic liberalism is ultimately an economic and political philosophy that aims to appeal to moderate or centrist democratic voters—who see liberalism as having both real strengths and weaknesses, and who have concerns about the rejection of liberal principles inherent in both democratic socialism and economic nationalism. Thus, for example, our vision of a green jobs corps is quite different from the version envisaged by many democratic socialist advocates, or proponents of a Green New Deal, who would see a green jobs corps as a backdoor means of increasing the minimum wage and/or replacing large numbers of existing low-paid private sector jobs. Instead, we suggest, a jobs guarantee should aim to promote a form of "subsidiarity" principle, which encourages private sector work wherever possible and therefore offers decent wages and benefits, but ones just below that offered by a private sector, full-time minimum wage job.

Some readers may still rightly question how realistic our ideas are. And they are right to do so. Like Rutger Bregman and others, we seek to offer new and challenging ideas that can advance the debate and inspire change.[1] That means that, while too modest for some, for others those ideas will be far too radical to contemplate—at least under current conditions.

How "realistic" our proposals are will also ultimately depend a great deal on the ingoing economic and political conditions in a society. In many European countries, there is already a well-developed social welfare state, which would mean that expanding it to create universal basic benefits or a universal jobs guarantee would not be a large step politically. It would also have modest, incremental economic costs. The same could be said for a range of other countries—including Canada, New Zealand, Australia, and indeed a range of Asian countries with a more mixed liberal and communitarian tradition, such as Singapore.

In the United States, in contrast, there is very little existing state support for work, wages, or benefits—and creating such programs would require a lot more politically and economically. But as recent US political experience shows, the greater the gap between voter aspirations and needs, and current policies, the more unpredictable the outcome. Biden's "American Jobs Plan" specifically contemplates increased wages for those engaged in the care economy, creating new jobs in the building of physical infrastructure (such as highways, bridges, ports, and airports) as well as green energy, in addition to the more traditional path of making it easier for workers to unionize and collectively bargain.[2]

The degree to which our ideas are economically realistic likewise depends on the degree to which there is a political willingness to consider a range of new approaches to tax—that preserve commitments to markets and liberalism but effectively expand the revenue available to fund democratic liberal policies. We acknowledge that policies such as a jobs guarantee, place-based policies, an earned income tax credit, wage earner equity subsidy, universal healthcare, childcare, and basic leave benefits are likely to be costly for governments and in some cases involve a significant investment that requires a concomitant increase in taxes. But we contend that there are changes to the tax system that are themselves consistent with democratic liberalism but that will generate significant additional revenues. We eschew ideas like a "wealth tax" as being neither consistent with liberalism nor likely to raise as much revenue as its advocates suggest. But we highlight how capital taxes could be increased to some degree, and outline the concept of a "progressive value added tax" along with various increased compliance efforts, reliance on progressive income taxes, and a meaningful competitive corporate tax rate. In some countries, there is also likely to be a genuine willingness to consider such proposals, whereas in others there is little or no appetite for tax reform.

Similarly, the extent to which our ideas are politically realistic may depend on the degree to which there is an existing commitment within a country to fair economic *and* political markets. As noted in Chapter 3, fair political markets (i) address concerns about access and equality of access among citizens in the political process, (ii) regulate the existence and exercise of monopoly power, and (iii) internalize externalities. This also translates into a range of electoral regulations or reforms—for instance, broad-ranging forms of campaign finance regulation designed to ensure access to and influence over democratic political process for all citizens regardless of wealth or income; the importance of processes for electoral redistricting that limit the exercise of political monopoly power—or the capacity for temporary political monopolies to reduce future electoral competition and "lock in" their hold on power by partisan forms of gerrymandering; and measures designed to encourage widespread voter participation as a means of discouraging the kind of strategic extremism among parties and representatives that can deprive many voters of true electoral choice. This could also involve a range of carrots and sticks designed to encourage voter registration and turnout, including automatic voter registration, increased access to vote-by-mail, and even an Australian-style model of compulsory voting.

Some of these "fair market" political reforms are quite modest and do not require a revolution in the conduct and nature of elections. They simply require that a number of "blockages" in the democratic process be removed.[3] These blockages involve partisan political actors and small but influential special interest groups possessing an outsized and unwarranted say in both who gets elected and what policies are ultimately enacted.

The practice of gerrymandering, for instance, has a long history. It occurred in the United States as early as 1740, in favor of the Quaker minority in the colony of Pennsylvania. The term "gerrymander" comes from the infamous instance in 1812, when then Governor Elbridge Gerry of Massachusetts (and later vice-president of the United States) signed a reapportionment bill favoring his Democratic-Republic party with a district in Essex Country that was said to resemble a salamander—giving rise to the portmanteau "Gerrymander." It has also become a ubiquitous part of modern political practice in the United States and in an increasing number of constitutional democracies elsewhere.[4]

Among the various ills that gerrymandering causes, it is widely acknowledged that it leads both to less long-run political competition and more extreme positions on the part of those who are elected. In many cases, it is also both a reflection of, as well as source of, the development of electoral monopoly power.[5]

A fair markets approach, therefore, favors limiting the scope for incumbent political actors to exercise this form of political market power—by attempting to impose legal standards limiting the role of partisan considerations in the redistricting process and/or giving the task to some kind of independent agency or "fourth branch" institution.[6]

Similarly, if people can choose not to vote, politicians have to worry not only about getting those who vote to vote for them, but also about turnout—that is, getting people to vote in the first place. Glaeser et al. have shown this gives rise to the concept of "strategic extremism" whereby it is optimal for politicians to make their platforms more extreme than they would otherwise be in order to drive turnout.[7] This, in turn, imposes an externality on other voters by depriving them of the opportunity to vote for candidates with a more moderate platform. So, some people choosing not to vote is not simply about individual choice; it indirectly affects other citizens, and in a potentially significant way.

Similarly, in terms of polarization, McCarty, Poole, and Rosenthal have famously documented the divergence between the average ideology of congresspeople and senators in the Republican and Democratic parties over time.[8] This polarization makes it harder for voters who want a centrist alternative to find it, thereby imposing an externality upon them.

A fair markets approach, therefore, is one that encourages widespread turnout among voters—through offering both carrots and sticks for large-scale voter turnout. Basic logic dictates that a necessary condition for being allowed to vote is being registered to vote. Without voter registration, various requirements about who is permitted to vote, such as citizenship and age requirements, cannot be ensured. But there can be significant barriers to voter registration, even for those who are voting-age citizens who are entitled to vote.[9] One potential response to this is also for the state to encourage "automatic voter registration" whereby registration is based on an "opt out" rather than "opt in" model, using other government agency records and information.[10] As the Brennan Center at New York University has shown, measures of this kind can both increase the number of registered voters and lead to a more accurate register of voters.[11]

Another is to make voting itself less costly—by providing appropriate alternatives to in-person voting and holding elections on weekends or public holidays, when a smaller proportion of the population are likely to be working.

However, other reforms—such as widespread campaign finance regulation or a system of compulsory voting—require a more significant rethink in the relationship between commitments to liberalism and democracy. Liberal democracy, as Chapter 3 notes, involves a commitment to freedom, dignity, and equality for all individuals. But there is significant scope for debate as to the relative priority of these commitments. Classical liberals in this context tend to argue for a strict priority for liberty as a value, or individual choice as paramount—at least absent demonstrable harm to others. This, for instance, was the logic behind John Stuart Mill's famous "harm principle": limits on individual freedom were only permissible, according to this principle, in order to prevent harm to third parties.[12]

Neoliberals also often place greater emphasis on individual liberty—even in the face of externalities, they argue for a form of libertarian or laissez faire approach by governments, which protects individual freedoms and leaves social costs or harms unaddressed.

Democratic liberalism, however, suggests that freedom, dignity, and equality should all receive similar weight, and be carefully balanced in a given context. Similar to a capabilities approach, a democratic liberal approach suggests that all citizens should have "the right of political participation, protections of free speech and association" and the right "to participate effectively in political choices that govern one's life." This also means that political rights and freedoms, including free speech, must be understood within in broader concern for equal and effective participation for all.[13] And this means recognizing the need for governments both to support the preconditions for effective participation, and respond to potential market failures in the political marketplace for ideas.

This also has direct implications for measures such as campaign finance regulations. One role that money can play in politics is to facilitate information provision to the electorate. Much as one perspective on commercial advertising is that is helps provide information to consumers, so too one perspective on money in politics is that it leads to a more informed electorate who can make better choices among candidates.[14] In this sense it can be seen to have a potentially pro-competitive effect. If voters know a lot about the candidates, then weak candidates are going to have a tough time getting elected, just as companies that manufacture defective cars have a tough time selling their products. For example, candidates might have past voting records, and advertising could provide information about this largely verifiable fact that gives voters a better understanding of candidates' ideology and policy preferences.

But the nexus between money and information in politics is not all that clear. Even before the term "fake news" became part of the zeitgeist, it was common for observers of politics to question whether political advertising was informative. In most advanced economies, there are also long-established rules concerning commercial advertising that make it unlawful to make misleading or deceptive claims about one's own products or those of competitors. In the United States, companies are held to "truth in advertising" standards and are regulated by the Federal Trade Commission, but for constitutional reasons no such regulation occurs for political advertising.[15] Many other countries, however, have broader regulations on political speech and the marketplace for ideas. They also have broader regulations of the role of money in politics.

One rationale for limitations on campaign contributions is corruption or the appearance of corruption. In the United States, this was a central consideration in elements of the Federal Election Campaign Act of 1971, and the Supreme Court in *Buckley v Valeo* upheld limits on direct contributions to candidates specifically by recognizing a government interest in preventing *quid pro quo* corruption.[16] The Court went further in *Austin v Michigan Chamber of Commerce* recognizing a governmental interest in preventing "the corrosive and distorting effects of immense aggregations of corporate wealth that have little or no correlation to the public's support for the corporation's political ideas," although it was precisely this precedent that was overturned in *Citizens United*.[17] But another rationale is that regulations of this kind help address the danger of a non-level political playing field, or inequalities in the economic sphere spilling over into the democratic sphere. If one candidate or type of candidate has a lot more money than another, they are more likely to win an election. And as we noted in Chapter 2, this kind of "inequality externality" is antithetical to the commitment to democratic equality. Many courts worldwide have also accepted this kind of democratic liberal justification for campaign finance regulation.[18]

Although it might be seen as anathema in the United States, a number of democracies have a system of compulsory voting.[19] In fact, 24 countries have some form of compulsory voting regime. For instance, in Australian elections at all levels of government (federal, state, and local) voting is compulsory for all citizens 18 and over, and has been since 1924. Indeed, failing to vote is punishable by a fine of around A\$80 per election. Other countries that have compulsory voting include Argentina, Belgium (although the law is not enforced), Egypt, Singapore, Turkey, and one canton in Switzerland.

Voting enrolment and participation rates are also consistently high in these countries. At the 2016 federal election, for example, more than 95% of eligible Australians were enrolled to vote (up from 92.4% at the 2013 election), and turnout was around 91% (compared to 92.3% at the 2013 election). This puts the proportion of the eligible voting population who voted at the last two federal elections at around 86.2%.[20] And it compares to turnout of roughly 60% in presidential elections in the United States, 60% in the United Kingdom, Germany, and Spain,[21] 67% in France, and 52% and 39% in Japan and most of Switzerland.[22]

Reforms of this kind should clearly be designed to as to promote respect for individual liberty. Campaign finance regulations, for example, should be carefully designed to preserve maximum individual freedom to express support for a political candidate and to communicate that support to other voters. And a system of compulsory voting should be designed so as to minimize compulsion, while still sending a clear message that voting is a civic opportunity and responsibility that must be accommodated and encouraged in social and economic life.

The Australian model of "compulsory voting," for instance, involves modest fines, strong social support for voting (scheduling elections on weekends and making polling stations enjoyable places to spend time), and the option of not completing a valid ballot paper—thereby voting "informally" or casting a so-called donkey vote. This combination means that, in effect, individuals' freedom not to express a political viewpoint is protected and preserved, even while citizens are strongly encouraged to show up to a polling station. This is also one reason many scholars suggest it would be possible—even though unlikely—that such a model could be adopted in countries such as the United States, with an especially strong tradition of protecting rights to free speech, including freedom from "compelled speech."[23]

Some democracies would also have more to do than others to make these regulations a reality. In the United States, for instance, it would likely involve quite wide-ranging political—and even potentially constitutional—reform. In other countries, it might involve far more incremental reform. While no country has a perfect system in this regard, various countries have components of such a system. Some countries have compulsory voting, and others have ranked-choice voting. Many countries have cabined the role of money in politics, and many more have ensured that nonpartisan commissions rather than politicians themselves draw electoral boundaries. There is, therefore, both empirical evidence on the workability and plausibility of many of these fair political market reforms.

There is also potentially a more contingent, empirical connection between the existence of fair political and economic markets. Liberal democracies do not necessarily have a monopoly on the adoption of democratic liberal policies. Indeed, one the of challenges for liberal democracies is that would-be authoritarian actors have sometimes been *more* willing than democratic ones to adopt democratic liberal policies, and gained substantial popular support as a result.

Good examples are the kind of broad, cash-based welfare schemes adopted by the Thai governments of Thaksin and Yingluck Shinawatra, and the PiS government in Poland. One of the central tenets of democratic liberalism is that economic and social policies should be sustainable, both in the economic and environmental sense. They cannot simply involve large-scale expenditures with no long-term benefit or investment potential, which are funded out of debt to be repaid by future generations. But if payments are sustainable, because they can be financed through the kinds of measures discussed in the Chapter 8, democratic liberalism suggests there is often good reason to favor a mix of public and private provision, universal and targeted forms of welfare, and cash as well as in-kind benefits. Doing so can often promote efficiency, inclusion, and public support for such schemes, and promote individual choice and welfare.[24]

From a democratic liberal perspective, it may thus be a mistake to identify all subsidies or child benefits as inherently illiberal: they may not be social democratic, but they may be consistent with democratic liberalism. In many cases, therefore, the problem will not be one of mistaken policy, but what one of us (with David Landau) has called "abusive constitutional borrowing": democratic liberal policies are being adopted in this context by regimes with patently antidemocratic or authoritarian aims.[25]

In Thailand, for example, both Thaksin Shinawatra and his sister Yingluck promised rice farmers substantial subsidies for their harvests. Yet one policy (Thaksin's) simply increased the profitability of rice farmers' sales, whereas Yingluck's—which involved buying millions of tons of rice at double the market value—left the government with large amounts of surplus rice after the world price for rice fell dramatically. It was clearly not sustainable, led to widespread theft, large amounts of rotten rice, and ended up costing billions of dollars.

Similarly, in Poland, one of the most popular policies adopted by PiS has been the child benefit program, which gives families 500 Polish zloty (approximately $US133) monthly for every child after their second child (and for low-income families, for every child).[26] Many Polish economists criticize the policy as diverting funds away from investments in critical social and physical infrastructure. But they also concede that the program is affordable, based on current Polish growth and tax rates. And the policy has several key democratic liberal hallmarks: it seeks to promote a generous social minimum to all, through a mix of public and private provision, universality, and means testing. While the policy may be ill-advised (as putting too much weight on current consumption over future investment), it is certainly not inherently illiberal. Rather, it is a debatable democratic liberal policy being adopted in the service of illiberal, antidemocratic ends—and, based on recent Polish presidential elections, with some success.

Why? Because in many countries, democratic liberal policies are not only good economics. They often enjoy broad public support. And this suggests that if a fair markets approach promotes true democratic competition, it is likely to lead elected officials to be more willing to adopt fair market economic policies.

Debates over healthcare reform in the United States are a good example. The center-right think tank the Heritage Foundation argued in a 1989 report[27] that the American healthcare system was "on the critical list and in need of intensive care." The report pointed out that—at the time—the United States spent 11% of GNP on healthcare, but "the system does not deliver the services that Americans expect." They pointed to the fact that at the time of the report, 37 million Americans were without healthcare and 89% of Americans believed that the system needed "fundamental changes."

At the core of their proposal to reform healthcare in America was an "individual mandate." This would require all Americans to have health insurance, and would provide subsidies for those unable to afford it. It would involve, as the report put it, "a contract between government and citizens: a commitment by government to provide aid to any family genuinely unable to afford health care; a legal obligation on all families to obtain a minimum level of protection against health care costs."

This formed a key basis of the health reforms implemented in Massachusetts by Mitt Romney as governor, and also formed the core of the Obama administration's healthcare policy, the Affordable Care Act (ACA). Yet, despite the intellectual history of these ideas, the Republican Party has consistently campaigned against the ACA. Every Republican presidential primary contender (including Mitt Romney) has argued against the law, and there have been countless attempts in congress to repeal the ACA. This is despite the fact that the law has the support of around 54% of American voters, and only around 17% of voters favor repeal of the act.

This is, in part, caused by the need to court donors, gerrymandered congressional districts, and strategic extremism to drive turnout. Courting donors like Sheldon Adelson (and others) who were strongly against the ACA no doubt led some candidates to adjust their policy positions. Gerrymandered political districts can lead to politicians adopting more extreme policy positions, pushing them away from supporting the relatively centrist ACA. And, as discussed previously, the need to drive turnout leads to strategic extremism, pushing politicians away from centrist positions.

It is, of course, hard to know whether compulsory voting would lead to a different approach by the Republican Party, but the individual mandate, and the ACA more generally, does seem like an issue that fits well with the strategic extremism paradigm. It is an issue—serious change or outright repeal of the ACA—with very strong support among the Republican base. The net favorability rating of the ACA with Republican voters was consistently in the -63%/-64% range from 2016 through 2019.[28] This compares to +67% among Democrats and +10% among Independents. As such, it is a strong turnout motivator.

The ACA is also extremely unpopular with Republican donors. Moderate Republican Senator Dean Heller (R-NV), changed from being a public critic of repeal efforts to a strong supporter of the Graham-Cassidy repeal bill, apparently after he came under scrutiny by Sheldon Adelson and Steve Wynn, two billionaire Republican donors who have a strong presence in his home state.

This does not mean, however, that there is any obvious path to adopting structural changes of this kind in systems where political markets are less competitive or well-regulated. This is the classic "insider–outsider" problem that often faces those seeking to adopt any kind of democratic reform: the very need for such political reforms, as a means of promoting democratic liberal economic and social policies, suggests the difficulty in adopting these political reforms in the process.[29] Witness the experience with attempts to end partisan gerrymandering, which have been blocked by those with the most to lose.[30]

The only true solution to this problem is political mobilization and pressure; and while ideas of the kind may help provide a rallying point for such mobilization, they are no substitute for it.

It should also be clear that we do not offer a panacea for all the ills of liberalism. We do not suggest how relationships and community can be valued and built beyond the accommodation of those social arrangements in how we design work wages and tax policy.

We do not consider how the global liberal order can be better designed to promote equality among as well as within nations, more effective global regulation of externalities and market power, and a truly global dignified minimum for all.

Nor do we explain how our account is best reconciled with debates over entry—or immigration—within liberal states. In one view, a commitment to liberalism entails a commitment to at least relatively open borders. But others argue that shoring up support for the democratic state, and especially its role in guaranteeing universal access to the social minimum, requires much stricter immigration policies. One proposed solution, which seems compatible with the idea of democratic liberalism, is that (to use a phrase developed by Thomas Friedman, not Donald Trump)—democratic states should have a "high wall, and big gate."[31] But we do not attempt in the book to explore this question or provide anything like a definitive answer.

We also offer only a partial account of how liberalism can tackle the rising challenge of economic inequality. At a theoretical level, we note the importance of a commitment in a democratic liberal approach to equality—not just sufficiency or adequacy—in relation to access to education, life-preserving healthcare, and proximate and decent housing. And we stress equality as a guiding value in the design of a public baseline system for healthcare. We likewise emphasize throughout the book the importance of guaranteeing a generous social minimum. We also suggest the value of attempts to broaden access to capital—the growth of which is argued to be one of the key drivers of increasing economic equality—for ordinary workers and citizens. And we emphasize the importance of the tax and transfer system in helping address inequality, including the importance of taxes such as progressive personal tax rates, a tax on capital, and "progressive VAT," that can effectively raise revenue *and* redistribute income from high-income to lower-income households. But the latent concern about inequality is not one that Covid-19 has offered any answers to, and therefore not one that we have focused on as directly as some other challenges.

The main aim of the book, however, is to show that far from being beyond redemption, liberalism can and should be reimagined in a post Covid-19 world. Coming out of the Covid-19 crisis we must remember the imperfections in liberalism that it has exposed. And we must look at which of the measures taken to battle the economic impact of the crisis should be kept after the crisis, and which should be wound back.

The crisis, when it is ultimately finished, will have taken a terrible toll in terms of human life, economic harm, and psychological suffering. It has to mean something. And one of the most important ways in which it can mean something is to help liberalism continue to renew and improve itself.

The alternative is either a return to the imperfect liberalism—in terms of economics and politics—of the pre-Covid-19 era, a lurch toward a kind of democratic socialism that fails to utilize the power of markets, or an ominous turn to the economic nationalism that Steve Bannon used to help elect Donald Trump President of the United States.

Acknowledgments

The authors thank Robert Akerlof, Adam Chilton, Evelyn Douek, Cynthia Estlund, Brent Neiman, Eric Posner, Ganesh Sitaraman, Betsey Stevenson, Mark Tushnet, and Luigi Zingales for helpful comments on previous drafts, Melissa Vogt for outstanding research assistance, and the Manos Foundation for research support. Thanks are also due to American Affairs for permission to reprint parts of https://americanaffairsjournal.org/2020/02/a-public-baseline-the-australian-health-care-model/ in chapter 5.

Notes

Chapter 1

1. https://inequality.org/facts/income-inequality/#income-inequality
2. This was sufficiently unexpected—in fact, quite the opposite of the kind of austerity that some predicted—that economist John Quiggin wrote, "When I agreed to write *The Economic Consequences of the Pandemic* for Yale UP, with a target date of May 2021, the idea was that it would be a polemic against austerity along the lines of Keynes' *The Economic Consequences of Mr Churchill*, and the *The Economic Consequences of the Peace*. In view of the rapid resurgence of austerity politics after the Global Financial Crisis, about which Henry and I wrote here, it seemed like a safe bet that this would be a hot topic in 2021. Even when Joe Biden won the election, and then the voters of Georgia gave the Dems a wafer-thin Senate majority, it still seemed likely that we would see, at best, a half-baked "compromise" along the lines of the Republican counter-proposal to the American Recovery Program.

   "But here we are, a couple of months later. Not only has the ARP passed with the only significant cutback being the exclusion of the $15 minimum wage rise, but the Administration is already talking about an additional $3 trillion in infrastructure expenditure." Available at: https://johnquiggin.com/2021/03/23/the-economic-consequences-of-mr-biden/.
3. Kahneman, Daniel, Jack L. Knetsch, and Richard H. Thaler. 1991. "Anomalies: The Endowment Effect, Loss Aversion, and Status Quo Bias." *Journal of Economic Perspectives* 5: 193.
4. Hochschild, Arlie, and Anne Machung. (2012). *The Second Shift: Working Families and the Revolution at Home*. New York: Penguin Books.
5. Compare Krygier, Martin 2016. "The Rule of Law: Pasts, Presents, and Two Possible Futures." *Annual Review of Law and Social Sciences* 12:199–229; Gutmann, Amy, and Dennis Thompson. 2004. *Why Deliberative Democracy*. Princeton: Princeton University Press; Habermas, Jürgen. 1994. "Three Normative Models of Democracy." *Constellations* 1(1): 1–10; Habermas, Jürgen. 1998. *Between Facts and Norms: Contributions to a Discourse Theory of Law and Democracy*, translated by William Rehg. Cambridge, MA: MIT Press; Ackerman, Bruce, and James S. Fishkin. 2005. *Deliberation Day*. New Haven, CT: Yale University Press.
6. Dixon, Rosalind, and David Landau. 2016. "Competitive Democracy and the Constitutional Minimum Core," in Tom Ginsburg and Aziz Huq (eds.) *Assessing Constitutional Performance*. Cambridge, UK: Cambridge University Press.
7. See Rawls, John. 1999. *A Theory of Justice*, revised edition. Cambridge, MA: Belknap Press; Rawls, John. 2013. *Political Liberalism*, expanded edition. New York: Columbia University Press; Dworkin, Ronald. 2008. *Is Democracy Possible Here? Principles for a New Political Debate*. Princeton: Princeton University Press.
8. See Rawls 1999, 2013.
9. See Sen, Amartya. 1985. *Commodities and Capabilities*. Amsterdam. Nussbaum, Martha. 1988. "Nature, Functioning and Capability: Aristotle on Political Distribution." *Oxford Studies in Ancient Philosophy* (Supplementary Volume) 6: 145–84.

10. See, e.g., Rawls. Contrast Pogge, Thomas W. 1989. *Realizing Rawls,* Ithaca, NY: Cornell University Press..

11. Greene, T. M. 1957. *Liberalism: Its Theory and Practice.* Austin: University of Texas Press; Hobhouse, L. T. 1964. *Liberalism.* New York: Oxford University Press.

12. https://www.kff.org/health-reform/poll-finding/5-charts-about-public-opinion-on-the-affordable-care-act-and-the-supreme-court/

13. We share some similarities but also important differences with Giddens, Anthony. 1988. *The Third Way: The Renewal of Social Democracy.* Cambridge, UK: Polity Press. Our notion of a "third way" in economics and politics differs from the ideas developed by Anthony Giddens in the 1990s. Giddens placed greater emphasis than we do on citizen participation in the design of policies and institutions, and notions of responsibility as well as rights in a liberal democratic context. But we share the same aim of creating a new way of understanding the relationship between liberalism and democracy that transcends current left–right political or ideological divides.

14. See Stiglitz, Joseph E. 2019. *People, Power, and Profits: Progressive Capitalism for an Age of Discontent.* New York: W.W. Norton.

Chapter 2

1. https://www.theguardian.com/business/2016/oct/09/the-world-bank-and-the-imf-wont-admit-their-policies-are-the-problem

2. Matthews, Dylan. 2019. "AOC's Policy Adviser Makes the Case for Abolishing Billionaires." *Vox,* July 9, 2019. https://www.vox.com/future-perfect/2019/7/9/20681088/alexandria-ocasio-cortez-dan-riffle-billionaire-policy-failure

3. https://www.nrdc.org/stories/paris-climate-agreement-everything-you-need-know

4. Dixon, Rosalind. 2008. "Feminist Disagreement (Comparatively) Recast." *Harvard Journal of Law & Gender* 31: 277.

5. See Nedelsky, Jennifer. 2011. *A Relational Theory of Self, Autonomy, and Law.* New York: Oxford University Press . See also https://plato.stanford.edu/entries/feminism-autonomy/.

6. See, e.g., Holley, Cameron and Clifford Shearing (eds.) 2017. *Criminology and the Anthropocene.* New York: Routledge..

7. Gygli, Savina, Florian Haelg, and Jan-Egbert Sturm. 2018. "The KOF Globalisation Index – Revisited." KOF Working Paper, No. 439, available at https://kof.ethz.ch/en/forecasts-and-indicators/indicators/kof-globalisation-index.html. Other indices of globalization include: Lockwood, B., and M. Redoano. 2005. "The CSGR Globalisation Index: An Introductory Guide." Technical Report 155 (04), CSGR Working Paper; Dreher, A., N. Gaston, and P. Martens. 2008. *Measuring Globalisation—Gauging its Consequences.* New York: Springer; Caselli, M. 2012. "Trying to Measure Globalization, Experiences, Critical Issues and Perspectives." *Springer Briefs in Political Science*; Figge, L. and P. Martens. 2014. "Globalisation Continues: The Maastricht Globalisation Index Revisited and Updated." *Globalizations* 7731 (April):1–19; Ghemawat, P. and S.A. Altman. 2016. "DHL Global Connectedness Index 2016—The State of Globalization in an Age of Ambiguity."

8. http://www.worldbank.org/en/news/feature/2016/06/08/ending-extreme-poverty

9. See, for instance, Paul Krugman, "The Increasing Returns Revolution in Trade and Geography." Nobel Lecture, December 8, 2008. Available at https://www.nobelprize.org/nobel_prizes/economic-sciences/laureates/2008/krugman_lecture.pdf.

10. https://www.forbes.com/sites/joelkotkin/2018/05/23/where-u-s-manufacturing-is-thriving-in-2018/#7885d4253b3e

11. Bureau of Labor Statistics, available at https://www.bls.gov/cps/cps_htgm.htm.

12. Munro, Mark. 2016. "Manufacturing Jobs Aren't Coming Back." *MIT Technology Review,* November 18, 2016. Available at https://www.technologyreview.com/s/602869/manufacturing-jobs-arent-coming-back.

13. Autor, David. 2018. "Trade and Labor Markets: Lessons from China's Rise." *IZA World of Labor* (February 2018):431.

14. Acemoglu, Daron, David Autor, D. Dorn, Gordon H. Hanson, and B. Price. 2016. "Import Competition and the Great US Employment Sag of the 2000s." *Journal of Labor Economics* 34:S141–98.

15. Autor, David, David Dorn, and Gordon Hanson. 2013. "The China Syndrome: Local Labor Market Effects of Import Competition in the United States." *American Economic Review* 103(6): 2121–68.

16. Hakobyan, Shushanik, and John McLaren. 2016. "Looking for Local Labor Market Effects of NAFTA." *Review of Economics and Statistics* 98(4):728–41.

17. Hakobyan and McLaren (2016).

18. OECD. 2018. "Putting Faces to the Jobs At Risk of Automation." Available at http://www.oecd.org/employment/future-of-work/.

19. Frey, Carl Benedikt, and Michael A. Osborne. 2013. *The Future of Employment: How Susceptible Are Jobs to Computerisation?*, available at https://www.oxfordmartin.ox.ac.uk/downloads/academic/future-of-employment.pdf.

20. PWC, *Will Robots Steal Our Jobs?* (UK Economic Outlook, Mar 2017), available at https://www.pwc.com/hu/hu/kiadvanyok/assets/pdf/impact_of_automation_on_jobs.pdf.

21. Bowles, J. 2014. "The Computerisation of European Jobs." Blog Post, Bruegel, July 24, available at http://bruegel.org/2014/07/the-computerisation-of-european-jobs/.

22. Brynjolfsson, Erik, and Andrew McAfee. 2014. *The Second Machine Age*. Cambridge, MA: MIT Press, p.11.

23. Autor, David H. 2015. "Why Are There Still So Many Jobs? The History and Failure of Workplace Automation." *Journal of Economic Perspectives* 29(3):3–30.

24. https://money.cnn.com/2015/06/18/investing/robo-advisor-millennials-wealthfront/?iid=EL

25. Autor, David H. 2015. "Why Are There Still So Many Jobs? The History and Future of Workplace Automation." *Journal of Economic Perspectives* 29(3): 3–30.

26. https://www.gallup.com/workplace/240929/workplace-leaders-learn-real-gig-economy.aspx

27. Weil, David. 2017. *The Fissured Workplace*. Cambridge, MA: Harvard University Press..

28. Estlund, Cynthia. 2018. "What Should We Do After Work? Automation and Employment Law." *Yale Law Journal*. 128:254.

29. https://www.bls.gov/news.release/union2.nr0.htm

30. https://stats.oecd.org/Index.aspx?DataSetCode=TUD

31. Azar, José, Ioana Marinescu, Marshall Steinbaum, and Bledi Taska. 2018. "Concentration in US Labor Markets: Evidence from Online Vacancy Data." IZA Discussion Paper No. 11379.

32. Azar, José Ioana Marinescu, Marshall Steinbaum. 2018. "Labor Market Concentration." NBER Working Paper No. 24147 (updated 2019).

33. Benmelech, Efraim, Nittai Bergman, and Hyunseob Kim. 2018. "Strong Employers and Weak Employees: How Does Employer Concentration Affect Wages?" Northwestern University Working Paper, available at https://www.kellogg.northwestern.edu/faculty/benmelech/html/BenmelechPapers/BBK_2018_January_31.pdf.

34. Eric A. Posner, E. Glen Weyl, and Naidu, Suresh. 2018. "Antitrust Remedies for Labor Market Power." *Harvard Law Review* 536.

35. https://www.engadget.com/2014/03/24/emails-reveal-that-steve-jobs-angrily-called-sergey-brin-over-go/

36. *United States v. Adobe Systems, Inc., et al.* Proposed Final Judgment and Competitive Impact Statement. See DOJ: https://www.justice.gov/opa/pr/justice-department-requires-six-high-tech-companies-stop-entering-anticompetitive-employee.

37. "U.S. Labor Markets Aren't Truly Free." October 21, 2018. Available at https://www.bloomberg.com/opinion/articles/2018-10-21/free-markets-could-make-workers-better-off.

38. Star, Evan, J.J. Prescott, and Norman Bishara. 2015. "Noncompetes in the U.S. Labor Force," University of Michigan Law & Econ Research Paper No. 18-013 (revised 2019).

39. For a discussion of the hold-up problem in economics see Aghion, Philippe, and Richard Holden. 2011. "Incomplete Contracts and the Theory of the Firm: What Have We Learned over the Past 25 Years?" *Journal of Economic Perspectives* 25(2):181–97.

40. Autor, David, David Dorn, Lawrence F. Katz, Christina Patterson, and John Van Reenen. 2017. "The Fall of the Labor Share and the Rise of Superstar Firms." NBER Working Paper No. 23396. Available at https://www.nber.org/papers/w23396.

41. Autor, David, David Dorn, Lawrence F. Katz, Christina Patterson, and John Van Reenen. 2017. "The Fall of the Labor Share and the Rise of Superstar Firms." NBER Working Paper 23396. Available at http://www.nber.org/papers/w23396.

42. See Table 1 of Eggertsson, Gauti B., Jacob A. Robbins, and Ella Getz Wold. 2018. "Kaldor and Piketty's Facts: The Rise of Monopoly Power in the United States." NBER Working Paper 24287. Available at http://www.nber.org/papers/w24287

43. https://promarket.org/are-markups-increasing/

44. https://www.brookings.edu/blog/up-front/2019/06/25/six-facts-about-wealth-in-the-united-states/

45. https://inequality.org/facts/wealth-inequality/

46. See *Capital*. Some economists have raised doubts about Piketty's analysis. See, e.g., Summers. But even if one does not fully subscribe to the Piketty thesis, it is hard to escape the conclusion that inequality will increase if the majority of workers continue to be compensated for their labor, while highly skilled employees at the top of the income distribution earn returns to capital.

47. As Larry Summers put it: "This rather fatalistic and certainly dismal view of capitalism can be challenged on two levels. It presumes, first, that the return to capital diminishes slowly, if at all, as wealth is accumulated and, second, that the returns to wealth are all reinvested. Whatever may have been the case historically, neither of these premises is likely correct as a guide to thinking about the American economy today.

"Economists universally believe in the law of diminishing returns. As capital accumulates, the incremental return on an additional unit of capital declines. The crucial question goes to what is technically referred to as the elasticity of substitution. With 1%

more capital and the same amount of everything else, does the return to a unit of capital relative to a unit of labor decline by more or less than 1%? If, as Piketty assumes, it declines by less than 1%, the share of income going to capital rises. If, on the other hand, it declines by more than 1%, the share of capital falls.

"Economists have tried forever to estimate elasticities of substitution with many types of data, but there are many statistical problems. Piketty argues that the economic literature supports his assumption that returns diminish slowly (in technical parlance, that the elasticity of substitution is greater than 1), and so capital's share rises with capital accumulation. But I think he misreads the literature by conflating gross and net returns to capital. It is plausible that as the capital stock grows, the increment of output produced declines slowly, but there can be no question that depreciation increases proportionally. And it is the return net of depreciation that is relevant for capital accumulation. I know of no study suggesting that measuring output in net terms, the elasticity of substitution is greater than 1, and I know of quite a few suggesting the contrary." See http://larrysummers.com/2014/05/14/piketty-book-review-the-inequality-puzzle/.

48. https://www.oecd.org/officialdocuments/publicdisplaydocumentpdf/?cote=ECO/WKP(2017)85&docLanguage=En

49. https://www.nytimes.com/2020/10/28/us/politics/2020-race-money.html

50. https://www.scientificamerican.com/article/discovery-of-global-warming/

51. Broecker, Wallace. 1975. "Climatic Change: Are We on the Brink of a Pronounced Global Warming?" *Science* 189:460–63.

52. National Academy of Science. 1979. "Carbon Dioxide and Climate." Washington, D.C. Available at https://www.nap.edu/read/12181/chapter/1.

53. https://www.sealevel.info/1988_Hansen_Senate_Testimony.html

54. https://www.bbc.com/news/science-environment-15874560

55. https://www.ipcc.ch/report/climate-change-the-ipcc-1990-and-1992-assessments/

56. See https://www.bbc.com/news/science-environment-24021772

57. National Geographic, *Climate Change*, available at https://www.nationalgeographic.com/environment/topic/climate-change; NASA, *The Consequences of Climate Change*, available at https://climate.nasa.gov; Union of Concerned Scientists, *Global Warming Impacts*; WHO, *Climate Change*, available at https://www.who.int/heli/risks/climate/climatechange/en/.

58. https://johnquiggin.com/2021/04/30/17752/

59. Currie, Janet, and Hannes Schwandt 2020. "The Opioid Epidemic Was Not Caused by Economic Distress But by Factors that Could Be More Rapidly Addressed." NBER Working Paper No. 27544, July 2020.

60. https://www.nytimes.com/interactive/2020/04/17/us/coronavirus-testing-states.html

61. https://www.nytimes.com/2020/06/14/business/media/media-executives-hamptons.html

62. Compare Nussbaum (1988).

63. https://www.cdc.gov/nchs/nvss/vsrr/covid_weekly/index.htm

64. https://www.nytimes.com/2020/04/14/opinion/coronavirus-racism-african-americans.html?referringSource=articleShare

65. https://www.cdc.gov/coronavirus/2019-ncov/need-extra-precautions/racial-ethnic-minorities.html

66. https://www.nytimes.com/2020/06/23/world/americas/coronavirus-brazil-mexico-peru-chile-uruguay.html?referringSource=articleShare

67. https://budget.gov.au/2019-20/content/bp1/download/bp1_bs6.pdf

68. https://www.quandl.com/data/ODA/USA_GGXWDN_NGDP-United-States-General-Government-Net-Debt-of-GDP

69. https://tradingeconomics.com/spain/youth-unemployment-rate; https://tradingeconomics.com/italy/youth-unemployment-rate

70. Kahn, Lisa. 2010. "The Long-Term Labor Market Consequences of Graduating from College in a Bad Economy." *Labour Economics*, 17(2):303–16.

71. https://www.theguardian.com/business/2020/jun/02/uk-electricity-coal-free-for-first-month-ever

72. https://www.forbes.com/sites/jeffmcmahon/2020/03/29/a-dirty-economic-restart-risks-more-lives-than-the-coronavirus/#798726b53d53

73. https://www.smh.com.au/environment/climate-change/carbon-emissions-will-drop-but-experts-fear-revenge-pollution-20200327-p54eft.html

74. https://www.forbes.com/sites/nishandegnarain/2020/05/19/what-canada-is-getting-right-with-its-covid-19-economic-response-plan/#7d0b3c3c5357

75. https://www.epa.gov/regulations-emissions-vehicles-and-engines/safer-affordable-fuel-efficient-safe-vehicles-final-rule

76. https://www.theguardian.com/environment/2020/mar/31/trump-epa-obama-clean-car-rules-climate-change

77. https://www.greentechmedia.com/articles/read/eu-green-deal-should-now-be-canceled-says-czech-pm

78. Stiglitz. John. 2020. *People, Power, and Profits: Progressive Capitalism for an Age of Discontent*. London: Penguin.

79. Harvey. David. 2005. *A Brief History of Neoliberalism*. New York: Oxford University Press..

80. The idea that there could only be a "market" or "government" solution to the problem of common-pool resource management was critiqued by Elinor Ostrom and gave rise to her Nobel Prize in Economic Sciences. Ostrom's contribution throughout her career was to highlight the poverty of this binary distinction and to document and illustrate a range of different organizational forms for governing common-pool resources. See https://www.nobelprize.org/uploads/2018/06/ostrom_lecture.pdf.

81. See Sitaraman, Ganesh. 2019. *The Great Democracy*. New York: Basic Books..

Chapter 3

1. See also Sperling, Gene. 2020. *Economic Dignity*. New York: Penguin.

2. World Bank. 2018 "Decline of Global Extreme Poverty Continues But Has Slowed." Available at https://www.worldbank.org/en/news/press-release/2018/09/19/decline-of-global-extreme-poverty-continues-but-has-slowed-world-bank.

3. Barzilay, Arianne Renan, and Anat Ben-David. 2017. "Platform Inequality: Gender in the Gig Economy." *Seton Hall Law Review* 47:393.

4. Hobhouse, Leonard Trelawn. 1964. *Liberalism*. Oxford, UK: Oxford University Press. pp.15–16.

5. See Sen, Amartya. 1985. *Commodities and Capabilities*. Amsterdam: North-Holland; and Nussbaum, Martha C. 2007. *Frontiers of Justice: Disability, Nationality, Species Membership*. Cambridge, MA: Harvard University Press.

6. This is an idea first articulated clearly by Hayek in his classic 1945 article, "The Use of Knowledge in Society." Hayek, F.A. 1945. "The Use of Knowledge in Society." *American Economic Review* XXXV(4):519–30.

7. De Loecker, Jan, and Jan Eeckhout. 2018. "Global Market Power." NBER Working Paper 24768. Available at http://www.nber.org/papers/w24768.

8. https://www.ftc.gov/system/files/documents/reports/fy-2020-congressional-budget-justi-fication/fy_2020_cbj.pdf

9. Calabresi and Melamed suggest it may still apply if transaction costs are asymmetric, or it is clear which party is the "least cost avoider": see note 10.

10. Calabresi, Guido, and A. Douglass Melamed. 1972. "Property Rules, Liability Rules, and Inalienability: One View of the Cathedral." *Harvard Law Review* 85(6).

11. https://www.nobelprize.org/prizes/economic-sciences/2016/summary/

12. See https://www.nobelprize.org/prizes/economic-sciences/2018/nordhaus/facts/

13. See https://web.archive.org/web/20080102015009/http://www.amazon.com/Libertarian ism-Against-Craig-Duncan/dp/0742542599 and https://www.oxfordscholarship.com/view/10.1093/acprof:oso/9780190468538.001.0001/acprof-9780190468538

14. Rahman, K. Sabeel. 2016. *Democracy Against Domination*. New York: Oxford University Press.

15. Schumpter, Joseph A. 1942. *Capitalism, Socialism and Democracy*. New York: Harper. Compare also von Hayek, Friedrich. 1944. *The Road to Serfdom*. Chicago: University of Chicago Press.

16. Issacharoff, Samuel, and Richard H. Pildes. 1988. "Politics As Markets: Partisan Lockups of the Democratic Process," *Stanford Law Review* 50(3):643–717.

17. Ibid.

18. Some of the following discussion is based on an article by one of the authors in *The Conversation*, available at https://theconversation.com/vital-signs-victorias-privatised-quarantine-arrangements-were-destined-to-fail-143169.

19. Smith, Adam, and E. Cannan. 2003. *The Wealth of Nations*. New York: Bantam Classic: II, 184–85.

20. Hart, Oliver, Andrei Shleifer, and Robert Vishny. 1997. "The Proper Scope of Government: Theory and an Application to Prisons." *Quarterly Journal of Economics* 112(4):1127–61.

21. EFTA. 2001. *Fair Trade in Europe 2001*. Maastricht: EFTA; FINE: 2001, see www.eftafairtrade.org/definition.asp.

22. Miller, David. 2010. "Fair Trade: What Does It Mean and Why Does It Matter?" CSSJ Working Paper Series, SJ013, November 2010.

23. Low, William, and Eileen Davenport. 2005. "Postcards from the Edge: Maintaining the 'Alternative' Character of Fair Trade." *Sustainable Development* 12.; Smith, Alastair. 2011. "Fair and Ethical Trade: An Explanation." *WIEGO* working paper,.

24. Moore, Geoff. 2004. "The Fair Trade Movement: Parameters, Issues and Future Research." *Journal of Business Ethics* 53:73–86. See p. 74.

25. Ibid.

26. Stiglitz, Joseph E. 2019. *People, Power, and Profits: Progressive Capitalism for an Age of Discontent*. New York: W.W.Norton.

27. https://berniesanders.com/issues/

28. https://berniesanders.com/issues/free-college-cancel-debt/

29. https://berniesanders.com/issues/housing-all/

30. https://www.congress.gov/bill/116th-congress/house-resolution/109/text

31. Naidu, Suresh, Eric A. Posner, and E. Glen Weyl. 2018. "Antitrust Remedies for Labor Market Power." *Harvard Law Review* 132: 536–601.

32. Romer, P.M. 1986. "Increasing Returns and Long-Run Growth." *Journal of Political Economy* 94:1002.

33. https://berniesanders.com/issues/free-college-cancel-debt/

34. https://berniesanders.com/issues/housing-all/

35. Smith, Adam. 1776. *The Wealth of Nations.* Book I, Chapter XI.

36. Hicks, J.R. 1935. "Annual Survey of Economic Theory: The Theory of Monopoly." *Econometrica* 56(3): 1–20.

37. Leibenstein, Harvey. 1966. "Allocative Efficiency vs. X-Efficiency," *American Economic Review* 56:392–414).

38. On the theoretical side see: Hart, Oliver D. 1983. "The Market Mechanism as an Incentive Scheme." *Bell Journal of Economics* 14:366–82; Hermalin, Benjamin E. 1992. "The Effects of Competition on Executive Behavior." *RAND Journal of Economics* 23:350–65; Martin, Stephen. 1993. "Endogenous Firm Efficiency in a Cournot Principal-Agent Model." *Journal of Economic Theory* 59:445–50; Nalebuff, Barry J., and Joseph E. Stiglitz. 1983. "Information, Competition and Markets." *American Economic Review* 73:278–83; Nickell, Stephen J. 1996. "Competition and Corporate Performance." *Journal of Political Economy* 104:724–46; Raith, Michael. 2003. "Competition, Risk and Managerial Incentives." *American Economic Review* 93:1425–36; Scharfstein, David. 1988. "The Disciplinary Role of Takeovers." *Review of Economic Studies* 55:185–99; Scharfstein, David. 1988. "Product Market Competition and Managerial Slack." *RAND Journal of Economics* 19:147–55; Schmidt, Klaus. 1997. "Managerial Incentives and Product Market Competition." *Review of Economic Studies* 64:191–213).

    On the empirical side, see: Nickell, Stephen J. 1996. "Competition and Corporate Performance." *Journal of Political Economy* 104:724–46; Cunat, Vicente, and Maria Guadalupe. 2005. "How Does Product Market Competition Shape Incentive Contracts?" *Journal of the European Economic Association* 3:1058–82; Galdon-Sanchez, Jose E., and James A. Schmitz Jr. 2002. "Competitive Pressure and Labor Productivity: World Iron-Ore Markets in the 1980s." *American Economic Review* 38:1222–35.

39. https://www.wsj.com/articles/steve-bannon-and-the-making-of-an-economic-nationalist-1489516113

40. Helpman, Elhanan. 1988. "Growth, Technological Progress, and Trade." National Bureau of Economic Research (Cambridge, MA), Working Paper 1145.

41. Cerdeiro, Diego, and Andras Komaromi. 2017. "Trade and Income in the Long Run: Are There Really Gains, and Are They Widely Shared?" IMF Working Paper, available at https://www.imf.org/en/Publications/WP/Issues/2017/11/07/Trade-and-Income-in-the-Long-Run-Are-There-Really-Gains-and-Are-They-Widely-Shared-45341.

42. So-called non-tariff barriers include quotas for foreign goods, price floors for domestic goods, and a range of other measures that have an equivalent effect to an ad-valorem tariff.

43. http://nationalhumanitiescenter.org/pds/livingrev/politics/text2/hamilton.pdf

44. Leonnig, Carol D. 2012. "Battery Firm Backed by Federal Stimulus Money Files for Bankruptcy." *Washington Post*, October 16. Available at https://www.washingtonpost.com/politics/decision2012/battery-firm-backed-by-federal-stimulus-money-files-for-bankruptcy/2012/10/16/89611566-17c6-11e2-8792-cf5305eddf60_story.html?utm_term=.b7fc5cdb919e.

45. Scales, Bill. 2017. "The Rise and Fall of the Australian Car Manufacturing Industry." *Australian Financial Review*. October 19. Available at https://www.afr.com/opinion/col

umnists/bill-scales-the-rise-and-fall-of-the-australian-car-manufacturing-industry-20171018-gz3ky4.

46. Broadberry, Stephen, and Tim Leunig. 2013. "The Impact of Government Policies on UK Manufacturing since 1945." LSE Working Paper, October 2013. Available at https://assets. publishing.service.gov.uk/government/uploads/system/uploads/attachment_data/file/277158/ep2-government-policy-since-1945.pdf.

47. Ibid.

48. As the US Department of Treasury put it, the paycheck protection program "provides small businesses with funds to pay up to 8 weeks of payroll costs including benefits. Funds can also be used to pay interest on mortgages, rent, and utilities. The Paycheck Protection Program prioritizes millions of Americans employed by small businesses by authorizing up to $349 billion toward job retention and certain other expenses." https://home.treasury. gov/policy-issues/cares/assistance-for-small-businesses. See also https://home.treasury. gov/policy-issues/cares/preserving-jobs-for-american-industry: "Employers of all sizes that face closure orders or suffer economic hardship due to COVID-19 are incentivized to keep employees on the payroll through a 50% credit on up to $10,000 of wages paid or incurred from March 13, 2020 through December 31, 2020."

49. https://home.treasury.gov/policy-issues/cares/state-and-local-governments

50. https://www.wsj.com/articles/what-is-in-the-900-billion-covid-19-aid-bill-11608557531

51. https://www.bbc.com/news/world-us-canada-56364944

52. https://www.quandl.com/data/ODA/USA_GGXWDN_NGDP-United-States-General-Government-Net-Debt-of-GDP

53. https://www.nytimes.com/2021/04/28/us/politics/biden-american-families-plan. html?searchResultPosition=4

54. https://www.gov.uk/government/news/chancellor-announces-workers-support-package

55. https://www.forbes.com/sites/tedreed/2020/05/08/after-win-at-united-labor-looks-to-change-delta-and-jetblue-cares-act-policies/#5957362421a7

56. https://www.theguardian.com/politics/2020/may/06/chancellor-unions-cliff-edge-end-furlough-rishi-sunak-coronavirus-wage-subsidies

57. https://euobserver.com/coronavirus/147827

58. https://theconversation.com/coronavirus-how-uk-job-retention-plan-borrows-from-collectivist-europe-134194

59. https://www.smh.com.au/politics/federal/union-deal-clears-way-for-130-billion-wage-subsidy-20200406-p54hjj.html

60. https://www.afr.com/politics/federal/ir-lifeboat-needed-for-rough-economic-seas-20200405-p54h7f

61. https://www.attorneygeneral.gov.au/media/transcripts/doorstop-parliament-house-6-april-2020

62. https://www.federalreserve.gov/newsevents/pressreleases/monetary20200409a.htm

63. https://www.japantimes.co.jp/news/2020/04/03/national/cash-stimulus-coronavirus/#.XpkHaC17Hys

64. https://www.imf.org/en/Topics/imf-and-covid19/Policy-Responses-to-COVID-19.   Of course, many countries that are not liberal democracies did similarly; a more complete list is: Australia, Belgium, Brazil, Canada, Costa Rica, the Dominican Republic, El Salvador, India, Indonesia, Iran, Japan, Kazakhstan, South Korea, Malaysia, Mauritania, Mongolia, Morocco, Peru, the Philippines, Samoa, Singapore, Sudan, Tunisia, and Zimbabwe.

65. https://www.americanprogress.org/issues/economy/news/2020/03/06/481394/economic-impact-coronavirus-united-states-possible-economic-policy-responses/

66. https://www.imf.org/en/Topics/imf-and-covid19/Policy-Responses-to-COVID-19

67. https://www.theguardian.com/environment/2020/apr/11/positively-alpine-disbelief-air-pollution-falls-lockdown-coronavirus

68. https://www.smh.com.au/environment/climate-change/could-a-reborn-cruise-industry-be-a-better-environmental-steward-20200409-p54iqo.html

69. https://www.nytimes.com/interactive/2021/03/31/upshot/whats-in-bidens-infrastructure-plan.html?searchResultPosition=2

70. Dixon, Rosalind, and Richard Holden. 2019. "A Public Baseline: The Australian Health Care Model." *American Affairs*, available at https://americanaffairsjournal.org/2020/02/a-public-baseline-the-australian-health-care-model/.

71. https://www.theguardian.com/business/ng-interactive/2015/apr/29/the-austerity-delusion

72. Indeed, as John Quiggin has noted, "Like Keynes' Londoner in the aftermath of the Great War, we are emerging from the pandemic into a world where the certitudes of the past have crumbled into dust. Balanced budgets, free trade, credit ratings, financial markets, above all free markets; these ideas have ceased to command any belief.

    "The failure of these ideas has been evident since the GFC and, in many respects, since the beginning of the 21st century. It has sunk in gradually, as the neoliberal political class formed in the 1980s and 1990s has passed from the scene, replaced by younger people whose experience of financialised capitalism is almost entirely negative.

    "But it is only with the shock of the pandemic that the thinking of the past has completely lost its grip on the great majority. The absence of any serious resistance to Biden's stimulus and infrastructure package reflects the fact that hardly anyone seriously believes the old verities of balanced budgets and free markets." Available at: https://johnquiggin.com/2021/04/30/17752/.

Chapter 4

1. Hart, Oliver, Andrei Shleifer, and Robert W. Vishny. 1997. "The proper scope of government: theory and an application to prisons." *The Quarterly Journal of Economics* 112.4: 1127–1161.

2. See, for instance, https://www.npr.org/2018/05/08/609091985/likely-2020-democratic-candidates-want-to-guarantee-a-job-to-every-american. See also Way, L. Randall. 2018. "A Consensus Strategy for a Universal Job Guarantee Program." *Levy Economics Institute*, Policy Note 2018/3.

3. The precise quote is as follows: "If the Treasury were to fill old bottles with banknotes, bury them at suitable depths in disused coalmines which are then filled up to the surface with town rubbish, and leave it to private enterprise on well-tried principles of laissez-faire to dig the notes up again (the right to do so being obtained, of course, by tendering for leases of the note-bearing territory), there need be no more unemployment and, with the help of the repercussions, the real income of the community, and its capital wealth also, would probably become a good deal greater than it actually is. It would, indeed, be more sensible to build houses and the like; but if there are political and practical difficulties in the way of this, the above would be better than nothing." Book 3, Chapter 10, Section 6, p. 129, *The General Theory of Employment, Interest and Money*.

4. See Tcherneva, Pavlina R. 2020. *The Case for a Job Guarantee*. Cambridge, UK: Polity Press, pp. 94–96.

5. See ibid., pp. 114–17 and references therein.

6. Way, L. Randall. 2018. "A Consensus Strategy for a Universal Job Guarantee Program." Levy Economics Institute, Policy Note 2018/3.

7. https://www.infoplease.com/business-finance/labor-and-employment/annual-federal-minimum-wage-rates-1955-2015

8. https://www.thebalancecareers.com/2018-19-federal-state-minimum-wage-rates-2061043

9. Pramuk, Jacob 2019.. "2020 Democrats Embrace a $15 US Minimum Wage As They Target Trump's Economy." *CNBC*, June 9, available at https://www.cnbc.com/2019/06/09/2020-election-news-democrats-embrace-15-minimum-wage-against-trump.html.

10. https://edition.cnn.com/2021/04/28/politics/biden-joint-address-fact-check/index.html

11. https://www.cnn.com/2021/04/27/politics/minimum-wage-federal-contractors-biden/index.html

12. For the etymology of the latter term and an outstanding summary of the issues, see Angrist, Joshua, and Jorn-Steffen Pischke. 2010. "The Credibility Revolution in Empirical Economics: How Better Research Design is Taking the Con out of Econometrics," *Journal of Economic Perspectives* 24(2):3–30. https://pubs.aeaweb.org/doi/pdfplus/10.1257/jep.24.2.3.

13. One example comes from *New York Times* columnist Paul Krugman after Krueger's premature death: https://www.nytimes.com/2019/03/19/opinion/alan-krueger-dies.html, but other examples both before and after Krueger's passing abound.

14. Neumark, David. 2018. "The Econometrics and Economics of the Employment Effects of Minimum Wages: Getting from Known Unknowns to Known Knowns." NBER Working Paper 25043.

15. See recent work by Cengiz, Doruk, Arindrajit Dube, Attila Lindner, and Ben Zipperer. 2019. "The Effect of Minimum Wages on Low-Wage Jobs." *Quarterly Journal of Economics* 134(3):1405–54. The authors suggest that modest minimum wage increases do not appear to have a material effect on the level of employment for low-wage workers in non-tradeable sectors.

16. Banerjee, Abhijit, and Esther Duflo. 2019. *Good Economics for Hard Times*. New York: Penguin.

17. Ibid.

18. Tcherneva, Pavlina R. 2020. *The Case for a Job Guarantee*. Cambridge, UK: Polity Press, pp. 97–100.

19. https://www.ceps.eu/system/files/PI2017-23_KL%20et%20al%20EUBS.pdf

20. https://www.aboutunemployment.org/faqs/best-and-worst-states-for-unemployment-benefits/

21. https://ec.europa.eu/employment_social/empl_portal/SSRinEU/Your%20social%20security%20rights%20in%20Italy_en.pdf

22. See https://japantoday.com/category/features/lifestyle/understanding-japanese-unemployment-insurance

23. https://www.arbeitsagentur.de

24. Government of Canada. "EI Regular Benefits: How Much You Could Receive." See https://www.canada.ca/en/services/benefits/ei/ei-regular-benefit/benefit-amount.html; Government of Canada. "EI Premium Rates and Maximums." https://www.canada.ca/

en/revenue-agency/services/tax/businesses/topics/payroll/payroll-deductions-contributions/employment-insurance-ei/ei-premium-rates-maximums.html.

25. https://www.humanservices.gov.au/individuals/services/centrelink/newstart-allowance

26. Australian Government. "Work for the Dole Information for Job Seekers." https://www.dese.gov.au/work-dole/work-dole-information-job-seekers.

27. Van Parijs, Philippe, and Yannick Vanderborght. 2017. *Basic Income: A Radical Proposal for a Free Society and a Sane Economy.* Cambridge, MA: Harvard University Press.

28. "Mark Zuckerberg's Commencement Address at Harvard." 2017. *The Harvard Gazette,* https://news.harvard.edu/gazette/story/2017/05/mark-zuckerbergs-speech-as-written-for-harvards-class-of-2017/.

29. https://www.cnbc.com/2018/06/18/elon-musk-automated-jobs-could-make-ubi-cash-handouts-necessary.html

30. See, for instance, Bregman, Rutger. 2017. *Utopia for Realists* (De Correspondent); Lowrey, Annie. 2018. *Give People Money.* (Crown,); and Stern, Andy. 2016. *Raising the Floor* (Hachette, 2016).

31. https://basicincome.ycr.org/our-plan

32. https://www.ontario.ca/page/ontario-basic-income-pilot

33. http://www.yang2020.com/policies/the-freedom-dividend

34. https://www.ubicenter.org

35. See https://taxfoundation.org/andrew-yang-value-added-tax-universal-basic-income/

36. https://rooseveltinstitute.org/wp-content/uploads/2017/08/Modeling-the-Macroeconomic-Effects-of-a-Universal-Basic-Income.pdf

37. Elster, Jon. 1986. "Comment on Van der Veen and Van Parijs," *Theory and Society* 15(5):709–21, p. 719; also quoted in Van Parijs and Yannick Vanderborght (2017).

38. Dixon, Rosalind, Richard Holden, and Lachlan Peake. 2019. "Saving (and) Care: Closing the Gender Gap in the Australian Superannuation System." New Economic Policy Initiative Report, UNSW Sydney.

39. https://podcasts.apple.com/us/podcast/the-daily/id1200361736?mt=2

40. https://www.economist.com/united-states/2018/11/24/the-earned-income-tax-credit-almost-pays-for-itself

41. https://drive.google.com/file/d/1GbBeeQzfGH9fF9Y1u5rS55Sn3eStBWE7/view

42. Bastian, Jacob. 2020. "The Rise of Working Mothers and the 1975 Earned Income Tax Credit." *American Economic Journal: Economic Policy* 12(3):44–75.

43. https://fas.org/sgp/crs/misc/R44787.pdf

44. https://fas.org/sgp/crs/misc/R44787.pdf

45. https://d3n8a8pro7vhmx.cloudfront.net/broadbent/pages/7073/attachments/original/1519312305/Canada%27s_Working_poor_and_the_Working_Tax_Benefit_-_Report.pdf?1519312305

46. https://www.cbpp.org/research/federal-tax/american-rescue-plan-act-includes-critical-expansions-of-child-tax-credit-and

47. https://www.cnbc.com/2018/01/22/heres-how-much-ceo-pay-has-increased-compared-to-yours-over-the-years.html

48. See *Capital.* Some economists have raised doubts about Piketty's analysis. See, e.g. Summers. But even if one does not fully subscribe to the Piketty thesis, however, it is hard to escape the conclusion that if the majority of workers continue to be compensated for their labor, while highly skilled employees at the top of the income distribution earn returns to capital.

49. OECD. 2017. "R&D Tax Incentive: United States," Available at https://www.oecd.org/sti/RDTax%20Country%20Profiles%20-%20USA.pdf

50. The United States is, broadly speaking, one example of this general approach (OECD, 2017), as is Australia (see https://www.ato.gov.au/business/research-and-development-tax-incentive/about-the-program/).

51. https://home.kpmg/cn/en/home/insights/2016/11/china-tax-alert-34.html

52. Accumulation indices assume that dividends are reinvested, since returns on stocks include both dividend income and capital gains.

53. Naturally, this makes overall earnings more volatile as well, with a standard deviation of 1.4%.

54. For average weekly earnings data as of November 2018, see https://www.abs.gov.au/ausstats/abs@.nsf/mf/6302.0?opendocument&ref=HPKI.

55. Kahneman, Daniel, Jack L. Knetsch, and Richard H. Thaler. 1991. "Anomalies: The Endowment Effect, Loss Aversion, and Status Quo Bias." *Journal of Economic Perspectives* 5:193 ().

56. Richard Holden and Anup Malani. 2019. "The ICO Paradox: Transaction Costs, Token Velocity, and Token Value," NBER Working Paper. http://www.nber.org/papers/w26265.

57. Kline, Patrick, and Enrico Moretti. 2014. "People, Places, and Public Policy: Some Simple Welfare Economics of Local Economic Development Programs." *Annual Review of Economics* 6:629–62.

58. Kline and Moretti (2014).

59. See Kline and Moretti (2014) *People, Places*, p. 631; Kline, Patrick, and Moretti, Enrico. 2014. "Local Economic Development, Agglomeration Economies, and the Big Push: 100 Years of Evidence from the Tennessee Valley Authority," *The Quarterly Journal of Economics* 129(1):275–331 .

60. http://www.spatialeconomics.ac.uk/textonly/SERC/publications/download/sercdp0191.pdf

61. Kazekami, Sachiko. 2017. "Evaluating Place-Based Job Creation Programs in Japan," *IZA Journal of Labor Policy* 6:1.

62. Lu, Yi, Jin Wang, and Lianming Zhu. 2018. "Place-Based Policies, Creation, and Agglomeration Economies: Evidence from China's Economic Zone Program." *American Economic Journal: Economic Policy* 11(2):325–360.

63. For instance, see Catalano, Ralph, Sidra Goldman-Mellor, Katherine Saxton, Claire Margerison-Zilko, Meenakshi Subbaraman, Kaja LeWinn, and Elizabeth Anderson. 2011. "The Health Effects of Economic Decline", *Annual Review of Public Health* 32:431–50, for an excellent survey. They note that "Research shows that undesirable job and financial experiences increase the risk of psychological and behavioral disorder, including violence and suicide," although it is fair to say that the literature that they summarize has had less success in pinning down the channels involved.

64. Akerlof, Robert, and Richard Holden. 2016. "Movers and Shakers." *Quarterly Journal of Economics* 131(4):1849–74. For an application to community investment, see Holden, Richard 2016. "Turnbull Needs Community of Believers for Northern Growth." *The Australian*, January 11 available at http://research.economics.unsw.edu.au/richardholden/assets/aus-jan-11-2016.pdf.

Chapter 5

1. Baumol, William J., and William G. Bowen. 1966. *Performing Arts, The Economic Dilemma: A Study of Problems Common to Theater, Opera, Music, and Dance*. Cambridge, MA: MIT Press.

2. Shleifer, Andrei. 1985. "A Theory of Yardstick Competition," RAND *Journal of Economics* 16:319.

3. For a general discussion of public options in healthcare and other aspects of the economy, see Sitaraman, Ganesh, and Anne L. Alstott. 2019. *The Public Option: How to Expand Freedom, Increase Opportunity and Promote Equality*. Cambridge, MA: Harvard University Press.

4. https://edition.cnn.com/2019/01/29/politics/bloomberg-medicare-for-all/index.html

5. https://www.johndelaney.com/issues/health-care/

6. See, in particular, Dixon, Rosalind, Richard Holden, and Melissa Vogt. 2019. "(Un)taxing Child Care." New Economic Policy Initiative report, October 2019, on which parts of this chapter are based.

7. http://www.oecd.org/education/school/2476019.pdf

8. "Daycare." *The Village*, <https://www.thevillage.be/daycare/>.

9. "Child Care." Handbook Germany, <https://handbookgermany.de/en/live/childcare.html>.

10. "Child Care Deduction." *Norwegian Tax Administration*, <https://www.skatteetaten.no/en/person/taxes/tax-return/find-item/3/2/10/>; Anne Lise Ellingsaeter. 2012. "Cash for Childcare: Experiences from Finland, Norway, and Sweden." (Friedrich Ebert Stiftung, 2012).

11. "Australia: Individual – Deductions." *PWC*, <http://taxsummaries.pwc.com/ID/Austria-Individual-Deductions>.

12. Lagerquist, Jeff. 2018. "With Fewer Tax Breaks for Child-Care, What's Left for Canadian Parents?" *CTV News*, April 2, 2018, available at <https://www.ctvnews.ca/5things/with-fewer-tax-breaks-for-child-care-what-s-left-for-canadian-parents-1.3864569>.

13. Crandoll-Hollick, Margot L. 2016. "The Child Tax Credit: Current Law and Legislative History." Congressional Research Service Report, <https://fas.org/sgp/crs/misc/R41873.pdf>; McCormack, Shannon Weeks. 2019, "America's (D)evolving Childcare Tax Laws." *Georgia Law Review* 53:1093–1168..

14. KPMG. 2017. "France – Income Tax." Available at <https://home.kpmg/xx/en/home/insights/2011/12/france-income-tax.html>; Lundberg, Claire. 2012. "Trapped by European-style Socialism – And I Love It!" *Slate*, available at <https://slate.com/human-interest/2012/11/socialist-child-care-in-europe-creche-ecole-maternelle-and-french-child-care-options.html>.

15. Shleifer, Andrei. 1985. "A Theory of Yardstick Competition." *RAND Journal of Economics* 16 (3):319–27.

16. https://www.whitehouse.gov/briefing-room/statements-releases/2021/04/28/fact-sheet-the-american-families-plan/

17. https://elizabethwarren.com/plans/universal-child-care

18. https://www.telegraph.co.uk/politics/2018/04/25/labour-will-ban-uber-airbnb-minister-warns-says-tories-party/

19. https://www.engadget.com/2018/04/02/new-york-surcharge-uber-lyft-manhattan/

20. https://www.smh.com.au/politics/nsw/1-rideshare-levy-nets-34m-for-state-but-taxis-are-losing-money-20181218-p50mvm.html

21. http://research.economics.unsw.edu.au/richardholden/assets/professor-holden_compensation_report_final.pdf

22. https://www.nytimes.com/2019/05/19/nyregion/nyc-taxis-medallions-suicides.html

23. https://www.nytimes.com/2018/12/02/nyregion/taxi-drivers-suicide-nyc.html

24. https://www.supremecourt.gov/opinions/17pdf/16-285_q8l1.pdf

25. See Reuters, "EU Seeks More Protection for Uber-style Jobs, September 25, 2017. Available at https://www.reuters.com/article/us-eu-workers-gigeconomy/eu-seeks-more-protection-for-uber-style-jobs-idUSKCN1BZ0OU

26. To see an illustration of this competitive advantage in a particular strategic context, consider a market where two firms compete in quantities (i.e., a "two-firm Cournot oligopoly") and, for simplicity, they have constant marginal cost determined solely by their labor costs. If one firm has access to a lower labor-cost technology (e.g., not having to pay annual leave but having access to workers who have the same productivity as other firms), two things happen: (i) the direct effect is that the lower-cost firm finds it optimal to set a higher quantity; and (ii) the competing firm finds it optimal to set a lower quantity. Thus, in equilibrium, the lower-cost firm benefits from the *direct effect* of lower costs and also the *strategic effect* of having lower costs. This gives the lower-cost firm greater market share and larger profits. Moreover, the strategic effect in this type of environment is first-order (in a formal sense) and can be large.

27. Cutler, David M., and Richard J. Zeckhauser. 1998. "Adverse Selection in Health Insurance." *Frontiers in Health Policy Research* 1:1–32. ().

28. Cardon, James H., and Igal Hendel. 2001. "Asymmetric Information in Health Insurance: Evidence from the National Medical Expenditure Survey." *RAND Journal of Economics* 32:408.

29. Akerlof, George A. 1970. "The Market for 'Lemons': Quality Uncertainty and the Market Mechanism." *Quarterly Journal of Economics* 84:488.

30. https://www.census.gov/data/tables/2019/econ/school-finances/secondary-education-finance.html

31. https://www.privateschoolreview.com/tuition-stats/private-school-cost-by-state

32. https://www.privateschoolreview.com/tuition-stats/new-york/elementary

33. https://taipd.org/node/307

34. https://www.bbc.com/news/education-49798861

Chapter 6

1. World Bank. 2019. "5-Bank Asset Concentration for United States," retrieved from FRED, Federal Reserve Bank of St. Louis; see https://fred.stlouisfed.org/series/DDOI06USA156N WDB, September 3, 2019.

2. Posner, Richard A. 1978. "The Chicago School of Antitrust Analysis." *University of Pennsylvania Law Review* 127:925–48.

3. Andrews, Suzanna. 2011. "The Woman Who Knew Too Much." *Vanity Fair*, available at https://www.vanityfair.com/news/2011/11/elizabeth-warren-201111.

4. https://www.consumerfinance.gov

5. https://www.washingtonpost.com/business/2019/05/09/bernie-sanders-ocasio-cortez-want-cap-credit-card-interest-rates-percent/

6. https://twitter.com/AOC/status/1126499462107607040

7. See, for instance https://www.politico.com/story/2019/07/18/elizabeth-warren-wall-street-2020-1421826

8. https://www2.deloitte.com/au/en/pages/financial-services/articles/open-banking.html

9. See, for instance, the work of Daniel Kahneman and Amos Tversky encapsulated in Kahneman's Nobel lecture (https://www.nobelprize.org/prizes/economic-sciences/2002/kahneman/lecture/), and of University of Chicago economist Richard Thaler in his Nobel lecture (https://www.nobelprize.org/prizes/economic-sciences/2017/thaler/lecture/).

10. https://www.creditcards.com/credit-card-news/rate-report.php https://www.creditcards.com/credit-card-news/rate-report.php

11. https://www.fdic.gov/bank/analytical/qbp/2018dec/qbp.pdf

12. https://www.nytimes.com/2019/07/25/technology/chris-hughes-facebook-breakup.html

13. https://www.nytimes.com/2019/05/09/opinion/sunday/chris-hughes-facebook-zuckerberg.html

14. See, for instance, Kahn, Lina. 2017. "Amazon's Antitrust Paradox," *Yale Law Journal* 126(3):710–805; and Kahn, Lina. 2018. "The New Brandeis Movement: America's Antimonopoly Debate." *Journal of European Competition Law & Practice* 9(3):131–32.

15. https://elizabethwarren.com/plans/break-up-big-tech

16. A relatively recent literature focuses on harm to sellers through monopsony, or through reduced bargaining power as the result of mergers. For a notable example of this line of argument, see Hemphill, C. Scott, and Nancy L. Rose. 2018. "Mergers that Harm Sellers." *Yale Law Journal* 127(7):2078–2109 The following example from the paper captures their main argument nicely: "Courts have found that a merger of sellers that enables such a transfer by reducing competition—for example, a merger of two hospitals that worsens an insurer's outside option—is unlawful. A symmetric injury to the competitive process can arise on the buy side—for example, a merger of two insurers that worsens a hospital's outside option and thereby reduces the price paid. We conclude that such a bargaining-based harm suffered by a hospital or other input provider is equally actionable."

17. https://elizabethwarren.com/plans/promoting-competitive-markets

18. https://www.wsj.com/articles/google-uses-its-search-engine-to-hawk-its-products-1484827203. See also reporting in *Fortune* magazine, available at https://fortune.com/2017/01/20/google-search-engine-advertising-ads/.

19. See, for instance, Douek, Evelyn, The Rise of Content Cartels (Feb 2020). Knight First Amendment Institute at Columbia, 2020, Available at SSRN: https://ssrn.com/abstract=3572309 or http://dx.doi.org/10.2139/ssrn.3572309

20. Hughes, Chris. 2019. "It's Time to Break Up Facebook." *New York Times*, May 9, 2019, https://www.nytimes.com/2019/05/09/opinion/sunday/chris-hughes-facebook-zuckerberg.html.

21. https://research.chicagobooth.edu/-/media/research/stigler/pdfs/market-structure-report.pdf?la=en&hash=E08C7C9AA7367F2D612DE24F814074BA43CAED8C

22. Akerlof, Robert, Richard Holden, and Luis Rayo, "Network Externalities and Market Dominance." Available at http://research.economics.unsw.edu.au/richardholden/assets/ahr-networks-december-15-2018.pdf.

23. As Akerlof, Holden, and Rayo put it: "We are particularly interested in understanding three features of the new economy. First, winning firms serve a disproportionate share of their

markets, with a large size gap between them and their closest rivals. For instance, Google's current share of web, mobile, and in-app searches is 90.8% while Amazon's share of the US e-book market is 83%. Second, it is difficult to become a winner and yet success is so fragile that it can vanish overnight. The difficulties of becoming popular (going from being "out" to being "in") are illustrated by Microsoft's search engine Bing, which despite years of sizeable investments remains much smaller than the current superstar Google.

"The ease with which a successful firm can suddenly fail (go from "in" to "out") is illustrated by the web browser Netscape, which despite its initial dominant status was overtaken quite suddenly by Microsoft's Internet Explorer. Finally, despite their seemingly-dominant position, winners are not asleep. They tend to continuously raise quality (for example, by purchasing new startups) while at the same time keeping their prices low, sometimes even below average cost. For example, despite serving around 70% of the US ridesharing market, Uber invests heavily in its mapping technology and, at the same time, has kept its prices so low that it has been unable to recoup its costs. Similarly, Google invests heavily in its search algorithm to fend off wealthy, though much smaller, rivals like Microsoft Bing."

24. https://www.cfr.org/in-brief/coronavirus-disrupt-us-drug-supply-shortages-fda
25. https://www.drugs.com/article/drug-expiration-dates.html
26. https://www.nytimes.com/2020/07/05/business/china-medical-supplies.html?action=click&module=Top%20Stories&pgtype=Homepage

Chapter 7

1. Eilperin, Juliet. 2013. "Obama Makes a Moral Case for Action on Climate Change." *Washington Post*, January 22, https://www.washingtonpost.com/national/health-science/obama-makes-a-moral-case-for-action-on-climate-change/2013/01/22/1d33ea98-64cf-11e2-9e1b-07db1d2ccd5b_story.html; McDonald, Matt. 2013. "Rudd and the Failed Promise of Climate Security." *The Conversation*, July 11, https://theconversation.com/rudd-and-the-failed-promise-of-climate-security-15460.
2. https://www.ipcc.ch/sr15/
3. https://www.carbonbrief.org/paris-2015-tracking-country-climate-pledges
4. https://joebiden.com/climate-plan/
5. The White House. 2012. "Obama Administration Finalizes Historic 54.5 MPG Fuel Efficiency Standards." (Press Release, August 28, 2012), https://www.washingtonpost.com/national/health-science/obama-makes-a-moral-case-for-action-on-climate-change/2013/01/22/1d33ea98-64cf-11e2-9e1b-07db1d2ccd5b_story.html; The White House. 2016. "Fact Sheet: The Recovery Act Made the Largest Single Investment in Clean Energy in History, Driving the Deployment of Clean Energy, Promoting Energy Efficiency, and Supporting Manufacturing" (Press Release, February 25, 2016), https://obamawhitehouse.archives.gov/the-press-office/2016/02/25/fact-sheet-recovery-act-made-largest-single-investment-clean-energy.
6. Joe Biden. "The Biden Plan for a Clean Energy Revolution and Environmental Justice." https://joebiden.com/climate-plan/. See also, https://www.nhtsa.gov/press-releases/fuel-economy-standards-2024-2026-proposal
7. Abnett, Kate. 2020. "EU Considers Tax, Emissions Trading for Carbon Border Plan." *Reuters*, July. 23, https://www.reuters.com/article/us-climate-change-eu-carbon-idUSKCN24O1IM; Shankleman, Jess. 2021, "U.K.'s Boris Johnson Considers G-7 Bid on

GreenBorder Levies." *Bloomberg*, February 5, https://www.bloomberg.com/news/articles/2021-02-04/u-k-s-boris-johnson-considers-g-7-bid-on-green-border-levies.

8. Chiu, Dominic. 2021. "The East Is Green: China's Global Leadership in Renewable Energy." Center for Strategic and International Studies, https://www.csis.org/east-green-chinas-global-leadership-renewable-energy.

9. The idea was originally proposed by the Climate Leadership Council. See https://clcouncil.org.

10. See Lange, Oskar. 1936. "On the Economic Theory of Socialism: Part One," *Review of Economic Studies* 4(1):53–71; Taylor, Fred M. 1929. "The Guidance of Production in a Socialist State." *American Economic Review* 19(1):1–8; Hayek, Friedrich A., ed. 1935. *Collectivist Economic Planning.* London: Routledge & Kegan Paul; Lerner, A.P. 1934. "Economic Theory and Socialist Economy." *Review of Economic Studies* 2(1):51–61.

11. Obama, Barack. 2020. *A Promised Land.* Crown: NewYork. Chapter 21.

12. Ibid.

13. https://www.reuters.com/article/us-usa-autos-emissions-idUSKBN21I25S

14. Holden. Richard, and Rosalind Dixon. 2018. "The Australian Carbon Dividend Plan." Available at https://www.auscarbondividend.com

15. Leonnig, Carol D. 2012. "Battery Firm Backed by Federal Stimulus Money Files for Bankruptcy." *Washington Post*, October 16. Available at https://www.washingtonpost.com/politics/decision2012/battery-firm-backed-by-federal-stimulus-money-files-for-bankruptcy/2012/10/16/89611566-17c6-11e2-8792-cf5305eddf60_story.html?utm_term=.b7fc5cdb919e

16. Statement available at https://epic.uchicago.edu/sites/default/files/Greenstone%20SCC%20testimony%20022717.pdf.

17. See Michael Greenstone and Tamma Carleton, "Updating the United States Government's Social Cost of Carbon." Available at https://bfi.uchicago.edu/wp-content/uploads/2021/01/SCC-1-pager.final_.pdf

18. See, for instance, Michael Greenstone and coauthors, "Valuing the Global Mortality Consequences of Climate Change Accounting for Adaptation Costs and Benefits." Available at https://papers.ssrn.com/sol3/papers.cfm?abstract_id=3224365&mod=article_inline.

19. Andersson, Julius J. 2019. "Carbon Taxes and CO_2 Emissions: Sweden as a Case Study." *American Economic Journal: Economic Policy* 11(4): 1–30.

20. Lazard. 2019. "The Renewable Energy Revolution Is Here." Available at https://www.lazardassetmanagement.com/de/en_uk/references/social/2020-q2/renewable-energy-revolution.

21. https://www.forbes.com/sites/energyinnovation/2020/01/21/renewable-energy-prices-hit-record-lows-how-can-utilities-benefit-from-unstoppable-solar-and-wind/?sh=2a8776a62c84

22. Cramton, Peter, and Steven Stoft. 2008. "Forward Reliability Markets: Less Risk, Less Market Power, More Efficiency." *Utilities Policy* 16(3): 194–201.

23. https://www.iso-ne.com/about/what-we-do/in-depth/

24. https://www.auscarbondividend.com

25. Climate Leadership Council. 2017. "The Conservative Case for Carbon Dividends." Available at https://www.clcouncil.org/media/TheConservativeCaseforCarbonDividends.pdf.

26. In the CLC plan, this would amount to approximately US$2000 in dividends for a family of four in the first year. The CLC suggests this be administered by the Social Security Administration, and the dividends would go to anyone with a valid Social Security number.

27. Horowitz, John et al. 2017. "Methodology for Analyzing a Carbon Tax." Department of the Treasury, Office of Tax Analysis, Working paper no. 115, https://www.treasury.gov/resou rce-center/tax-policy/tax-analysis/Documents/WP-115.pdf.

28. The World Trade Organization recognizes measures may be implemented to achieve legitimate policy objectives, including protection of the environment. Such measures must still be consistent with WTO rules: see WTO, "Environmental Requirements and Market Access: Preventing 'Green Protectionism.'" Available at <https://www.wto.org/english/tratop_e/envir_e/envir_req_e.htm>.

29. Oliver, Alex. 2016. "2016 Lowy Institute Polling." Lowy Institute, June 21, 2016, https://www.lowyinstitute.org/publications/2016-lowy-institute-polling-us-presidential-elect ion-asylum-seeker-policy-and-methods.

30. Greenstone, Michael. 2016. "Americans Appear Willing to Pay for a Carbon Tax Policy." *The New York Times*, September 15, https://www.nytimes.com/2016/09/15/upshot/americ ans-appear-willing-to-pay-for-a-carbon-tax-policy.html?mcubz=0; Graham, Karen. 2017. "New Yale Study: Majority of Americans Support a Carbon Tax." *Digital Journal*, September 14, http://www.digitaljournal.com/news/politics/new-yale-study-majority-of-americans-support-a-carbon-tax/article/502458; Rabe, Barry G., and Christopher P. Borick. 2010. "The Climate of Belief: American Public Opinion on Climate Change." *Issues in Governance* 31 STUD. 1-15..

31. Mildenberger, Matto et al. 2016. "The Distribution of Climate Change Public Opinion in Canada." PLOS 11 ().

32. https://www.civicfed.org/civic-federation/blog/exploring-downtown-congestion-fee-chi cago

33. For the classic starting point of the vast literature on this subject, see Manne, Henry. 1966. *Insider Trading and the Stock Market*. New York: The Free Press.

34. Buffett's full quote in Berkshire Hathaway's 2002 annual shareholder letter reads: "In our view, however, derivatives are financial weapons of mass destruction, carrying dangers that, while now latent, are potentially lethal."

Chapter 8

1. See https://www.brookings.edu/wp-content/uploads/2019/03/On-Falling-Neutral-Real-Rates-Fiscal-Policy-and-the-Risk-of-Secular-Stagnation.pdf.

2. Sarin, Natasha and Summers, Lawrence H. 2020. "Understanding the Revenue Potential of Tax Compliance Investment." NBER Working Paper 27571, https://www.nber.org/papers/w27571.

3. www.oecd.org

4. https://podcasts.google.com/?feed=aHR0cHM6Ly9yc3Muc2ltcGxlGxlY2FzdC5jb20vcG9kY 2FzdHMvMzk5OC9yc3M&episode=ZTRkMGQxYjktNzg3MC00ZDY4LTg4ZGUtNjlk M2MxZWUwNmU5&hl=en&ved=2ahUKEwjp2v3WofHoAhUWgp4KHUvKDxcQieU EegQICxAE&ep=6

5. An exception to the point that taxes are distortionary are so-called Pigouvian taxes, named after British economist Arthur Pigou who first wrote about them in 1913. Pigouvian taxes

are designed to "internalize externalities" into the price mechanism and thus make sure that the market-clearing role the price mechanism plays in equilibrating supply and demand in a given market takes account of the social cost of activities not otherwise included in market prices. The classic example is pollution of various kinds, and the leading application is a carbon tax to balance the costs (climate change) and benefits (economic living standards) of carbon dioxide emissions.

6. https://www.brookings.edu/wp-content/uploads/2019/03/On-Falling-Neutral-Real-Rates-Fiscal-Policy-and-the-Risk-of-Secular-Stagnation.pdf

7. http://larrysummers.com/category/secular-stagnation/

8. http://larrysummers.com/2016/02/17/the-age-of-secular-stagnation/

9. Ibid.

10. Keane puts it this way: "When I simply average the Hicks elasticity across twenty-two well-known studies of males, I obtain 0.31. Several studies have shown that such a value is sufficient to induce substantial efficiency losses from progressive income taxation. Furthermore, if one weighs studies by features I argued are desirable, such as (i) use of direct rather than ratio wage measures, or (ii) accounting for human capital, one gets a larger value of the Hicks elasticity."

11. https://www.cnbc.com/2019/02/12/bill-gates-supports-wealth-tax-like-aoc-but-income-is-a-misfocus.html

12. https://taxfoundation.org/publications/corporate-tax-rates-around-the-world/#_ftn2

13. https://taxfoundation.org/publications/corporate-tax-rates-around-the-world/#_ftn2

14. https://www.npr.org/2021/04/05/984461923/janet-yellen-proposes-bold-idea-the-same-minimum-corporate-tax-around-the-world

15. See, for instance Chamley, Christophe. 1986. "Optimal Taxation of Capital Income in General Equilibrium with Infinite Lives." *Econometrica* 54(3):607–22, and Mankiw, N. Gregory, Matthew Weinzierl, and Danny Yagan. 2009. "Optimal Taxation in Theory and Practice." NBER Working Paper 15071. See also, Atkinson, Anthony, and Joseph E. Stiglitz, 1976, "The Design of Tax Structure: Direct Versus Indirect Taxation." *Journal of Public Economics* 6:55–75, which showed that when agents have preferences that can be represented by a utility function that is additively separable in consumption and leisure, and assuming the existence of an optimal income tax, it cannot be optimal to have any positive level of commodity taxation. By treating consumption at different dates as different commodities—which is consistent with the Arrow-Debreu model of general equilibrium—an immediate corollary of the Atkinson–Stiglitz theorem is that it cannot be optimal to have a positive level of taxation on interest income.

16. For a model considering a richer economic environment than the ones used to obtain the "zero capital taxation" results. see Stiglitz, Joseph E. 2017. "Pareto Efficient Taxation and Expenditures: Pre- and Re-distribution." NBER Working Paper No. 23892.

17. In Australia they are exactly half the ordinary income rate, by means of a specific deduction in capital income of 50% that is then taxed at an individual's marginal personal income tax rate.

18. https://www.irs.gov/newsroom/questions-and-answers-on-the-net-investment-income-tax

19. See https://www.treasury.gov/resource-center/tax-policy/tax-analysis/Documents/Taxes-Paid-on-Capital-Gains-for-Returns-with-Positive-Net-Capital-Gains.pdf for the raw data.

20. https://www.irs.gov/pub/irs-pdf/p5332.pdf

21. Sarin, Natasha, Lawrence H. Summers, Owen M. Zidar, and Erick Zwick. "Rethinking How We Score Capital Gains Tax Reform." NBER Working Paper 28362.

22. https://www.cnbc.com/2021/04/28/biden-american-families-plan-whats-in-it.html

23. https://www.oecd.org/tax/tax-policy/revenue-statistics-highlights-brochure.pdf

24. https://www.urban.org/policy-centers/cross-center-initiatives/state-and-local-finance-initiative/projects/state-and-local-backgrounders/sales-taxes

25. This involves linearly extrapolating the $310 billion CBO estimate of the revenue raised by a 5% VAT to $930 billion for a 15% VAT—which involves a variety of embedded assumptions that may or may not be fully justified—and then deducting the $377 billion and $182 billion in general and selective sales taxes from this amount.

26. See https://www.nytimes.com/2019/10/11/opinion/sunday/wealth-income-tax-rate.html.

27. See https://www.census.gov/quickfacts/fact/table/US/PST045218.

28. https://www.federalreserve.gov/paymentsystems/fednow_about.htm

29. See https://www.imf.org/en/Publications/WP/Issues/2018/01/25/Shadow-Economies-Around-the-World-What-Did-We-Learn-Over-the-Last-20-Years-45583 and https://www.imf.org/external/pubs/ft/issues/issues30/.

30. Existing personal income tax collection data from https://stats.oecd.org/Index.aspx?DataSetCode=REVUSA.

31. See https://www.bostonglobe.com/opinion/2019/03/28/broader-tax-base-that-closes-loopholes-would-raise-more-money-than-plans-ocasio-cortez-and-warren/Bv16zhTAkuEx08SiNrjx9J/story.html?p1=Article_Inline_Text_Link.

32. Mankiw summarized his own position in public remarks to the National Press Club while CEO chair. Available at http://scholar.harvard.edu/files/mankiw/files/npc.pdf.

33. As Mankiw notes: "Unfortunately, the same insights have not been applied to the estate tax. Under what circumstances would the estate tax actually fall only on the decedent? That would happen if the tax prompted the decedent to reduce his consumption during his lifetime, so that he could satisfy the tax obligation without diminishing the after-tax bequests left to his loved ones. In other words, the estate tax would have to reduce lifetime consumption and promote estate accumulation.

    "Simply stating this assumption casts doubt upon it. A good rule of thumb is that when you tax an activity, you get less of it. The estate tax makes estate building less attractive and probably reduces the size of bequests. Empirical research confirms that, in fact, the estate tax reduces the amount that decedents accumulate and pass on to their heirs. As a first approximation, it would make more sense to distribute the burden of the tax to the estate's beneficiaries rather than to the decedent.

    "What would happen if we allocated the estate tax burden to heirs rather than decedents? At first blush, one might think that it would not make much difference. After all, are not the children of rich people rich?

    "It turns out that the answer is 'not always.' A number of economists have taken a careful look at this difficult question, using a variety of data sets and methodological approaches. Their results are roughly similar. The correlation between the lifetime earnings of successive generations is around 0.4 or 0.5. Even adding in inheritances, the figure increases to only about 0.7. This is nowhere near a perfect correlation. And the correlation is far smaller when we look at the link between grandparents and grandchildren, and probably smaller still if we consider nephews, nieces, and other possible heirs. The bottom line is, once we move away from the standard assumption that the entire burden falls on the decedents, the tax appears much less progressive than one might have guessed."

34. See the classic papers of Kaplow, Lous. 2001. "A Framework for Assessing Estate and Gift Taxation," in W. Gale, J. Hines, and J. Slemrod, eds. *Rethinking Estate and Gift Taxation*. Washington, DC: Brookings Institution Press, and Farhi, Emmanuel, and Ivan Werning 2010. "Progressive Estate Taxation." *Quarterly Journal of Economics* 125(2):635–73.

35. See Piketty, Thomas, and Emmanuel Saez. 2013. "A Theory of Optimal Inheritance Taxation." *Econometrica* 81(5):1851–86.

36. Piketty and Saez restrict attention to linear taxes, unlike Farhi and Werning, who consider the fully optimal suite of tax instruments.

37. Piketty and Saez (p. 1866) note: "As our analysis makes clear, however, the Farhi–Werning (2010) two-period model only provides an incomplete characterization of the bequest tax problem because it fails to capture the fact that lifetime resources inequality is bi-dimensional, that is, individuals both earn and receive bequests. This key bi-dimensional feature makes positive bequest taxes desirable under some redistributive social welfare criteria."

38. See http://gabriel-zucman.eu/files/saez-zucman-wealthtax-warren.pdf.

39. https://www.washingtonpost.com/opinions/2019/06/28/be-very-skeptical-about-how-much-revenue-elizabeth-warrens-wealth-tax-could-generate/

40. https://www.washingtonpost.com/opinions/2019/06/28/be-very-skeptical-about-how-much-revenue-elizabeth-warrens-wealth-tax-could-generate/

41. https://www.washingtonpost.com/opinions/2019/04/04/wealth-tax-presents-revenue-estimation-puzzle/

42. See again Van Parijs and Vanderborght (2017), Chapter 6.

43. Van Parijs and Vanderborght (2017).

44. See again Van Parijs and Vanderborght (2017), Chapter 6.

45. See discussion in Van Parijs and Vanderborght (2017).

46. For a notable popular account, see Kelton, Stephanie. 2020. *The Deficit Myth*. New York: Public Affairs.

47. Edmond, Chris, Richard Holden, and Bruce Preston. 2020. "Should Governments Obsess about Debt? Yes, Say Traditionalists. No, Says the Theory." *Crikey*, July 7, available at https://www.crikey.com.au/2020/07/07/should-governments-worry-about-debt/.

Chapter 9

1. Bregman, Rutger. 2017. *Utopia for Realists*. London: Bloomsbury.

2. https://www.whitehouse.gov/briefing-room/statements-releases/2021/03/31/fact-sheet-the-american-jobs-plan/

3. Dixon, Rosalind. Forthcoming. "Democracy and Dysfunction: Towards a Responsive Theory of Judicial Review." See also Dixon, Rosalind. 2017. "The Core Case for Weak-Form Judicial Review." Cardozo Law Review 38(6):2193–2232

4. Friedman, John N., and Richard T. Holden. 2008. "Optimal Gerrymandering: Sometimes Pack But Never Crack." *American Economic Review* 98(1):113–44. Re Hungary, see: https://www.nytimes.com/2018/03/25/world/europe/hungary-election-viktor-orban.html.

5. Issacharoff, Samuel. 2002. "Gerrymandering and Political Cartels." *Harvard Law Review* 116:593; Stephanopoulos, Nicholas O. 2017. "The Causes and Consequences of Gerrymandering." *William & Mary Law Review* 59:2115.

6. Tushnet, Mark. 2020. "Institutions Protecting Constitutional Democracy: Some Conceptual and Methodological Preliminaries." *University of Toronto Law Journal* 70:95.

7. As Glaeser, Ponzetto, and Shapiro emphasize, this is a necessary but not sufficient condition for strategic extremism. As they put it: "But the existence of strategic extremism requires more than just a second intensive margin. Politicians who deviate from the median gain more support from their own supporters, but they also energize their opponents' supporters. For extremism to be an equilibrium, a move from the center must increase turnout among a politician's supporters more than among his opponent's supporters."

8. McCarty, Nolan, Keith T. Poole, and Howard Rosenthal. 2016. *Polarized America: The Dance of Ideology and Unequal Riches*. Cambridge, MA: MIT Press.

9. https://www.brennancenter.org/our-work/research-reports/automatic-voter-registration-summary

10. https://www.brennancenter.org/our-work/research-reports/automatic-voter-registration-summary

11. "Automatic Voters Registration," Brennan Center for Justice, https://www.brennancenter.org/issues/ensure-every-american-can-vote/voting-reform/automatic-voter-registration. See also Bhatt, Rachana, Evgenia Dechter, and Richard Holden. 2020. "Registration Costs and Voter Turnout: Evidence from a Natural Experiment." *Journal of Economic Behavior & Organization* 196:91–104 .

12. Mill, John Stuart. 1859. *On Liberty*. London: John W. Parker and Son.

13. See Nussbaum (1988) and Dixon, Rosalind, and Martha Nussbaum. 2011. "Children's Rights and a Capabilities Approach: The Question of Special Priority." *Cornell Law Review* 97:549–94.

14. For the classic economic analysis of informative advertising, see Grossman, Gene, and Carl Shapiro. 1984. "Informative Advertising with Differentiated Products." *Review of Economic Studies* 51:63–81.

15. https://www.ftc.gov/news-events/media-resources/truth-advertising

16. It is worth noting that the Court invalidated the expenditure ban in §608(e) of the Act because it "fail[ed] to serve any substantial governmental interest in stemming the reality or appearance of corruption in the electoral process."

17. *Unions NSW v New South Wales* [2019] HCA 1 *29 January 2019* S204/2018. *Buckley v. Valeo,* 424 U.S. 1 (1976). *Austin v. Michigan Chamber of Commerce,* 494 U.S. 652 (1990). *Citizens United v. Federal Election Commission,* 558 U.S. 310 (2010). *McCloy v New South Wales* [2015] HCA 34 *7 October 2015*.

18. *McCloy v New South Wales* [2015] HCA 34 *7 October 2015; Harper v Canada (AG)*, [2004] 1 SCR 827, 2004.

19. https://www.nytimes.com/2018/10/22/world/australia/compulsory-voting.html?searchResultPosition=5

20. https://www.aph.gov.au/About_Parliament/Parliamentary_Departments/Parliamentary_Library/pubs/BriefingBook45p/FederalElection2016

21. http://www.ukpolitical.info/Turnout45.htm

22. https://www.independent.co.uk/news/world/europe/french-election-turnout-emmanuel-macron-parliament-france-victory-fn-marine-le-pen-national-front-a7785366.html

23. See, e.g., Matsler, Sean. 2003. "Compulsory Voting in America." *Southern California Law Review* 76:953–78 and (2007) "Notes: The Case for Compulsory Voting in the United States." *Harvard Law Review* 121:591–612.

24. There is a large literature in development economics on the efficacy of so-called conditional cash transfer. See, for instance, Gertler, Paul. 2004. "Do Conditional Cash Transfers

Improve Child Health? Evidence from PROGRESA's Control Randomized Experiment," *American Economic Review* 94(2): 336-341.

25. Dixon, Rosalind, and David Landau. 2021. *Abusive Constitutional Borrowing.* Oxford: Oxford University Press.

26. https://www.france24.com/en/20190507-poland-woos-voters-controversial-child-benefits-scheme-european-union

27. https://www.heritage.org/health-care-reform/report/national-health-system-america

28. https://fivethirtyeight.com/features/does-trying-to-repeal-obamacare-actually-increase-its-appeal/

29. See Posner, Eric, and Adrian Vermeule. 2013. "Insider or Outside the System?" *University of Chicago Law Review* 80:1743–97. Available at https://chicagounbound.uchicago.edu/cgi/viewcontent.cgi?article=7879&context=journal_articles.

30. See, for instance, https://www.detroitnews.com/story/news/politics/2019/07/30/republicans-sue-block-michigan-redistricting-commission/1860829001/.

31. See Friedman, Thomas, https://www.nytimes.com/2018/11/27/opinion/immigration-republicans-democrats-climate-change.html.

About the Authors

Rosalind Dixon is professor of law at UNSW Sydney. She was previously on the faculty at the University of Chicago Law School, and holds an LLM and SJD from Harvard Law School.

Richard Holden is professor of economics at UNSW Sydney. He was previously on the faculty at the University of Chicago and Massachusetts Institute of Technology, and holds a PhD in economics from Harvard University.

Index